Pictorial History of

Protestantism

Books by Vergilius Ferm

Pictorial History of Protestantism

A PANORAMIC VIEW OF
WESTERN EUROPE AND THE UNITED STATES

by Vergilius Ferm, PH. D.

Former President, American Theological Society

PHILOSOPHICAL LIBRARY • NEW YORK

Printed in the United States of America

To

ADAM ELLIOTT ARMSTRONG, D.Sc.

Table of Contents

Introduction

The name "Protestant" is a battle-name, *Kriegsname* — so writes a German professor in Bonn. In the light of the days of the Reformation, this, indeed, is what Protestantism over-all came to mean. The times were bad, politically, religiously, ethically, socially — and especially in the precincts of the holy church. One must never forget the almost incredible abyss of tyranny, superstition, cold formalism, bigotry, sanctified authoritarianism, intolerance, corruption, into which the Roman church had slumped, nor fail to remember and appreciate the heroism of those who stood out so boldly against everything that was sentimentally dear, even against the corporate promise of eternal salvation of the soul — if one is to understand what Protestantism originally meant.

It is true, that we now like to stress the word "Protestant" as meaning a positive "witness" to a faith. But such charity must not offset the historical realism of the genesis of the Reformation. All institutions with time get set into frozen patterns of belief and behavior and even Protestants suffer from this inexorable law of potential stagnation and decay. It is a law of life that life moves toward death; and it is a corollary law that if life is to retain itself it must undergo vigorous regeneration.

The Catholic church in its own Counter-Reformation has acknowledged some of the mistakes and evils of that day and would now wish that Luther had had better handling by Pope Leo X, so as to have averted the tragedy (to itself) of the split from its ranks. But the Reformation was deeper than that. It cut at roots, not branches. It would individualize man before his God and remove some of the machinery that stood in the way in expressing his own inner conscience. It was a fearful and yet a great day in the history of Christianity. We shall perhaps not see again the likes of such heroes who fought so willingly with their lives for the recovery of the spirit of the common man.

Protestantism itself, as time went on, proved to be no angel of reform since it took up, in many instances, the very tools of iniquity which plagued those early in the strife. We do well not to extol the warriors of reform unduly for they, too, were men of their times. It would be folly to quote them indiscriminately and approvingly for everything they did. The appeal to their writings and sayings as proof-texts is the appeal to authority all over again, a lack of remembrance that the life of the spirit has continually to be recharged as men come to see the errors of the past and to reach out for further illumination in the things that matter most.

Protestantism means fundamentally, then, eternal vigilance against all the forces which encase the human spirit. It remains a "battle-name" in the core of its heritage and in the essential mission of its general point-of-view. It means protesting not alone against Catholicism but a protesting against any form of Protestantism itself which usurps power over individual conscience and over the spirit of freedom in the realm of man's inner life. It means this today as much as any yesterday. It means reforms, if necessary, down to the roots, of its own traditions. There continued to be

Protestants protesting against Protestants after the first guns were fired and its own history is full of the tragic accounts of martyrs within its own household.

This book, it is hoped, will create the impression — and historical it is — that other than being a witness to something (which it was) the Protestant spirit essentially is a battle-name against unwholesome infringements (be they of creeds, councils, books, catechisms, theology, ecclesiastical polity, confessions, heroes) against the onmoving forces of the spirit of life itself. The battle is never finished and we must be prepared for neo-Protestants of whatever kind in the days to come — if we are of this historic tradition or pretend to be.

In the preparation of this volume there are sources of help almost innumerable. One does not attempt such a huge subject without having through the years sampled much in one's reading from the dramatic stories of Reformation history. The subject has been of particular personal fascination. History is the teacher of perspectives (along with philosophy) and without a perspective one inclines to myopic dogmatism of opinion.

The publisher, Dr. Dagobert D. Runes, has generously surrounded me with appropriate literature bearing on almost the whole gamut of modern and recent history, some of which has come directly from European sources. Mrs. Rose Morse of the Philosophical Library staff has helped with practical suggestions which only those who sit in editorial offices seem to be in possession of. A recent visit to the Boston University, Yale University and the New York City libraries has helped in the accumulation of tools. Public relation officers, denominational librarians and officials in various churches have gone out of their way to supply samples representative of their particular groups, drawing from their precious historical files. I have approached practically all denominational officials seeking their help; if there is a void here and there in this volume, not all of it, I must protest, is due to negligence on my part. Some officials have turned my request aside although I did stress its importance. Some officials have written me courteously that they are in no sense of the Protestant tradition and the omission of their ecclesiastical bodies stems, therefore, from their own interpretation of their church (rightly or wrongly). The usual testimony is that they are but the continuing expression of primitive Christianity or that they are purely Biblical.

For textual quotations from Luther and for a sense of the chronology in his life as well as for accuracy of information in this area I am indebted to Professor Roland H. Bainton, a life-long student of Luther, whose books on that period remain incomparably authoritative and readable as well. It was he, I seem to recall, who stimulated me to further interests in the field of Reformation history — his seminar at Yale (in which I once in the long ago was a member) being one of the academic classics in the graduate school.

The running commentaries and the sequences of illustrations as well as the selections are here forthright acknowledged as mine, for better or for worse. This being a panoramic view precludes any attempt for every detail of importance.

It is unfortunate that the candid-camera was not invented along with the printing press to have made more accurate the scenes of an earlier day. And yet, artists are not always to be mistrusted, especially if they show professionalism in their art and if they were contemporaneous with what went on (as in the cases of Holbein and Cranach). Cartoons and paintings of that earlier day reflect history as much as the printed word, when properly understood. Wherever available, photostatic copies of the written and printed word have been secured and they need no apology for authentication.

To the Trustees of The College of Wooster I am indebted for another sabbatical year (1956-1957) during which time this and other publications have been completed.

To Adam E. Armstrong of Three Rivers, Michigan, I would in appreciation dedicate this book. A layman in the Protestant church to which he has devoted himself both by interest in big causes and by generous sharing in their fulfilment, a professional in American industry, his spirit I have come to know as representative of the meaning of the word "Protestant." His mind strikes deep at the roots of conventionalism and his mature thought has evolved for him a conviction of a philosophy of the Universe which, though it slides against the grain, is commanding the attention of many other free spirits. I am indebted to him for his encouragement to make a pilgrimage to some of the major shrines of Europe in the summer of 1956 which gives to me a peculiar feeling for the authenticity of many of the pictures in this volume, particularly of the Reformation scenes.

It would not be amiss to suggest to the reader of this volume to note that there were Protestants before and during the German and Swiss Reformation and that there were Protestants protesting against Protestants after that period (Anabaptists, Quakers, Unitarians, Universalists, Methodists, Christian Scientists, and the like). And the reader will not fail to note how all along in the path of this story, institutionalism and the priests settle in their foundations only to be provoked and even unsettled anew by some prophetic Protestant spirits.

VERGILIUS FERM

Mercer Lake
Mercer, Wisconsin

Pictorial History of
Protestantism

A PANORAMIC VIEW OF
WESTERN EUROPE AND THE UNITED STATES

Catholicism and Early Stirrings of Reform

The Council of Nicaea

The Roman Emperor Constantine (who furnished traveling expenses) called this great Council of Nicaea (325), the first assembly representing the entire Christian Church. Nicaea is south of Istanbul (Constantinople). Some 300 delegates were present and many visitors. The great majority of those who were to settle a theological-Christological controversy were themselves untrained theologians.

No official records of this great meeting are extant. We know that the Emperor (not then a full member of the Church) was interested primarily in peace rather than theology. When a creed was drawn up, he reinforced it by setting a penalty of political banishment upon any dissenter — a new chapter in the history of the Church. This served to set off anew many pathetic civil wars within the Church.

The Creed affirmed Jesus coequal in substance with God from all eternity, and also one Holy Spirit — a major creed in both Catholic and traditional Protestant churches.

Constantine the Great, Roman Emperor (274?-337) was baptized on his deathbed. A Mithraist at first, according to legend, he saw during a battle a cross in the sky. Taking this sign as an omen, he favored "religious toleration" and made Christianity a state religion by the Edict of Milan in 313. In 330 he dedicated the city of Constantinople on the site of Byzantium.

Iona is a very small island, about three miles long and one or more in breadth — in the setting of the blue Hebridean seas off the mainland of west highland Scotland.

This spot ranks with Rome and Constantinople as one of the most significant foci of missionary effort in the history of Christian Europe.

In 563 A.D. Columba came to the island and history began.

In the foreground is St. Martin's Celtic Cross (tenth century). Near the chapel is St. John's Cross (tenth century).

The cathedral is the Abbey Church in partial restoration. Its cemetery claims the remains of many famous names (King Duncan, Macbeth and other ancient kings).

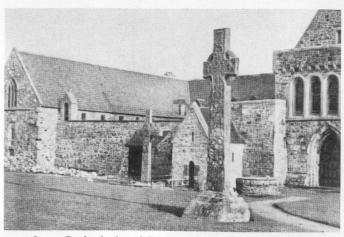

Iona Cathedral and St. Martin's Cross, Scotland

Baptizing the earliest converts in Britain. The conversion of the English began with Augustine's mission to Canterbury, 597.

Bede, the Venerable (673-735), English monk and scholar, author of *An Ecclesiastical History of the English People* (ca. 731).

Medieval scholars, like Bede, preserved the Bible through study and translation. Death overtook him, it is said, when he was beginning to dictate a vernacular translation into Anglo-Saxon of the Gospel of St. John (as pictured).

Named after the town of Albi in southern France, these people rebelled against the Roman Church authorities. Persecuted, they continued to criticize the priests of their day (eleventh to thirteenth centuries). Evil is matter and light is good, they said. "Eternal Light, Eternal Light" — an eighteenth-century hymn — characterizes their view of salvation. They were known — as were others — as the Cathari.

They were crushed by a Catholic crusade against them. The Inquisition followed, dealing sternly with heretics.

Pope Innocent III (rule: 1198-1216) summoned a council in Rome in 1215 which declared the universal authority of the bishop at Rome as Vicar of Jesus Christ — the high mark of papal theocratic government. Heretics could not be tolerated then and henceforth.

The Count of Bezieres, a powerful noble, was among those who supported the Albigenses. Bezieres was besieged and its inhabitants, some 30,000, were slain — the purpose of a papal army being to destroy the Albigenses.

The Albigensian Worshipers on the Banks of the Rhone

The Flight of the Waldenses

A certain rich Waldus of Lyons, France, founded in 1177 a society, "The Poor Men of Lyons," after a conversion and giving away his possessions. Itinerant preachers adopting the rule of poverty, these people were in the bad graces of the Catholic Church. They are precursors of the Reformation. In Italy they were popularly known as the Waldenses. The German group stood out against pilgrimages, indulgences, worship of images, wearing of clerical vestments, and suffered the tortures of persecution. Their appeal was to the New Testament Scriptures, and they were denounced by the Pope because the Scriptures (it was asserted) need to be interpreted by clerical authorities.

Simple folk they were. They laid claim to apostolic origin. Their ethical seriousness was their chief characteristic.

For more than two hundred years some of the Waldenses found refuge and lived in the valley country of Piedmont on the eastern slope of the Alps. Owing to the wild and rugged nature of this country they were able to continue to live undisturbed for a long time.

A Bookseller Burned with Two Bibles around His Neck for Selling Them in His Shop at Avignon, France

A drawing depicting the crime of selling French Bibles. This individual was charged with being one of the Waldenses.

The Catholic Bishop of Aix and some priests (so goes the story) were walking the streets of Avignon, stopped to purchase several obscene pictures, and met the bookseller who tried to sell his Bibles. They ordered his arrest.

Waldensian Missionaries in the Guise of Peddlers

The Waldenses take refuge in a cave and are smothered to death. More than a thousand bodies were found, including women and children, after the fires had spent themselves. The measure to crush the Waldenses had been determined by the Pope.

Dante Alighieri (1265-1321), Italian poet, author of the *Divine Comedy,* exiled in 1302, is regarded as the supreme interpreter of medieval thought in the area of symbolism and allusion. The story tells of Dante's imaginary trip through the world of after-death (he is pictured here in Purgatory with the poet Virgil) to Paradise, where he finally attains spiritual redemption.

John Tauler

A Dominican mystic and preacher, whose work was associated with the city of Strasbourg, Tauler (1300-1361) was a member of the mystical associates called "The Friends of God." His writings and sermons have influenced those for whom Christianity is essentially an experience of the inner life.

John Wycliffe

Wycliffe (*ca.* 1320-1384) began to attack the papacy and clerics vigorously and, though he belonged to the age of the Scholastics, he did herald the dawn of the Reformation in England. England, of course, was Roman Catholic, but there were strong stirrings against papal interference (e.g., the Statute of Provisors, 1351 and re-enacted in 1391, was a statute of Parliament against the appointment to any bishopric or the benefices in England by the Pope; or that of Praemunire, 1353, re-enacted in 1365 and 1393, which forbade any person to bring papal bulls or letters into England without the permission of the king, under penalty or interference by papal courts in the jurisdiction of civil law).

Against the ecclesiastics of his day he hurled such sharp words as "horned fiends to be damned in hell." He denied the Catholic view of the Lord's Supper (transubstantiation) and, with an intimate knowledge of Scripture and a mastery of language and learning, he stood up as a leader girded for battle against the Church of his day.

His contemporary, Chaucer, was the poet of the same age of stirrings. The Black Death had brought more misery to the people and papal demands had been too burdensome. The country was poor, but the Church rich. There was the complaint that the Pope received in taxes five times as much as the king. The Catholic mendicant friars preyed upon the people, providing worthless relics in return for gifts to them. To combat these intruders, Wycliffe sent out "Poor Preachers" who should model themselves after the ways of St. Francis.

He translated the Bible in full into English, then considered a too "vulgar tongue" for Sacred Scripture. Though threatened, his life was spared by powerful friends and he died peacefully while saying Mass as a Catholic.

Wycliffe's followers were called Lollards (the term means "mumblers of prayers and psalms," and was originally applied to a Dutch group). They grew in numbers until strong enough to petition the English Parliament to bring about church reforms. They were repulsed by the king and virtually wiped out under a statute, *De Heretico Comburendo,* in 1401. A new wave of horror entered into English life. Some Lollards persisted in secret and perhaps helped to pave the way in England for the sixteenth-century Reformation.

Pictured here is Wycliffe sending out his "Poor Preachers."

The Wycliffe Bible

The first Bible in English ("Middle English"), late in the fourteenth century.

Wycliffe's Bones Taken from the Grave and Burned

This occurred forty-one years after their interment "by the Papists." A London drawing (published in 1811).

John Hus

The Council of Constance brought to trial John Hus (1369-1415), leader of Czech reform. He was judged guilty by the Church ecclesiastics and burned at the stake on July 6, 1415 (see picture).

Hus studied the writings of John Wycliffe and became devoted to the cause of reforming the Catholic Church. Although he was no complete adherent of Wycliffe, he was so accused.

"Among the articles of John Hus," said Luther in his debate with Eck at Leipzig, "I find many which are plainly Christian and evangelical, which the Universal Church cannot condemn. . . . As for the article of Hus that 'it is not necessary for salvation to believe the Roman Church superior to all others,' I do not care whether this comes from Wycliffe or from Hus. I know that innumerable Greeks have been saved though they never heard this article. It is not in the power of the Roman pontiff or of the Inquisition to construct new articles of faith. No believing Christian can be coerced beyond Holy Writ."

To all this Eck replied with the zeal of a pious papal representative, "If you defend them [the alleged propositions of Hus], you are heretical, erroneous, blasphemous, presumptuous, editious and offensive. . . ."

Luther, spoken of as a new Hus by his accusers, retorted: "A simple layman armed with Scripture is to be believed above a pope or a council without it."

One of Many Hussite Monuments in Czechoslovakia Giving Prominent Place to the Communion Cup

Jerome of Prague

Jerome, a student under Hus, went to Oxford and became acquainted with the writings of Wycliffe. He began in 1407 to speak the views of Wycliffe openly in Prague. He came to the Council of Constance to assist Hus but was imprisoned. He at first recanted and later reaffirmed his convictions. In 1416 he was burned at the stake as a heretic — in the cause of a Reformation in Bohemia.

Jerome is pictured in the stocks.

Jerome Savonarola

Italian preacher and reformer (1452-1498). Besides attacking the morals of his day, he was a prophet of future events and leader of a theocratic government in Florence. The Pope excommunicated him. His denial of papal infallibility did not sit well with the ecclesiastical powers. A mob took him captive and he suffered martyrdom by burning.

9

The Martyrdom of Savonarola in Florence, Italy

This is the famous council of the Roman Catholic Church which defined the position against the Protestants.

The first council was held in 1545 at Trent (for two years) and then at Bologna. The second was held in 1551 (for two years). The third in 1562 (for two years).

In 1564 the creed of the Pope summing up its decisions was issued. Among the Catholic doctrines reaffirmed were: on the Holy Scripture, original sin, justification, the seven sacraments, baptism, confirmation, oral tradition (same level as Scripture), the right of interpretation confined to the Church. The doctrine of transubstantiation was adopted, penance declared valid, all sins must be confessed, the priest's absolution being judicial and whatever he enjoined was to the satisfaction of God's justice.

The Council of Trent

10

The Moravian Church

John Hus Standing Trial

Artist's conception of John Hus standing trial for heresy in 1415 in the Cathedral of Constance during the ecumenical council held in that city. In 1457, men and women influenced by the teachings of this great Bohemian reformer organized the Unitas Fratrum, or Moravian Church, at Kunwald in what is now Czechoslovakia. Painting by Vacslav Brozik, 1898.

John Amos Comenius

Known as an educational reformer, Comenius was born in south Moravia in 1592 and was educated first among the Unity of Brethren and later at Heidelberg University. While a refugee in Poland he published his *Janua linguarum reserata* which brought him fame. He worked for the unity of Christendom. He died in Amsterdam in 1670.

THE MORAVIANS

The genesis of the Moravian Church lies in the Bohemian Reformation led by John Hus. Hus's followers organized in 1457 and were called "Unitas Fratrum" ("Unity of Brethren"). In Peter Chelcicky (1390-1456) the Brethren found a devoted leader who required of his followers the repudiation of war, of political power, of human laws and of the papacy. The church must separate itself from the state, the clergy must accept poverty. The group withdrew to live according to its tenets but suffered cruel persecution. John Comenius (1592-1670) was their last bishop, and is known as the "father of modern education."

A small group of the Brethren from Moravia settled on the estates of Count Zinzendorf at Herrnhut in Saxony. Reorganized, the Unity of Brethren in 1722 became known as the Moravian Church.

The Kralitz Bible

A first-edition set of volumes of the Kralitz Bible, printed 1579-1593 on a press in Kralitz Castle which belonged to Baron Von Zerotin, a prominent member of the Unitas Fratrum or the Moravian Church. Painstakingly translated from the original Hebrew and Greek texts, this Bible did for the Czechs much of what Luther's version had done for Germany. Because extensive efforts to destroy this work were made during the Counter Reformation, copies of the Kralitz Bible are rare. The set shown is the property of the Moravian Archives, Bethlehem, Pennsylvania.

John Amos Comenius Bidding Farewell to Bohemia in 1628

When the Protestant forces were defeated in the Battle of White Mountain at the outset of the Thirty Years' War, the Moravian Church faced such opposition from the state that it could no longer maintain its organized activity in Bohemia or Moravia. Many of its members fled over the northern and eastern borders into Germany and Poland. This is an artist's conception of John Amos Comenius, noted educator, Moravian clergyman and later Bishop of the Unitas Fratrum, bidding farewell to Bohemia in 1628. Painting by J. F. Hettes.

THE MORAVIAN CHURCH

Count Nicholaus Ludwig von Zinzendorf (1700-1760) was instrumental in renewing the Moravian Church, though, as a Lutheran, he aimed at a "congregation of God in the Spirit," an interchurch society. A small group of Bohemian Brethren nestled on his estate, building the famous Herrnhut (Lord's Watch) community, attracting Christians from widely scattered sections.

The Count was interested in mission work among non-Christians and in interdenominational programs. From Herrnhut in 1732 missionaries were sent to the island of St. Thomas in the West Indies to convert the Negro slaves. To convert American Indians, missionaries came to Georgia in 1735. The Brethren there moved on to Pennsylvania, founding, in 1740, Bethlehem, the mother community of Moravians in America.

In 1957 the Moravian Church celebrated its five-hundredth anniversary at Bethlehem in Pennsylvania, when the world-wide Moravian Church met for the first time in the United States.

Zinzendorf as He Appeared in Early Manhood

A Count Zinzendorf Painting, a Benjamin Franklin Imprint, and a Zinzendorf Manuscript

Count Nicholaus Ludwig von Zinzendorf, a pious nobleman of Saxony, became an instrument in God's hand for the resuscitation of the Unitas Fratrum of the Moravian Church in the eighteenth century. Under his inspiration, the renewed Moravian Church began widespread foreign missionary activity in 1732.

The painting shown is thought to be the work of John Valentine Haidt, an eighteenth century Moravian clergyman, important as a painter in Colonial America. The manuscript shown is a hymn composed by Zinzendorf. The book is a Benjamin Franklin imprint containing an account of Zinzendorf's efforts to unite Protestants in Pennsylvania in one "Church of God in the Spirit." The tassel on the book is taken from Zinzendorf's cane sword.

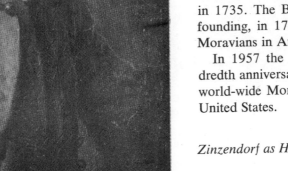

Ecce Homo

Zinzendorf was profoundly moved by this painting, especially by the Latin words: "This I have done for you. What have you done for me?"

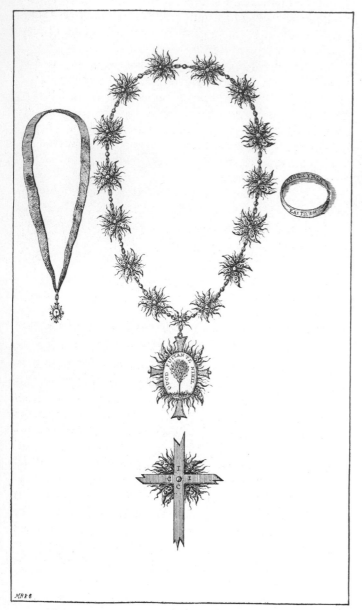

Insignia of the Order of the Grain of Mustard Seed

As a very young man, Zinzendorf attended the school of Halle under Francke. The insignia signified the conversion of like-minded youthful companions.

Count Zinzendorf

Devotional Manual of the Watchwords

Copies of 1733 edition of the *Watchwords* of the Moravian Church. This unique devotional manual has been published annually since 1731. It contains scripture texts drawn for each day by lot after the earnest prayer that these texts may serve Christ's people as watchwords for each day and thus become the source of light and strength for all who read them.

The lot was often resorted to by the Moravians in the eighteenth century as a means of ascertaining the Lord's will in many specific decisions which the church had to make. The picture shows different types of texts used as lots.

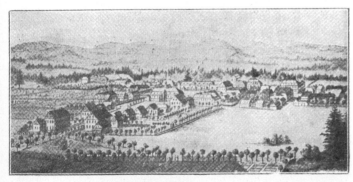

Herrnhut

Augustus Gottlieb Spangenberg

Bishop of the Moravian Church. As adjunct professor at Halle, he joined the Moravian Church in 1733. A capable organizer in England, the West Indies, Pennsylvania and North Carolina, he was an outstanding figure in his church. His dates: 1704-1792.

The Grave Marker of Count Zinzendorf

Moravian Church, Bethlehem, Pennsylvania

In 1740 Moravians purchased a large tract of land in eastern Pennsylvania, naming their city Bethlehem. The following year Count Zinzendorf arrived to give the colony leadership. A chapel, bishop's house and residence for Moravian Sisters were erected. The chapel dates back to 1742. In 1751 the chapel was expanded in the fast-growing community center. To its hospital came many strangers. General Lafayette was cared for here. Count Pulaski attended Moravian services in stately array. From here he carried a silk banner embroidered by the Sisters, a dramatic scene recorded by Longfellow in "The Hymn of the Moravian Nuns." This banner was carried in war and in ceremony.

Trombone Choir in the Church Cupola

Cupola of Central Moravian Church, Bethlehem, Pennsylvania, showing members of the trombone choir. Trombones were brought to Bethlehem in 1754. The choir plays hymn tunes to announce the festival days of the church and also to make known to all within hearing the decease of members of the church. The tunes played indicate whether the deceased was a child, a single man or woman, married person, or a widower or widow.

Central Moravian Church, Bethlehem, Pennsylvania

The Central Moravian Church, a Colonial-type building, was erected 1803-1806 as a central meeting place for members and friends of the area. When it was built, the community numbered less than 600. The sanctuary seats 1,000 persons today. It was in this building that the first Bach Festivals were held for Bethlehem music lovers in 1900.

Moravian College, Bethlehem, Pennsylvania

A part of the south campus of Moravian College, Bethlehem, Pennsylvania, with Christmas illumination. The central building, "Colonial Hall," was erected in 1748 as the "Brethren's House" for the home of the single men of the community. During the Revolutionary War, the building saw use as a hospital for the sick and wounded Colonial soldiers.

The John Vogler House, Winston-Salem

The John Vogler House, Salem Square, Winston-Salem, North Carolina now restored by "Old Salem, Inc." to its original appearance. This building was long the home of John Vogler, a noteworthy Moravian silversmith.

John Vogler's Silversmith Workshop, Winston-Salem

The silversmith's workshop in the John Vogler house, Salem Square, Winston-Salem, North Carolina. Other trades during the early days of the town were gunsmith, baker, potter and carpenter.

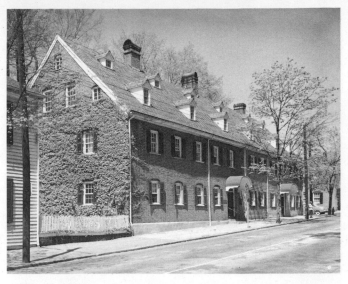

The Brothers' House, Winston-Salem, North Carolina

The Brothers' House, Salem Square, Winston-Salem, North Carolina. The frame section to the right was built in 1769 as the "Brethren's House" of Salem, home of the single men of that community. It is one of the buildings to be acquired by "Old Salem, Inc."

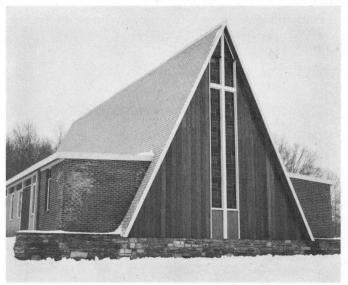

Moravian Church, Big Oak, Pennsylvania

A recently constructed Moravian Church, dedicated in 1956 and located at Big Oak, near Yardley, in Pennsylvania. It serves Moravians in the Morrisville area.

Home Moravian Church, Winston-Salem

Home Moravian Church on Salem Square, Winston-Salem, North Carolina, built in 1800. Winston-Salem is the center of the Moravian Church in the Southern Province. In the left foreground stands Salem Bookstore; the center building serves as office of the president of Salem College.

Luther and the German Reformation

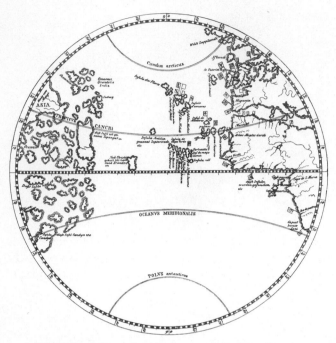

West Europe, Atlantic Ocean and America —
A Map of 1492 by Martin Behaim

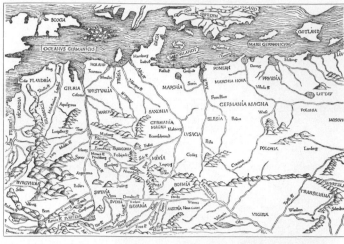

Map of Germany and Neighboring Countries, 1493

The limitations of the knowledge of geography are apparent in the coastal area.

A German Peasant Couple at Meal in Luther's Day

A "Wild Man" Preys upon Children
(Woodcut by Lucas Cranach)

It was an age filled with superstitions and fears in which children were indoctrinated.

The Drunken Devil at a Bier

A little book against drinking, Augsburg, 1534. Devils play with man's fate.

A Procession of Clergy According to Rank
(A woodcut of 1491)

Punishment for Unfaithfulness of Malicious-Tongued Servants

The clipping of the tongue.

A Peasant Breaks in upon a Monk Seeking His Daughter
(A woodcut, ca. 1523)

The monk attempts to silence the father by offering him cash. At the right, the mother is weeping. At the left, another monk is saying:

"This thing compels me to be still,
Although this is not my will."

A Printing Shop in the Sixteenth Century

Luther's Birthplace in Eisleben

TOP: The village and countryside.
BOTTOM: The Luther house.
Martin was the second son of Hans Luther, a miner of peasant stock. He was born on November 10, 1483.

Luther's Father, Hans Luther

A stocky, swarthy German peasant, who was brought up on a farm and went over to mining, and who came to own some six foundries.

Luther's Mother, Margaretta Luther

A devout woman of peasant stock.

The Parental Home of Luther in Mansfeld

Where Luther spent his early boyhood years.

O Er alt Barlaam antwurt dem künig vnd sprach. Die liebhaber der weltlichen wollu/ stigkeyten vnnd die durch die süssikeit diser welt verfürt werden vnd diß zergängklich fliessend

A Popular German Book in Luther's Time, Printed in Type, Augsburg, ca. 1475

Magdeburg

In 1497 Luther was sent to school in Magdeburg. Only fourteen years old, he there witnessed (as he later remarked) the emaciated Prince William of Anhalt, who as a begging friar "had so worn himself down by fasting and vigil that he looked like a death's-head, mere bone and skin." Here was monasticism on sickening exhibition.

Erfurt

Many-spired, where Luther carried on studies at the University, and earned his B.A. degree in 1504 and a year later his M.A. His studies were in the conventional classics, including the physics of Aristotle. He was preparing for the profession of law. It was during his student days at Erfurt (in 1505), while returning from a visit with his parents, that he was struck by lightning, which diverted his course, by a solemn resolution to serve God rather than the law and to enter a monastery.

The Registry of the University of Erfurt, in Which Martin Luther's Name Appears

Luther's Cell in the Augustinian Cloister in Erfurt

Luther's Rosary

In this monastery Luther learned the rigors of monastic life. The rules were severe: scant diet, rough clothing, poverty, the shame of begging, vigils by night and labor by day.

His father had violently opposed the decision of his son, but came to attend the first Mass said by the new celebrant. Hans Luther could not understand Martin's disobedience and his forsaking a promising career in the law.

Johann von Reuchlin

Great-uncle of Melanchthon, Reuchlin (1455-1522), a German humanist, was involved in a clash with the Church over the issue of freedom of scholarship. He was involved in a dispute with the fanatical Jewish convert, Pfefferkorn, a Dominican friar who had inspired an edict in 1509 to destroy the Talmud and other Hebrew writings. This edict was rescinded, thanks to Reuchlin's efforts. Reuchlin was a student of Hebrew and among his writings were a Hebrew grammar and dictionary. He stood for a fearless investigation of all literature in the search for truth. He pointed out the fact that there were errors in the authorized translation of the Bible, the Vulgate.

Shown here is the printed text from Reuchlin's *Rudiments of Hebrew* (1506).

Frontispiece from Reuchlin's De Rudimentis Hebreicis *(1506)*

Johann von Reuchlin

The City of Rome in the Sixteenth Century

In 1510 Luther made a pilgrimage to the Eternal City. As one of two representatives of the monastery of Erfurt, he was to ask for a settlement by the Pope on a current dispute.

He was not interested in the antiquities nor the Renaissance splendors of the city. There was, moreover, little time since it was a long journey. He remarked on the ignorance, immorality and frivolity of the Italian priests who jumbled through the Masses irreverently.

He climbed the Stairs of Pilate on hands and knees, kissing each step in the hope of helping someone to be delivered from Purgatory, as became a devout believer. Arrived at the top, he raised his head in doubt, to say, "Who knows whether it is so!"

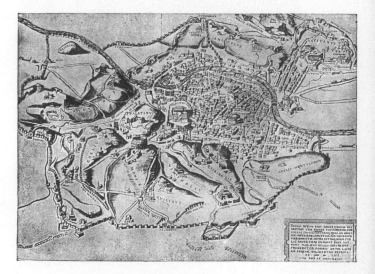

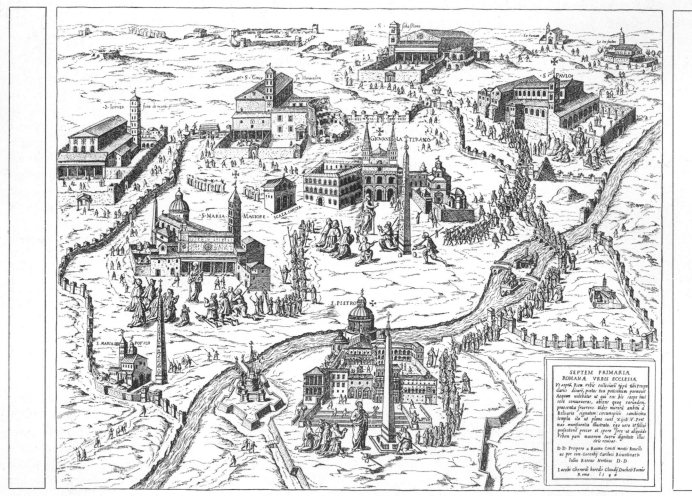

Rome, the Eternal City, in the Sixteenth Century

IOANNES STAVPITIVS D. THEOLOGIÆ ORDIN. S. AVGVSTINI EREMITARZ
EX DISPENSATIONE APLICA, ABBAS S. PETRI PRÆFVIT ANN. III MEXV. O ANNO M.D.XXIII

Johann von Staupitz

Vicar of the Augustinian order, it was he who recognized the awful distress of soul of the monk, Martin Luther. He chided Luther for grieving over little sins, suggesting jokingly that he ought to commit some major sin over which to suffer torment. It was he who recognized the usefulness of Luther in the area of preaching and teaching, even urging him to press on in his studies for a doctorate. Said Luther, "If it had not been for Dr. Staupitz I should have sunk in hell," so seriously had the monk become a monk. He and Luther were in correspondence until Staupitz's death in 1524, Staupitz admonishing, correcting and even encouraging his younger friend.

Luther and Philosophy

Martin Luther, an Augustinian Doctor of Theology

Luther was encouraged to study for a Doctor's degree by Staupitz, his superior, who recognized the young monk's unusual gifts. An earned Doctor's degree required much discipline in study in his day. The picture here shows a sixteenth-century ceremony of the conferring on a candidate of the ring and the doctor's hat.

Luther was justly proud of this distinctive achievement (1512), which entitled him to an academic chair. More than once he justified himself by pointing to his degree. "Although I am a doctor," he said, "I have to do just as a child and say word for word every morning and whenever I have time the Lord's Prayer and the Ten Commandments, the Creed and the Psalms." He once remarked that he would surrender his doctor's hat to anyone who could reconcile the writings of James in the New Testament with those of Paul.

Pictured here is a typical tribute to philosophy by the German Catholic humanist-poet, Konrad Celtes (born 1459). Against philosophy (and humanism) Luther came to react violently. For him speculation could not attain a knowledge of God. Reared in the teachings of the late Scholastics, Luther divorced theology as based on revelation from philosophy as based on human reason. In this he was like Tertullian, who was willing to believe even though reason held such belief impossible. Luther was disinterested in speculation as such, since his own problem lay in finding a religious commitment which would resolve his own inner conflict of spirit. He particularly hated Aristotle.

Luther's Doctor's Ring

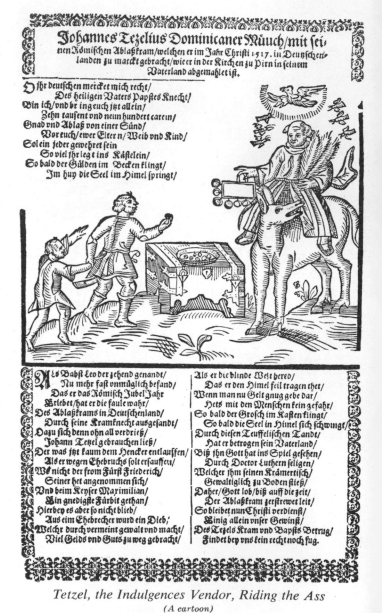

Luther, the Preacher

An altar painting by Lucas Cranach.

Johann Tetzel

Tetzel, the Indulgences Vendor, Riding the Ass
(A cartoon)

Tetzel, the vendor of indulgences, provoked Luther to wrath. He had been haranguing the populace with rash promises, armed with the approval of the Church of Rome. For coins dropped in the coffers there was the alleged assurance of complete pardon for sins and the release of beloved souls from Purgatory. Not allowed to come into Wittenberg — because Frederick the Wise would not give permission — Tetzel was vending his indulgences across its borders. The credulance of his parishioners was too much for Luther. There must be an outcry against such abuses. Luther posted his Theses in protest.

Scene in Front of All Saints Church, Wittenberg,
October 31, 1517

Luther challenges the Church powers to debate. Indulgences do not forgive sins! They bring a false peace to man's conscience! Albert of Hohenzollern, who paid a fee for the archbishopric of Mainz (a custom of the day) and another (of 10,000 ducats) for a further dispensation from Pope Leo X, was given papal permission to proclaim indulgences on his territories, with a split of income between himself and Rome. He appealed to the people for generous contributions for the construction of the basilica of St. Peter's. Remission of sins and release of friends from Purgatory, it was claimed, would be the reward for contributions.

Later the Pope made it clear that indulgences do not forgive sins but only remit penalties imposed by the Church. Indulgences concern remission of temporal punishment for sins imposed by the Church. The Roman Catholic Church taught that a sinner's guilt and eternal punishment are removed by the sacrament of penance. But there still remains punishment here and now and in Purgatory. These latter are relieved by the declaration and specific requirements of the Church through its chief bishop. The common people did not see this distinction and believed indulgences applied to contrition for sin.

The whole issue revolved around the abuse of the practice in the late medieval period.

The Luther Pulpit

Amore et studio elucidande veritatis: hec subscripta disputabitur Wittenberge. Presidente R. P. Martino Lutther: Artiu et S. Theologie Magistro: eiusdemq ibidem lectore Ordinario. Quare petit: vt qui non possunt verbis presentes nobiscu disceptare: agant id literis absentes. In noie dni nostri Jesu chri. Ame.

1 ¶Dominus et magister nr Jesus chrs dicendo. penitentiam agite. ze. omnem vitam fideliu penitentiam esse voluit.

2 ¶Qd verbu de penitetia sacramentali (id est confessiois et satisfactiois que sacerdotum ministerio celebratur) non pot intelligi.

3 ¶Non tn solam intendit interiore: immo interior nulla est. nisi foris operetur varias carnis mortificationes.

4 ¶Manet itaq pena donec manet odiu sui (id est penitentia vera intus) scz vsq ad introitum regnu celoz.

5 ¶Papa no vult nec pot vllas penas remittere. pter eas: quas arbitrio vel suo vel canonum imposuit.

6 ¶Papa no pot remittere vlla culpa nisi declarando et approbando remissam a deo. Aut certe remittendo casus reseruatos sibi: quib9 pteptis culpa prorsus remaneret.

7 ¶Nulli prorsus remittit deus culpa: quin simul eu subijciat: humiliatu in oibus: sacerdoti suo vicario.

8 ¶Canones penitetiales solu viuetibus sunt impositi: nihilq morituris fm eosd em debet imponi.

9 ¶Inde bn nobis facit spusctus in papa. excipiendo in suis decretis sp articulu mortis et necessitatis.

10 ¶Indocte et male faciut sacerdotes ii: qui morituris pnias canonicas in purgatoriu reseruant.

11 ¶Zizania illa de mutanda pena Canonica in penam purgatorij. vident certe dormientibus episcopis seminata.

12 ¶Olim pene canonice no post: sed ante absolutionem imponebantur: tanq tentamenta vere contritionis.

13 ¶Morituri: p morte omnia soluunt. et legibus canonu mortui iam sunt habentes iure earum relaxationem.

14 ¶Impfecta sanitas seu charitas morituri: necessario secum fert magnu timorem: tantoq maiorem: quato minor fuerit ipsa.

15 ¶Hic timor et horror satis est. se solo (vt alea taceo) facere penà purgatorij: cum sit primu desperatiois horror.

16 ¶Uidentur infernus: purgatoriu: celum differe: sicut desperatio: ppe desperatio. securitas differunt.

17 ¶Necessariu videt aiab9 in purgatorio: sicut minui horror. ita augeri charitatem.

18 ¶Nec pbatum videt vllis: aut roibus aut scripturis. q sint extra statum meriti seu agende charitatis.

19 ¶Nec hoc pbatu esse videt: q sint de sua btitudine certe et secure saltem oes. licz nos certissimi simus.

20 ¶Igitur papa p remissione plenaria oim penax. no simpliciter oim. intelligit: sed a seipso tantumodo impositax.

21 ¶Errant itaq indulgetiarii pdicatores. ii: qui dicut per pape indulgetias: hoiem ab oi pena solui et saluari.

22 ¶Quin nulla remittit aiabus in purgatorio: quà in hac vita debuissent fm Canones soluere.

23 ¶Si remissio vlla oim oino penax: pot alicui dari. certu est eà no nisi pfectissimis. i. paucissimis dari.

24 ¶Falli ob id necesse est: maiore parte popli: per indifferente illà et magnificam pene solute pmissionem.

25 ¶Quale ptatem hz papa in purgatorii gnaliter: talem hz quilibet Episcopus et Curatus in sua diocesi et parochia specialiter.

1 ¶Optime facit papa: q no ptate clauis (quà nulla hz) sed per modu suffragii dat aiabus remissionem.

2 ¶Holem predicat. qui statim vt iactus nummus in cistam tinnierit: euolare dicunt anima.

3 ¶Certu est: nummo in cistà tinnietante: augeri questu et auaricià posse. suffragium aut ecclesie: in arbitrio dei soli9 est.

4 ¶Quis scit, si oes aie in purgatorio velint redimi. sicut de. s. Seuerino et paschali factu narratur.

5 ¶Nullus est securus de veritate sue cotritiois. multominus de cosecutione plenarie remissionis.

6 ¶Q rar9 est ve penites: tà rar9 est ve indulgetias redimes. i. rarissim9

7 ¶Danabunt ineternu cu suis magistris: qui p lras veniax securos sese credunt de sua salute.

8 ¶Cauendi sunt nimio: qui dicut venias illas Pape: bonu esse illud dei inestimabile: quo reconciliat homo deo.

9 ¶Gratie em ille veniales: tantu respiciunt penas satisfactiois sacrametalis ab homie constitutas.

10 ¶Non christiana predicant: qui docent. q redemptorie aniae vel cofessionalia: no sit necessaria contritio.

11 ¶Quilibet christianus vere copunctus: hz remissione plenarià a pena et culpa. etiam sine lris veniax sibi dedita.

12 ¶Quilibet verus christianus: siue viuus siue mortu9: hz participatione oim bonox Chri et Ecclesie. etia sine lris veniax a dco sibi datam.

13 ¶Remissio tn et participatio Pape: nullo mo est ptemnenda. qi (vt dixi) est declaratio remissionis diuine.

14 ¶Difficilimu est: etià doctissimis Theologz simul extollere veniax largitatem: et contritiois veritate coram populo.

15 ¶Contritionis veritas penas querit et amat. Veniax aut largitas relaxat: et odisse facit saltem occasione.

16 ¶Laute sunt venie apstice pdicande. ne populus false intelligat. eas pferi ceteris bonis opibus charitatis.

17 ¶Docendi sunt christiani. q pape mens no est: redemptione veniax vlla ex parte coparandà esse opibus misericordie.

18 ¶Docendi sunt christiani. q dans paupi: aut mutuans egenti: meli9 facit q si venias redimeret.

19 ¶Quia p opus charitatis crescit charitas: z fit ho melior. sed p venias no fit melior: sed tmmodo a pena liberior.

20 ¶Docendi sunt christiani. q qui videt egenu: et neglecto eo. dat p venijs no indulgetias Pape: sed indignatione dei sibi vendicat.

21 ¶Docendi sunt christiani. q nisi supfluis abundent: necessaria tenent domui sue retinere: et nequaq pter venias effundere.

22 ¶Docez z sunt christiani. q redemptio veniaru est libera: no precepta.

23 ¶Docez z sunt christiani. q Papa sicut magis eget: ita magis optat in venijs dandis p se deuotam orationem: q promptam pecuniam.

24 ¶Docendi sunt christiani. q venie Pape sunt vtiles: si non in eas confidant. Sed nocentissime: si timorem dei per eas amittant.

25 ¶Docendi sunt christiani. q si Papa nosset exactiones venaliu pdicatorum mallet Basilica. s. Petri in cineres ire: q edificari. cute carne z ossibus ouium suax.

1 ¶Docendi sunt christiani. q Papa sicut debet ita vellet. etiam vendita (si opus sit) Basilica. s. Petri: de suis pecunijs dare illis: a quorum plurimis quidà cocionatores veniax pecuniam eliciunt.

2 ¶Vana est fiducia salutis p lras veniax. etià si Comissarius: immo papa ipse suà aiam p illis impigneraret.

3 ¶Hostes chri et Pape sunt ii: qui ppter venias pdicandas verbu dei in alijs ecclesijs penitus silere iubent.

4 ¶Iniuria fit verbo dei: du in codez sermone: equale vel longius tepus impenditur venijs q illi.

5 ¶Mens Pape necessario est. q si venie (qd minimum est) vna capana: vno pompis: et ceremonijs celebrant. Euangelium (qd maximu est) centu campanis: centu pompis: centu ceremonijs predicet.

6 ¶Thesauri ecclie vn Papa dat indulgetias: neq satis noiati sunt: neq cogniti apud ppim christi.

7 ¶Temporales certe no esse patet: q no tà facile eos pfundunt: sz tmmo colligunt multi concionatoz.

8 ¶Nec sunt merita Chri et sctoz. qi hec sp sine Papa operant gram hois interioris: et cruce: morte: infernumq exterioris.

9 ¶Thesauros ecclie. s. Lauret9 dixit esse: pauperes ecclie. sz locutus est vsu vocabuli suo tpe.

10 ¶Sine temeritate dicim9 claues ecclie (merito Chri donatas) esse thesaurum istum.

11 ¶Clax est em. q ad remissione penax et casuu sola sufficit ptas Pape.

12 ¶Verus thesaurus ecclie. est sacrosctm euangelium glorie et gratie dei.

13 ¶Hic aute est merito odiosissimus. qi ex primis facit nouissimos.

14 ¶Thesaurus aut indulgentiax merito est gratissimus. qi ex nouissimis facit primos.

15 ¶Igitur thesauri Euangelici rhetia sunt: quibus olim piscabant viros diuitiarum.

16 ¶Thesauri indulgentiax rhetia sunt: qbus nuc piscant diuitias viro.

17 ¶Indulgetie: quas cocionatores vociferant maximas gras. intelligunt vere tales quoad questum pmouendum.

18 ¶Sunt tamen re vera minime ad gram dei et crucis pietate compate.

19 ¶Tenent Epi et Curati veniax aplicaru Comissarios cu oi reuerentia admittere.

20 ¶Sed magis tenent oibus oculis intendere: oibus auribz aduertere: ne p comissione Pape sua illi somnia pdicent.

21 ¶Cotra veniax aplicax pietate q loquit. sit ille anathema z maledict9.

22 ¶Qui vero contra libidine ac licentià verboru cocionatoris veniaru curam agit: sit ille benedictus.

23 ¶Sicut Papa iuste fulminat eos: qui in fraudem negocij veniaru quacunq arte machinantur.

24 ¶Multomagis fulminare intendit eos: qui p veniaru pretextu in fraudem scte charitatis et veritatis machinant.

25 ¶Opinari veniax papales taras esse: vt soluere possint hoiez. etià si q p impossibile dei genitrice violasset. Est insanire.

1 ¶Dicimus contra. q venie papales: nec minimu venialium pctoz tollere possint quo ad culpam.

2 ¶Qd df. nec si. s. Petrus modo Papa esset: maiores gras donare possz est blasphemia in sctm Petrum et Papam.

3 ¶Dicimus contra. q etià iste z quilibet papa maiores hz. scz Euangelium: virtutes: gras curationu. ze. vt. i. Co. xij.

4 ¶Dicere. Cruce armis papalibus insigniter erecta: cruci christi equiualere: blasphemia est.

5 ¶Ratione reddent Epi: Curati: et Theologi. Qui tales sermones in populum licere sinunt.

6 ¶Facit hec licetiosa veniax pdicatio. vt nec reuerentià Pape facile sit: etià doctis vir redimere a calunijs aut certe argut questioib9 laicox.

7 ¶Scz. Qur Papa no euacuat purgatoriu ppter scissimà charitatez et summà aiarum necessitate: vt càm oim iustissimà. Si infinitas alias redimit. ppt pecunià funestissimà ad structurà Basilice: vt cà leuissimà.

8 ¶Ite. Cur pmanet exequie et annuersaria defunctoz: et no reddit aut recipi pmitti bnficia p illis instituta. cu sit iam iniuria p redept9 orare.

9 ¶Ite. Que illa noua pietas Dei et Pape. q impio et inimico ppter pecunià pcedit aiam pià z amicà dei redimere. Et tn ppter necessitate ipsiusmet pie et dilecte anie no redimunt eà gratuita charitate.

10 ¶Ite. Cur Canones pnitales re ipsa et no vsu: tà diu in semet abrogati z mortui: adhuc tn pecunijs redimunt per pcessione indulgetiax tanq viuacissimi.

11 ¶Ite. Cur Papa cui9 opes hodie sunt opuletissimis crassis crassiores: no de suis pecunijs magis q paupu fideliu struit vnà tmmo Basilicà sancti Petri.

12 ¶Item. Quid remittit aut participat Papa iis: qui p ptritione pfectaz ius habet plenarie remissionis et participationis.

13 ¶Item. Quid adderet ecclie boni maioris. Si Papa sicut semel facit: ita centies in die cuilibz fideliu has remissiones z pticipatioes tribuet.

14 ¶Ex quo Papa salute querit aiax: p venias magis q pecunias. Cur suspendit lras et venias iam olim pcessas: cu sint eque efficaces.

15 ¶Hec scrupulosissima laicox argumeta: sola ptate opescere: nec reddita ratione diluere. Est ecclesiam z Papà hostib9 ridendos exponere et infelices christianos facere.

16 ¶Si ergo venie fm spiritu et mente Pape pdicarentur: facile illa omnia soluerent: immo no essent.

17 ¶Valeat itaq oes illi pphe: q dicut ppfo Chri. Pax pax. et no est pax.

18 ¶Bn agat oes illi pphe: q dicut ppfo Chri. Crux crux. et non est crux.

19 ¶Exhortandi sunt Christiani: vt caput suu chrm per penas: mortes: infernosq sequi studeant.

20 ¶Ac si magis p multas tribulatioes intrare celu: q p securitate pacis confidant.

M.D.Xvij.
1517

Contemporary Placard of Luther's Famous Theses

The Castle Church in Wittenberg, in 1509

The Castle Church Door at Wittenberg

The famous church door upon which Luther posted his Ninety-Five Theses. Reconstructed in the nineteenth century. The Theses are reproduced.

The storm broke here. It had been declared only recently — before Luther's birth — by a pope that indulgences applied to Purgatory for both the living and the dead. The Church now claimed reduction of the time in Purgatory to those who availed themselves of the power of indulgences. The Castle Church of Wittenberg was given the privilege of dispensing indulgences. The first of November, the day of All Saints, was selected for the proclamation. Here were displayed some five thousand relics which Frederick the Wise had gathered to make it a special shrine.

Before 1517 Luther spoke up, questioning the indulgences practice. The traffic in indulgences was a source of revenue for the Church and the University.

The University Town of Wittenberg, 1550

Interior of the Castle Church in Wittenberg

The oldest known picture, from the eighteenth century.

Pope Leo X

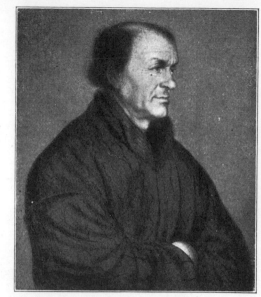

Printer Johann Froben

Johann Froben, besides printing the Ninety-Five Theses and other Luther writings, had in 1516 brought out Erasmus' New Testament in Greek. Luther was greatly influenced by this translation.

Printers risked not only their business but even their lives by undertaking the publication of the writings of heretics.

Informed of Luther's challenge and disturbance in Wittenberg (a copy of the Theses having been sent him by Albert of Mainz), Pope Leo is supposed to have made two comments: "Luther is a drunken German. He will feel different when he is sober." "Friar Martin is a brilliant chap. The whole row is due to the envy of the monks."

Leo X was a weak, indolent pope, interested in sports and in accumulating resources which he in turn squandered. His intent to complete the building of the new St. Peter's brought on the indulgences excesses, the revenues of which were to be the means of paying off debts and financing the St. Peter's project.

Luther's Theses and Reform Bring on a Violent Reaction of the Vested Interests
(A caricature from the early seventeenth century)

⟨Ein ſchöns tractetlein von dem
Götlichen/vñ römiſchen Ablas.vffs gegēwür-
tig Jübel ſar/yetzt zū Rom/gemacht durch
ein vngdärten Leyen. XVᶜ.XXV.

Johã.11.Herr ich glaub das du ſeyeſt Chriſtus desleberdigē gottes ſon.

Cartoon Depicting with Scales How Christ's Forgiveness Outweighs the Indulgences from the Pope

Eyn deutſch Theologia. das iſt
Eyn edles Buchleyn/von rechtem voiſtand/was
Adam vnd Chriſtus ſey/vnd wie Adam yn
vns ſterben/vnd Chriſtus erſteenſall.

Titel der von Luther 1518 herausgegebenen „Deutſchen Theologie".
(Weimarer Lutherausgabe 1, 376 A.)

A German Theology

Next to the Bible and St. Augustine, said Luther, an anonymous manuscript taught him more than any other writing. This he published in full with the above title in 1518. (The manuscript was issued by the Friends of God, in the late fourteenth century.) Some twenty different editions in German, and others in French and Latin, appeared in the sixteenth century. In 1621 it was declared a forbidden book by the Roman Church.

Georg Spalatin

In the days when Martin Luther had begun to disturb the peace of the Church, especially the hierarchy, Georg Spalatin served as an intermediary between Frederick the Wise and Luther. One significant result which Spalatin (died 1545), as court chaplain, helped to bring about was setting the hearing for Luther in Germany rather than at Rome. It would have been hopeless had Luther been forced to answer for himself in the precincts of the papal capital. Frederick's interests prevented his mingling directly with the German professor. Many of Luther's letters were directed to Spalatin, a trusted friend and counselor.

31

Cardinal Cajetan

Luther completely understood the warning that he would suffer some form of assassination by his enemies. He knew that a trip to Rome would be a one-way trip and he pressed his German protectors to prevent his summons to foreign parts. Even so, he traveled incognito to ecclesiastical meetings. After his Theses he began to write and circulate sermons in support of his reformatory views. Then Rome summoned him. Frederick the Wise, through Spalatin, negotiated with Cardinal Cajetan for Luther's appearance at a forthcoming diet in Augsburg — on German soil (1518).

Cajetan represented the Pope at the diet, having been instructed to secure Luther's recantation or to have him sent to Rome. After disputing with Cajetan over the merits of Christ as a treasure of indulgences and over the supremacy of the Pope to interpret Scripture, the meeting ended in a stalemate. Luther would not recant and Cajetan could not supersede the orders from headquarters. Cajetan would permit no lingering debate. With the connivance of friends, Luther left the city under the cover of darkness, knowing that the Cardinal had the authority and power to place the stubborn professor under arrest.

St. Ann's Church, Augsburg

This church, together with the cloister of the Carmelites, to which it belonged, was built in 1321. Jakob Fugger, the founder of the Fuggerei, and his brothers had a sepulcher chapel built in Renaissance style, consecrated in 1518 (the first Renaissance structure on German soil). In 1460 a great fire destroyed part of its convent. The church tower was built by Elias Holl in 1602.

When Luther was to defend his doctrines before Cardinal Cajetan, he stayed in the cloister of St. Ann's as the guest of the prior, Frosch (October 5-21, 1518). Frosch began to preach favorably on the Reformation — thus he was a pioneer at Augsburg.

In 1632 Gustavus Adolphus, King of Sweden, ordered his court chaplain, Fabricus, to hold a thanksgiving service in St. Ann's.

It is still a Protestant church.

Luther, the Undeterred German Professor, Standing Accused before Cardinal Cajetan, Representing the Pope

Johannes Eck

Luther in 1518

The name of Eck, of the University of Ingolstadt, is associated in Reformation history with the disputation in Leipzig in 1519. Dr. Eck represented the University of Leipzig, the rival of the University of Wittenberg. The former group supported the absolute claims of the papacy, the latter supporting Luther.

Carlstadt, Luther's senior, and Philip Melanchthon, young and promising colleague, were at Luther's side at Leipzig. Students and townspeople and learned doctors were in attendance. Pope Leo X had delayed dealing with Luther; Frederick the Wise had maneuvered to avoid sending Luther to Rome; Eck had challenged the Reformer; Luther had appealed to a council; it all added up to a public hearing.

Eck was an excellent debater and drew from Luther an admission that general councils could err in judgment (as one did in the case of Hus). Eck (who died in 1543) reported to Rome and Luther came away still farther removed in thought from his Mother Church.

The Leipzig Disputation

Scholars in the Sixteenth Century in a Disputation

The Coming of the Anti-Christ

The picture reveals the conception of Anti-Christ in the days of Martin Luther. Based on the Book of Revelation, it shows that before "the coming of the Messiah" there shall be an Anti-Messiah (a Jewish conception), accompanied by a horrible series of events. Two witnesses will testify for their faith (on the right in the pulpit) and suffer martyrdom. Michael the Archangel (at the top) smites the Anti-Christ with his sword. The Anti-Christ, with the Devil whispering in his ear, is beguiling the people (on the left). The Mount of Olives (in the center) is the place of Christ's ascension, from which the Anti-Christ is to be cast into an everlasting hell.

The idea of the Anti-Christ was popular in the Middle Ages. The followers of Wycliffe and Hus identified the evil popes as the Anti-Christ. Luther was pressed to say that the papacy itself was the Anti-Christ.

Cartoon Depicting Luther and Hus Serving Both Bread and Wine at Communion

Two of Luther's Primary Tracts, Published in 1520

On the left is the title page of his famous *The Babylonian Captivity,* and on the right that of his equally famous *The Freedom of the Christian Man.*

The first dealt with the sacraments, Luther claiming that the Scriptures authorized but two (instead of the traditional seven claimed by the Church). These two (baptism and the Lord's Supper) were instituted by Christ himself and were therefore valid. The attack here upon the Roman Church struck at the roots of its sacerdotal system and power.

The second pamphlet, issued late in the same year, asserted a fundamental principle of the Reformation: the priesthood of all believers. He said also in this tract that "Good works do not make a man good, but a good man does good works." A Christian becomes "a sort of Christ" to his fellow men even as "Christ gave himself for me."

Luther in 1520

Bulla contra errores Martini Lutheri z sequacium.

The Pope Acts Against Luther

The Seal of Pope Leo X

The Pope was pressed by Luther's enemies to bring condemnation. The universities of Cologne and Louvain pressed for action. Eck had given his Leipzig report. There were, however, complications. Frederick the Wise and even the Catholic vicar, Staupitz, stood off the threats of Rome against Luther. The Pope himself had other interests and why bother about the quarrels of German monks? Moreover, politics in that day were extremely delicate. And what charges should be leveled against this Martin Luther? Should he have another hearing? Should he only be warned? The Pope's advisers could not settle upon a unanimous opinion.

Finally Pope Leo issued the ban (known by its opening words, *"Exsurge Domine"*). Dated June 15, 1520, it gave Luther sixty days to capitulate. It took until October before Luther received the official notice.

The papal bull opened with these words: "Arise, O Lord, and judge Thy cause. A wild boar has invaded Thy vineyard."

Luther's Address to the German Nobility

Hieronymus Aleander

Along with John Eck, Hieronymus Aleander, a humanist and a former rector of the University of Paris, was assigned as a special inquisitor in securing the execution of the papal bull. Aleander pressed his assignment vigorously, appealing to the Holy Roman Emperor to bring the Reformer to punitive justice and protect the honor of the papacy. However, he had no easy time with his planned bonfire of Luther's books — the situation in Germany being unfavorable to easy conformity. The Edict of Worms was prepared by Aleander.

When it did not avail to appeal to Rome or to an ecclesiastical council, Luther turned to his countrymen. The nobility, from the emperor to the magistrates, were urged to protect their citizens against ecclesiastical powers. It was a daring move. There must be a thorough housecleaning from top to bottom, Luther counseled. The Church is corrupt and has made extravagant claims. Charles V was appealed to: "I appeal to Caesar . . . I ask that neither truth nor error be condemned unheard and unrefuted."

This was less a theological work than a folk appeal involving Germany as a nation. The issue was political as well as religious.

Ulrich von Hutten's Protest Against the Burning of Luther's Books at Mainz

Title page of a pamphlet, *ca.* 1520-1521.

Emperor Charles V

Charles V, Emperor of the Holy Roman Empire, occupied with a war in Spain, did not take an early hand in the current German uproar. Frederick the Wise was the key figure. When he returned, the papacy pressed him for action against Luther. Said Luther: "Would that Charles were a man and would fight for Christ against these Satans."

With pressures from both sides and vacillating in his decision, Charles finally declared that Luther should be given a hearing at a diet to be held in Worms. Reversing this order and under conflicting pressures, he renewed his command. Said Luther: "I will enter Worms under the banner of Christ against the gates of hell."

Luther as Hercules

A cartoon (*ca.* 1520) in which Luther is pictured as the German Hercules. The Pope is pictured as suspended from Luther's nose. An inquisitor is in his hand. The Devil disguised as a monk is fleeing (on the left). Luther is hammering away at such ancient and medieval stalwarts as Aristotle, Peter Lombard, St. Thomas, Duns Scotus and others — all at his feet.

Luther Burns the Papal Bull

When Luther's books were publicly burned, he retaliated by issuing an invitation to the Wittenberg faculty and students to assemble for a public burning of the canon law, scholastic books and the papal bull. "Since they have burned my books, I burn theirs." This was on December 10 in the year of the issue of the bull and at the completion of the sixty days granted for his submission to the Pope.

Luther, with a Dove Above His Head
(A cartoon of 1521)

Er hat funden ym tēpell vorkauffer/schaff/ ochßen vñ tawben
vñ wechsler sitzen/vñ hat gleich ein geyssel gemacht vō stricke
alle schaff/ochßen / taußē vñ wechßler außem tempell trieben/
das gelt verschüt/die zall biedt vmkart vñ zu den die tawben
no...ffen t...chen / ...euch h...mit di...en auf...ing

Hie sitzt der Antichrist ym tempell gots vñ erzeygt sich alß got
wie Paul⁹ vorkundet 2. Thessal 2. vorandert alle gotlich ord=
nung wie Daniel sagt vnnd vntherdruckt die heylig schrifft /
vorkeufft dispensacion/ Ablas pallia Bißthumb lehen/ erheßt
...o.h...../ ß...... T...d.... ...esch....die ...... Tant

Christ vs. Anti-Christ

A Reformation pamphlet. A wood engraving of 1521. Christ driving the money vendors, the Pope welcoming them.

Luther Before his Adversary Champions the Cause of the Reformation
(A cartoon of the times)

Luther at Worms (1521)

Two thousand persons followed the monk to his place of lodging at Worms. His popularity was enormous.

Before the Emperor and the princes of the Church and domains he stood in defense of himself. Another Eck plied him with questions, which Luther skillfully parried. He was termed a new Wycliffe and another Hus. Pressed for a simple answer, the famous reply came forth: "Since then Your Majesty and your lordships desire a simple reply, I will answer without horns and without teeth. Unless I am convicted by Scripture and plain reason — I do not accept the authority of popes and councils, for they have contradicted each other — my conscience is captive to the Word of God. I cannot and I will not recant anything, for to go against conscience is neither right nor safe. God help me. Amen."

When the printed reports came out, Luther was said to have exclaimed: "Here I stand, I cannot do otherwise."

Luther at Worms (1521)

Luther spoke in German first and then, by request, in Latin. On the second day of the hearing a large hall was engaged to accommodate the crowds.

The following day the report circulated that Luther had been declared a heretic. The Emperor so did declare first and then the majority of the electors ratified the royal opinion.

"I will have no more to do with him," said the Emperor. "He may return under his safe conduct, but without preaching or making any tumult. I will proceed against him as a notorious heretic."

The City of Worms as Drawn in 1574

The Luther Gate, Worms

Among the many Luther legends, the Luther Gate in the wall which surrounded Worms is the place through which Luther is supposed to have entered the city for his hearing and from which he departed in the darkness of night.

The Luther Monument in Worms

An imposing monument consisting of twelve statues, all over life-size. The Luther statue, standing in the center, depicts his witnessing in Worms. Erected in 1868 and designed by E. Rietschl. Among the figures surrounding him are those of Johann Reuchlin, Philip Melanchthon, Hus, Savanarola, Waldus, Wycliffe, Frederick the Wise and Philip of Hesse. There are twenty-four coats-of-arms representing "states," and statues symbolizing the towns of Speyer, Augsburg and Magdeburg.

The Plaque at Worms

This plaque modestly stands today, amidst the ruins of a recent war, not far from the cathedral.

The Cathedral at Worms

As it appears in modern times (before war damages), situated not far from the place where the diet was held.

Luther with Four of His Supporters

To the extreme left is Elector Frederick the Wise, prince in Luther's own Saxony. Working behind the scenes, Frederick sought to give his subject impartial hearings. After Luther's trial and defense at Worms, where he was put under the ban, Luther was taken captive by what turned out to be friends and hustled to Frederick's castle, the Wartburg, where he was put in secret retirement under Frederick's protection.

Pictured to the right of Frederick is Philip of Hesse, a young and politically minded leader who was so anxious to demonstrate his new loyalty to the Protestant faith that at the Diet of Speyer (1526) he ate forbidden meat on a Friday. He took a leading part in crushing the Peasants' Revolt in 1525. It was he who sought to bring Luther and Zwingli together, arranging for the famous meeting at Marburg in 1529.

Pictured to the far right is Ulrich von Hutten, a humanist, a knight and a hopeful nationalist in the days before German unification, who issued tirades against Roman imperialism and helped to champion Luther's cause. Said he, voicing a typical statement to arouse the public: "Everything could be had at Rome for money and nothing could be had there without it!"

To the right of Luther is Philip Melanchthon, Luther's right-hand man. It was he who drafted the Augsburg Confession. Luther was not present at the Diet of Augsburg in 1530 because he was under the ban of the Empire.

At the upper left corner of the picture is the Augustinian monastery at Erfurt. At the age of twenty-two Luther had vowed he would become a monk if spared death in a violent encounter with lightning in a thunderstorm.

At the upper right corner is Luther's Wartburg Castle room. At Wartburg Luther translated the entire New Testament from the original Greek into idiomatic German.

At the lower left corner, the Castle Church in Wittenberg, where Luther posted his Ninety-Five Theses for debate when the issue of indulgences had irked him to protest. The beginning of the Protestant Reformation is by many dated October 31, 1517, with this act of challenge.

At the lower right is the Luther study at Wittenberg. In 1508, as a priest of the Roman Church, he was transferred to the new University of Wittenberg, later becoming a professor of theology there.

45

Franz von Sickingen

Franz von Sickingen, a representative of German nationalism (along with Ulrich von Hutten), played a significant role in the cause of Luther's Reformation. He championed the poor and oppressed, even though he himself lived a privileged life (his castle was called the Ebernburg). He would go to arms to defend Luther, if called upon. He could have checked the Emperor had occasion demanded, since he controlled with might the valley of the Rhine. Luther dedicated one of his tracts to him.

Luther as Squire George
(A cartoon)

Luther called his exile at the Wartburg Castle "the Isle of Patmos." There he suffered loneliness, depression, insomnia and physical illness. He dressed as a knight and grew a full beard. Here he wrote many treatises, including a German vernacular of the New Testament which remains in use to this day. He returned to Wittenberg, after almost a year, in March, 1522.

Wartburg Castle

At the Wartburg Luther Works on the Translation of the New Testament

The Rioting Mob on Luther's Return to Wittenberg

When Luther returned to Wittenberg from the castle at Wartburg, he was incensed to find Frederick's relics still testifying to papal and court favors and to religious externals. Yet he shuddered to witness the destruction and abuse which had been heaped upon holy symbols and servants of the Church by students and townspeople. Revolution and iconoclasm were in the air. Freedom for the masses meant unbridled license. Priests had been driven from the parish church; statues had been broken; altars overturned. "Preach, pray, but do not fight," Luther exclaimed. Carlstadt had instituted reforms of worship, reforms extreme in nature. "Such haste and violence [against abuses of the Church]," said Luther, "betray a lack of confidence in God."

This painting depicts a rioting mob in the church sanctuary, with Luther calling a halt.

47

Thomas Münzer

The Revolt of Sectarians

Sectarians arose to plague Luther. They stressed an inward freedom and an external emancipation from all aids, such as music, sacraments, segregation — a restitution of primitive simplicity. Carlstadt had paved the way in Wittenberg. Thomas Münzer, who came from Zwickau, was more radical: he would abolish the whole of tradition and rely on the Spirit. Thousands flocked to his preaching in Alstedt. Iconoclasm was encouraged. Against all this, Luther, the conservative reformer, spoke out roughly.

A portrait of Thomas Münzer.

The Peasants' War

The peasants' uprising brought horror to Luther. Concentrated in the *Bundschuh* (the leather shoe worn by the peasants being the symbol of the revolt), these rebels attacked the government and priests, not the Roman Church. The peasants had been fomenting for years against taxes and civil infringements on their way of life. The upheaval came in 1524-1525.

Luther was regarded as their liberator. When by the Edict of Worms Lutheran ministers were arrested, the Bund moved in to their defense. Both Catholics and Protestants shared membership in the revolt. Luther cautioned against violence, but the peasants continued to plunder cloisters. Münzer's aggressive actions helped to fan the rebellion and provoked Luther the more.

When the situation was getting out of hand, Luther issued his famous tract, *Against the Murderous and Thieving*

Andreas Carlstadt

Professor and Luther's elder at Wittenberg. In 1521 he celebrated Mass officiating in plain clothes and omitting reference to sacrifice in the traditional liturgy. He gave the words of institution at the Lord's Supper in German and distributed both wine and bread to the communicants, passing the elements into their hands. He married a very young girl, asserting that priests should raise families. His reforms grew more radical when he left his professorship and assumed a parish.

Hordes of Peasants. Meanwhile, he counseled the princes to fight and stop the rebellion. "Let everyone who can, smite, slay and stab, secretly or openly, remembering that nothing can be more poisonous, hurtful or devilish than a rebel."

In the battle against them some five thousand were slain and Münzer was later taken captive, tortured and beheaded. The princes had moved in.

Luther's defense of government against the revolting *hoi polloi* brought him censure by both Catholics and his own followers. It was one of his darkest hours.

Pictured here is the pledging of allegiance to the Bund.

48

Three Peasants

The Peasants in Struggle with Soldiers

A Battle with the Peasants

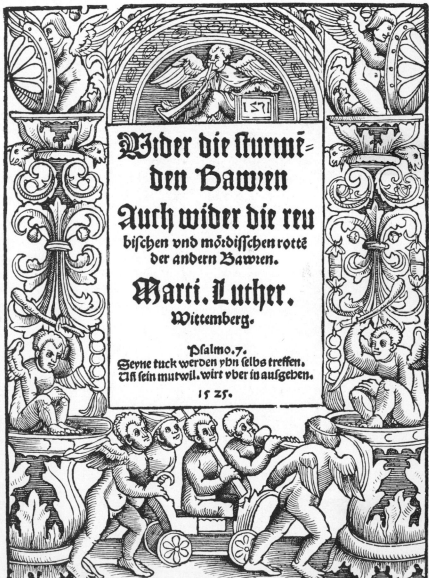

Luther's Tract Against the Violent Peasants (1525)

Von dem grossen
Lutherischen Narren wie in
docto: Murner beschworen hat.꙼.

*Cartoon Picturing the Reformer, "the Lutheran Fool,"
Being Attacked by Murner Dressed with the Cat Head*

This cartoon is a counterblast against Luther's own blast.

Singing Students

Luther had a strong bent for music. He played the lute and sang lustily. "Music," he said, "drives away the Devil and makes people gay; they forget thereby all wrath, unchastity, arrogance and the like. Next after theology I give to music the highest place and the greatest honor." The Devil, he thought, hated music because it led to gaiety.

In this respect he was in the spirit of the humanists of his time, for whom music was a part of formal instruction (as pictured).

The First Evangelical Hymnal

In 1524 Luther published a hymn book, pictured here in its title and first pages.

Lutherans took up singing with enthusiasm. After "catechism" singing followed in the family circle. Congregations, encouraged by Luther (who wrote both lyrics and music), came together during the week for rehearsals.

The Famous Battle Hymn of the Reformation by Luther

"A Mighty Fortress Is Our God," in Luther's handwriting. Based on the Vulgate version of the Forty-sixth Psalm, it was composed by him in the period of deep depression and appeared in a later hymn book.

51

Luther, the Groom, and Katherina von Bora, the Bride

"Good heavens! Monks too? They'll never give me a wife," exclaimed Luther when he learned at the Wartburg of monks getting married. He helped some nuns escape their convents, for whom he felt responsible to find homes and husbands. Katherina was one among those whom he helped and her eyes were set on Luther. Luther was not infatuated but did later propose marriage. "I would not exchange Katie for France or for Venice," he came to remark, "because God has given her to me and other women have worse faults."

In this marriage (1525) he claimed to have pleased his own father, to have brought spite to the Pope and the Devil, and to have given testimony to his Reformed faith before his expected martyrdom. One letter of invitation to a friend to come to his wedding read: "I am to be married on Thursday. My lord Katie and I invite you to send a barrel of the best Torgau beer, and if it is not good, you will have to drink it all yourself."

A banquet in the Augustinian cloister followed the ceremony in the parish church in Wittenberg, and then a dance in the town hall, followed by another dinner.

The Luther Family

The Luther home — Protestant parsonage, we would say now — turned out, in many respects, ideally. There was hospitality, laughter, mutual consolation, serious discussion, storytelling, six children and four orphans.

One of the most trying experiences was the death of his little daughter Magdalene (pictured here), who passed away in her early teens. Said Luther as she was buried: *"Du*

Liebes Lenichen, you will rise and shine like the stars and the sun. How strange it is to know that she is at peace and all is well, and yet to be so sorrowful."

Luther and His Children

He played and sang with his children, telling them fairy stories (of his own), writing to them in childish language when he was away from home, and composed songs for them (one of which, a Christmas carol, is still sung by children of today).

Luther in the Circle of His Family and Guests

The Luther household was also a home for transient guests — sometimes the number at table and overnight being as many as twenty-five.

After his death students issued a volume entitled *Table Talk,* in which Luther table conversations were recorded, ranging from God, the pope and end of the world to dogs, Noah, monks, politics, pregnancies, printing and many other subjects.

Luther possessed a mug with three rings around it, representing, he said, the Ten Commandments, the Apostles' Creed and the Lord's Prayer. He once bragged that he could drain it through the Lord's Prayer (outdoing some of his friends).

Luther's Catechisms

In 1529 Luther wrote his two Catechisms, the Large one for adults and the Small one for children.

These productions were meant for home use in particular. With these Catechisms were included lively Biblical illustrations. Once a week, it was recommended, fathers should conduct an examination of their children on the Catechism. Likewise of the servants.

Pictured here is the title page of Luther's Small Catechism.

Title Page of Luther's Large Catechism
(1529)

The Diet of Speyer, 1529

The name "Protestant" is usually dated from the occasion of this diet, which pronounced against Protestant freedom and gave bishops the right to depose preachers at will. The protestors appealed to a previous diet declaration: "In matters concerning God's honor and the salvation of soul each one must for himself stand before God and give account."

A drawing of the Elector of Saxony reading the protest at the Diet of Speyer.

Cartoon of Luther as a Seven-Headed Monster (1529)

One head symbolizes a fanatic with wasps in his hair.

Luther and Zwingli

At the famous conference in Marburg, 1529, matters of theology were discussed face to face by two of the leading Protestant leaders, the German Luther and the Swiss Zwingli. A surprising amount of agreement was found to exist. It was around the doctrine of the Lord's Supper that the chief dispute centered. How close they were: Luther insisted on the real presence of Christ in the Supper and agreed that the sacrament is of no value apart from the recipient's faith; Zwingli held the Lord's Supper to be a memorial, but conceded that there is a spiritual communion with Christ in its celebration. The Lutheran and Swiss Reformed theologians could not agree on a formula, and because of this the Swiss suggested a fraternal practice of intercommunion. It was Luther, egged on by Melanchthon, who stood aloof from reconciliation.

The issue was more than theology. There were underlying and important political alliances at stake. The split here was a major schism in Protestantism.

Marburg

Overlooking the capital city, its towers and the river, stood Philip of Hesse's picturesque castle, within which was held the famous conference of German and Swiss theologians. Philip hoped for a strong Protestant alliance and a common confession. The conference failed to unite on doctrine and no military alliance resulted.

Lutherans and Reformed Protestants went their separate ways, even though the leaders (Luther, Zwingli and others) had met face to face in an attempt at reconciliation.

The Old University Building at Basel, Switzerland

Basel has been the center of much culture. There Erasmus took up residence, and now lies buried in its old cathedral. At Basel the printer John Froben issued in a single edition the Ninety-Five Theses and other works of Luther, bringing the German Reformer to international attention.

In 1529 Basel became linked to the side of the Reformation. Representing Basel at the famous Conference of Marburg was Johannes Oecolampadius.

Martin Bucer

Bucer (1491-1551) was a leader in Strasbourg (later a theological professor at Cambridge, England). His role was that of a mediator between the Swiss and the Lutherans. He was completely dedicated to throwing off the power of the pope. The Scriptures were the final arbiter of doctrinal dispute. Predestination, he held, assures of salvation and it is proper for God to make elections.

Johann Oecolampadius

Swiss Reformer in Basel, a friend of both Erasmus and Zwingli, Oecolampadius (1482-1531) was a vigorous participant in the Marburg Conference. In the Lord's Supper he held "This is my *body*" means a *sign* (soma, sign).

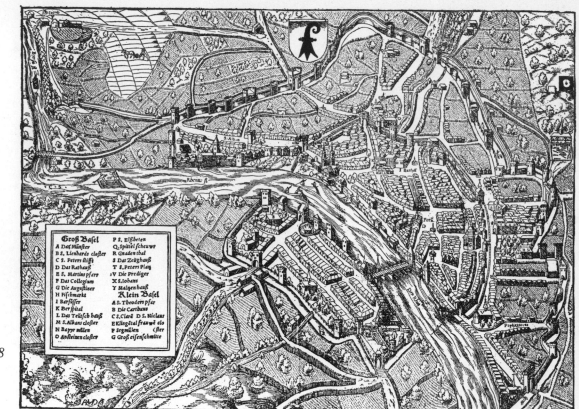

Basel in 1558

DESIDERIUS ERASMUS

Born in Rotterdam in 1466, Erasmus was apparently an illegitimate son, his father probably a priest. (His real name: Gerard Gerardson.) He early acquired a knowledge of Latin and much later the then less well-known Greek. Eight rather miserable years he spent in a monastery, becoming an Augustinian monk — a calling not of his own choosing. His restless spirit demanded freedom and he turned from his restricted life to university studies and intellectual companionship. John Colet (later Dean of St. Paul's) and Thomas More (future Lord Chancellor of England) were his close friends. His lifework, he came to see, was to rescue theology from outmoded medieval ideas. To achieve this, he gave himself to New Testament studies in Greek. From Cambridge he received his Bachelor of Divinity degree; from Turin his Doctor's degree. In Rome he was welcomed (in 1509) as an equal by its greatest scholars.

His *Adagia,* a collection of quotations from the classics, to aid scholars who desired to write well in Latin, was widely acclaimed and ran into sixty editions. His most famous Work, *Praise of Folly,* a satire on ignorance, stupidity and superstition, dealt wittily with the failings of men of all classes, including churchmen. Provocatively interesting, this work had considerable influence on the Reformation.

Cambridge still boasts of its "Erasmus· Tower," a turret in Queen's College where he lived while a tutor. There he began his work on the Christian Fathers and the Greek text of the New Testament for which he became increasingly famous.

His desire was to translate the New Testament in a manner for the layman's understanding and expressed the wish that it be translated into all tongues — to show by sound learning and common sense that the Church had departed from its real foundations.

Bitter feelings arose between him and his famous contemporary, Martin Luther. He kept his own course, unwilling to agree with the right of private judgment as over against obedience to the authority of the Church, holding that reforms must come *from within,* through knowledge and not under passion.

The remaining score of years were spent in Basel.

The year before his death the Pope offered him the rank of cardinal, which he refused. He died in 1536 and lies buried in the cathedral at Basel.

Desiderius Erasmus

A portrait by Hans Holbein. The works of Erasmus in the 1530's were placed upon the Index by the Mother Church.

A Note Written by Erasmus Within Six Weeks of His Death (1536) to a Merchant of Antwerp

A specimen of the handwriting of the period, with nearly all the letters of the Latin alphabet contained therein. Many abbreviations occur, usually at the end of words (sometimes in the middle).

The signature is *"Erasmus Rot aegra manu."*

An Hourglass Used by Erasmus

The use of this sort of timer dates back to the eighth century. Since the sixteenth century these hourglasses have been used in churches to limit the length of sermons. It is common to see such glasses mounted on pulpits in contemporary Protestant churches in Europe.

The Imperial Diet of Augsburg, 1530

Political considerations were fundamental to the calling of this diet. It was hoped that Lutheranism and Catholicism could come to some understanding. The Augsburg Confession was presenting the Reformers' views in the most acceptable form to the Mother Church. Justification by faith was stressed. The doctrine of transsubstantiation was denied. It was a confession of princes rather than theologians.

Today there is but a small and simple marker to call to remembrance this historic place. The marker is inscribed "Confessio Augustana," on the residence of the former bishop's palace, where the Confession was solemnly and publicly proclaimed by the civil powers to the assembled townspeople.

SI·DEVS·PRO·NOBIS· ·QVIS·CONTRA·NOS·

PLVRIMA·QVI·RELEGIS·DOCTI·MONVMENTA·PHILIPPI·
ILLIVS·HIC·ETIAM·QVÆ·SIT·IMAGO·VIDES·
LVSTRA·NOVÉ·VITÆ·DEMPTIS·TRIBVS·EGERAT·ANNIS·
TALIS·VBI·VVLTV·CONSPICIENDVS·ERAT·
PHILIPPVS·MELANTHON·
·M·D·XXXX·

IACTA ... IPSETE ENVTRIET·

ASSERVIT·CHRISTVM·DIVINA·VOSE·LVTHERVS·
CVLTIBVS·OPPRESSAM·RESTITVITQVE·FIDEM·
ILLIVS·ABSENTIS·VVLTV·HÆC·DEPINGIT·IMAGO·
PRÆSENTE·MELIVS·CERNERE·NEMO·POTEST·
MARTINVS· LVTHERVS·
·M·D·XXXX·

The Two Chief Reformers, Melanchthon Who Authored the First Protestant Confession, the Augsburg Confession of June 25, 1530, and Luther Who Gave His Approval

Lutheranism, by the Augsburg Confession, became a united front and set Protestantism distinctly over against Catholicism. The power of the Holy Roman Empire was broken at Augsburg.

The pictures are dated ten years later.

A Picture (1630) Commemorating the Augsburg Confession *(1530)*

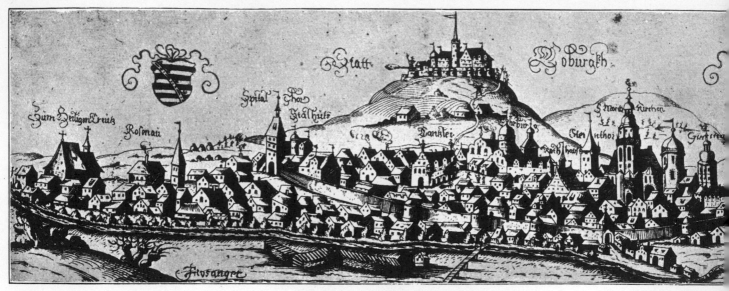

The City of Coburg

At the Castle of Coburg, Luther, under the ban, was held prisoner for six months (1530). From there he directed the cause of the Reformation, and turned to a further study of the Scriptures. The Reformation proceeded without his presence — even at Augsburg.

Two Worship Services Contrasted — The Reformers vs. the Catholics
(A cartoon)

On the left, a girl reads the Scriptures while listening to the Evangelical preacher. There is reverent attention on the part of the assembled.

On the right, a Catholic priest exhorts but the people are busy with their beads.

In the middle an elderly man points to both congregations.

The Castle of Coburg

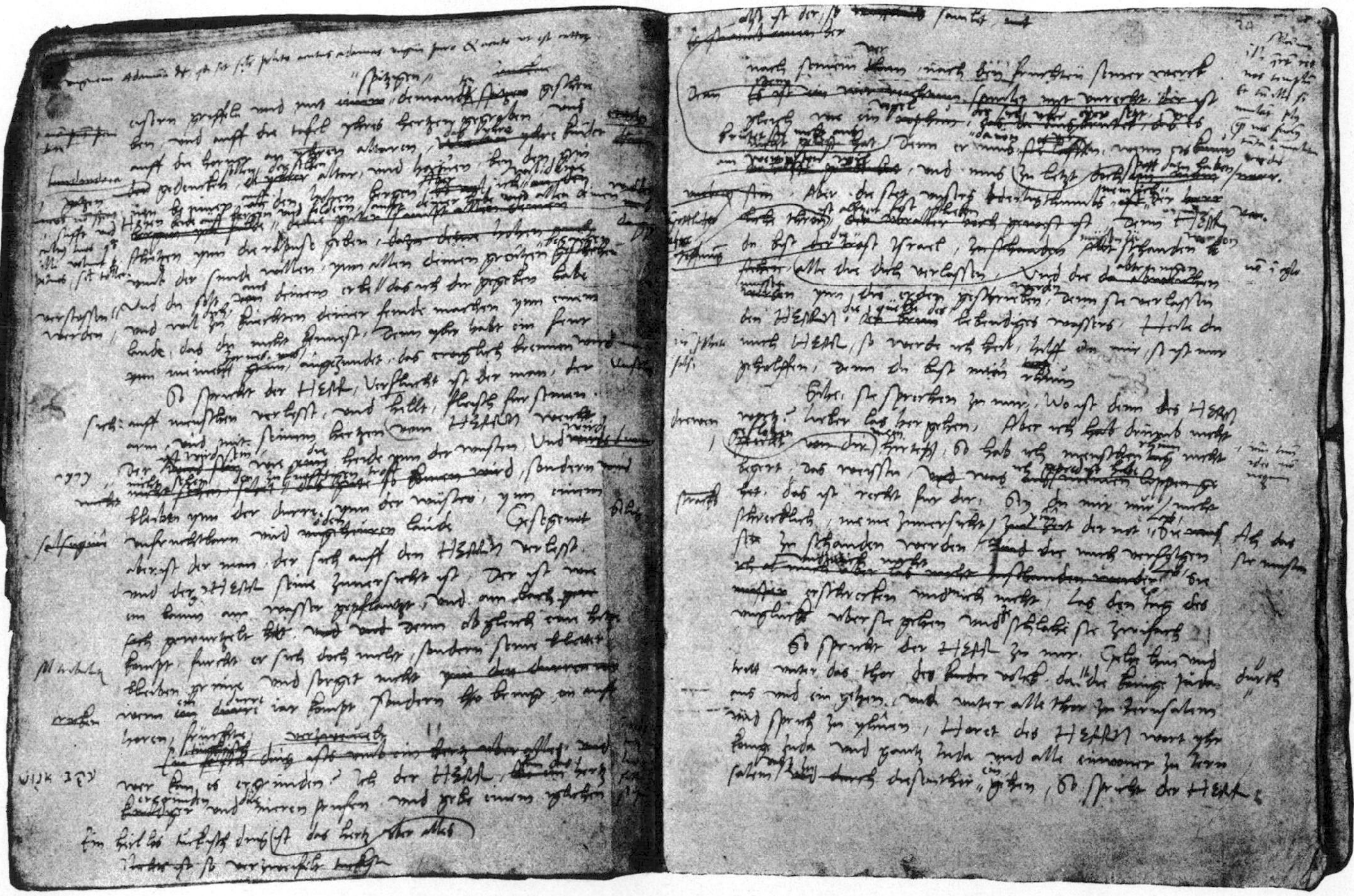

Luther's Translation of the Bible

The whole of the New Testament Luther completed while a captive in Wartburg Castle. His New Testament was first published in 1522 but he continued the work of revision until his death.

The Old Testament he began work upon after leaving Wartburg. By 1534 the entire Bible was completed (with the help of others) in German translation. "I endeavored," he said, speaking of his manner of translation, "to make Moses so German that no one would suspect he was a Jew."

The Luther Bibles (not the first translation of the Scriptures into German) contained many illustrations.

Here is a two-page copy of his written translation of a portion of Jeremiah.

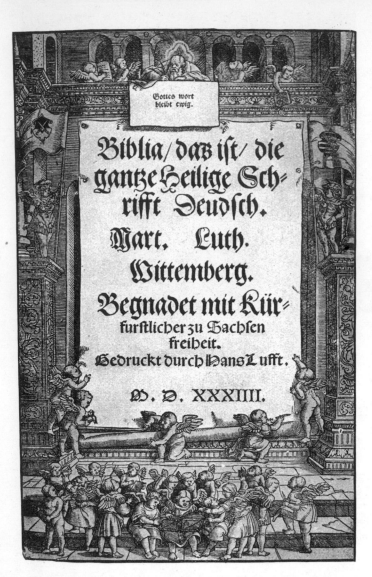

The Luther Bible

The first picture is the title page of the Luther translation, edition of 1534. The second is from the same edition, showing the First Book of Moses.

Luther's Handwriting

64

Hans Holbein

A self-portrait by the famous cartoonist and portrait painter of the Reformation period.

Lucas Cranach, the Painter

Lucas Cranach, artist and banker, has furnished posterity with many valuable illustrations from the days of Luther. Above is a self-portrait.

Eisleben — The House Where Luther Died (1546)

Luther's Last Great Blast Against the Papacy (1545)

Luther became increasingly bitter against the papacy as the years went on. Here pictured is the pope being swallowed up in hell, the Devil furiously at work.

The Reformers: Zwingli and Calvin

HVLDRYCHVS ZVINGLIVS
DVM PATRIÆ, QVÆRO PER DOGMATA SANCTA SALVTEM
INGRATO PATRIÆ GÆSVS AB ENSE CADO

OBIIT AÑO DÑI, M,D,XXXI, DCDOBX
ÆTATIS SVÆ XLVIII.

Ulrich Zwingli

One of the most influential reformers outside Germany, Zwingli was born in 1484 and died in 1531. A humanist in training and outlook, his point of view differed from that of Luther. He became a parish priest and a student of Greek, Hebrew and Church history. Especially did he apply himself to the study of the Scriptures.

In 1518 he became a priest at Zurich. He began his reform preaching in 1519, the date which marked the beginning of the German-Swiss Reformation. He began by attacking the Roman Church for its abuses, particularly fasting and celibacy. He protested a papal attack by producing 67 theses. When the City Council upheld him, the Reformation in his territory was sealed. With Luther he agreed in many respects. Political developments prompted him, as a Swiss patriot, to leadership in freeing his people from Catholic powers.

*The Zwingli House and
Its Environs*

Birthplace of Zwingli

Zwingli was born in the little parish of Wildhaus in the beautiful country of the Swiss Alps.

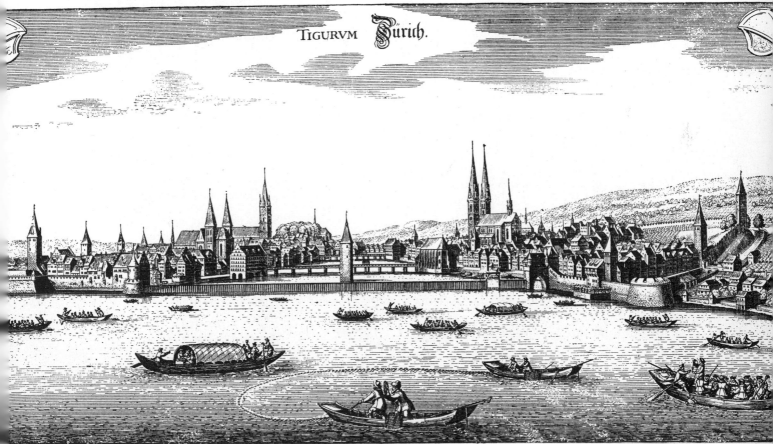

TIGURVM Zürich.

Zurich, the Center of the German-Swiss Reformation

Von erkiesen und fryheit der spysen. **Von ergernus vñ** verbösezung. Ob man gwalt hab die spysē zů etlichen zyten verbieten/ mey= nung Huldriché Zuing lis zů Zürich gepredi= get jm.M.D.XXII.Jar.

Christus Mathei.XI. Kümend zů mir alle die arbeitend vnd beladen sind/vnd ich wiluch rüw machen.

Deß walt Got:

Title Page of Zwingli's Tract on Freedom Concerning Food *(1521)*

Zwingli's Handwriting

In Zurich there was a union between church and democratic state. It was a form of theocracy, with the doctrine of election (predestination) as a religious tenet: Those who possess faith are of the elect. Catholics were barred from a share in the government. (Zwingli's debate with Luther at Marburg is elsewhere set down and pictured in this volume.) Neighboring Catholics and Swiss Protestants eyed each other suspiciously, and gave battle with each other. The Swiss were also suspicious of Lutherans, who seemed to them too Catholic. Zwingli was a passionate nationalist and believed in militarism to settle quarrels. In 1525 the Anabaptists, who renounced oaths and were pacifists, were made subject to the death penalty.

Zwingli was a Biblical preacher, departing from traditional selections and following the consecutive Greek text. Does the Bible prescribe image worship, fasting during Lent, celibacy?

On the question of eating during Lent, there were many in Zurich who flaunted the Catholic custom. Zwingli came to justify this freedom, in the tract pictured here.

In politically free Zurich there was a representative assembly which discussed and decided such questions. Zwingli sided with those who favored the abolishment of celibacy — there having been such prevalent violations of it by those who had taken vows. He opposed the iconoclasm which had arisen, and yet joined in recommending the abolition of many Catholic practices, such as the Mass and the use of images and liturgical accruements. Thus a kind of Puritanism ensued.

Herr Ulrich Zwingli leerbiechlein

wie man die Knaben Christlich vnterweysen
vnd erziehen soll / mit kurtzer anzayge
aynes gantzen Christlichen lebens.
M. D. xxiij

Zwingli's Little Manual of Christian Instruction for Youth,
Title Page (1524)

Zwingli wielded these weapons in the Kappel War, and in 1531 fell with sword in hand on the battlefield.

Monument to Zwingli Near Kappel, Erected in 1838

Monument to Ulrich Zwingli at Zurich

Heinrich Bullinger

Successor to Zwingli as the leader of the Reformation in Zurich after Zwingli's death, Bullinger (1504-1575) modified somewhat the views of his predecessor, being more conciliatory to the views of others. He had great ability as a preacher. He helped to bring about a better understanding with other Protestant leaders, participating in the Reformation cause in England. In 1566 he prepared the statement of faith known as the Second Helvetic Confession, which became widely adopted by the Continental Reformed Protestants and was translated into many languages. Calvin's views came to prevail over those of Zwingli.

(The First Helvetic Confession, 1536, a first Reformed statement, was an attempt to bring Lutherans and Zwinglians together. Bullinger, among its drafters, warned against making creeds more authoritative than the Bible.)

JOHN CALVIN

Born at Noyon, France, John Calvin (1509-1564) was a student from the start. His formal education was superior, at the University of Paris and at the famous law school of Orléans. He excelled in literary expression. Under the influence of humanism he wrote a commentary on Seneca (which was probably a veiled testimony of leniency toward Protestants). Under suspicion of leanings to Reformed views, he fled Paris and then experienced a new set of convictions which amounted to a conversion and dedication. By nature shy and stern, he was drawn to the life of a scholar, but circumstances brought him openly into the Protestant struggle.

Though young, he produced a work which became standard for the Reformed wing of Protestantism, his *Institutes*. It was Farel who enticed him to come to Geneva, Switzerland. Banished for a time from that city, he returned to assert more vigorous leadership. His marriage was brief.

His view of man was pessimistic: Man's intellect is vitiated and his morals depraved. Apart from revelation man cannot attain divine truth; apart from God's grace virtues are but vices. His whole thought revolves about the absolute sovereignty of God, who elects whom He wills to salvation and determines the destinies of all men (predestination). This is theocentrism. (Luther, in contrast, was Christocentric in emphasis.) God's chosen elect were first the Jews, and now a new Israel, the Christian Church. But the Church is not known to man and election can be known only by those through proper faith, with proper participation in the sacraments and in proper living. The latter is a strict Puritanism — no dancing, gambling, drunkenness, obscenity, card playing, theater participation, etc.

His passion was to set up a disciplined community in Geneva with the Church's commission asserting itself in state affairs and all committed to God in a covenant. A rigoristic regime was instituted and intolerance of opposition came to be the determined order. Punishment for offenders was made obligatory. The details of everyday life came under close scrutiny. The Council of Geneva even prohibited the traditional Catholic custom of giving to children the names of saints. The Old Testament had a better assortment to offer. All dissenters were requested to leave the city. Catholics were forbidden to hold office. Heretics were dealt with rigorously. Michael Servetus, anti-Trinitarian, an early acquaintance of Calvin's, refused to conform and by decree of Calvin's city suffered martyrdom. (Calvin himself defended the execution and his admirers have erected a monument [in 1903] to Servetus, charging Calvin with "an error which was that of his century.")

The influence of Calvin's thought and polity was enormous — overshadowing in many respects the freer and non-Puritanical views of his contemporary, Martin Luther.

John Calvin

Calvin's House in Noyon

72

Guillaume Farel

Farel (1489-1565) was a courageous reformer among the French Swiss, succeeding in 1535 in persuading the government in Geneva to adopt Protestantism and in enlisting John Calvin to help with the reforms in this center. In 1538 both Calvin and Farel were banished from this city, Farel spending his remaining years in Neuchâtel and Calvin returning by invitation to assume vigorous leadership again.

*Calvin and Farel, Reformation Leaders
in Geneva, Switzerland*

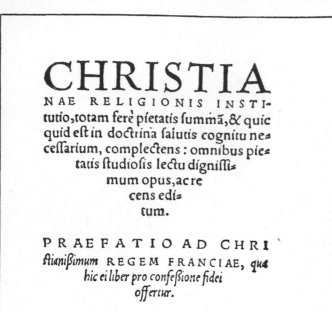

CHRISTIA

NAE RELIGIONIS INSTI-
tutio, totam ferè pietatis summā, & quic
quid est in doctrina salutis cognitu ne-
cessarium, complectens : omnibus pietatis studiosis lectu dignissi-
mum opus, ac re
cens edi-
tum.

PRAEFATIO AD CHRI
stianißimum REGEM FRANCIAE, qua
hic ei liber pro confessione fidei
offertur.

IOANNE CALVINO
Nouiodunensi autore.

BASILEAE,
M. D. XXXVI.

Title Page of the First Edition of Calvin's
Institutes of the Christian Religion (1536)

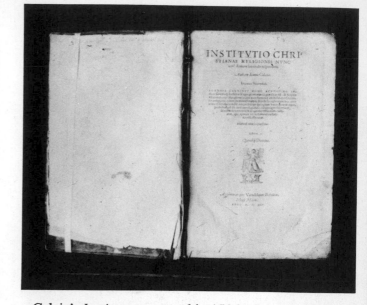

Calvin's *Institutes* appeared in 1536 when Calvin was in his twenty-seventh year. The work was subsequently enlarged and revised. It is regarded as "the clearest and most comprehensive statement of the Reformed faith produced during the Reformation," and is still a standard Protestant book.

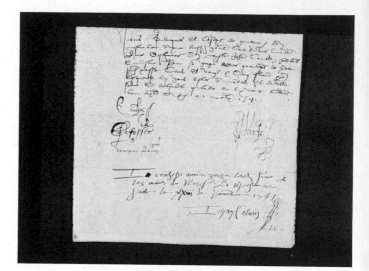

John Calvin's Signature

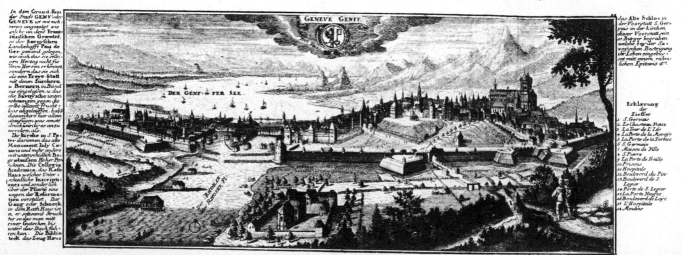

An Old View of Geneva

St. Peter's Cathedral, Geneva

When John Calvin, at twenty-seven, already famous by reason of his *Institutes,* came to Geneva, he found a church which had already adopted the Reformation principles. It lacked only organization and leadership. For thirty years Calvin preached in St. Peter's. Calvin was buried in the graveyard at Plainpalais as a simple citizen, requesting this place of burial without any stone marker. All that remains in St. Peter's which is peculiarly Calvin's is a chair on which he sat as he preached from the pulpit.

The cathedral dates from between 1160 and 1220. In Geneva citizens under the name *"amateurs de la Sainte Evangile"* gathered in the early sixteenth century to study the Bible — a popular movement. They welcomed French preachers, Farel among them. On May 21, 1536 the town council's action forbidding the Mass was confirmed and the Reformation had its birth in this citadel.

Pictured here is a painting by Lugardon of Calvin refusing the Lord's Supper to the libertines in St. Peter's Cathedral.

75

St. Peter's Cathedral as It Appeared in 1750

St. Peter's Cathedral as It Appears Today

Interior of St. Peter's Cathedral

In the foreground is Calvin's chair.

Psalm Set to Music from a Huguenot Psalter, Geneva, 1542

CHRISTIANI∙
SMI RESTITV∙
TIO.

Totius ecclesiæ apostolicæ est ad sua limina vocatio, in integrum restituta cognitione Dei, fidei Christi, iustificationis nostræ, regenerationis baptismi, et cœnæ domini manducationis. Restituto denique nobis regno, cælesti, Babylonis impia captiuitate soluta, et Antichristo cum suis penitus destructo.

בעת ההיא יעמוד מיכאל השר

καὶ ἐγένετο πόλεμος ἐν τῷ οὐρανῷ.

M. D. LIII.

Title and Page from Servetus' Restitution of Christianity
(1553)

734   APOLOGIA.

nima quædam, omnia in se contemplans, et lucide continens: mortalibus olim velata, et per Christum reuelata: quam et plerique dixerunt, fuisse ipsammet animam Christi. Sapientiam nos vere dicimus, instar animæ Christi, rationem diuinam de Christo, personalem Christi substantiam in Deo relucentem, et omnia continentem. In ea primaria luce esse reliqua omnia secundario relucentia, vt in anima tua relucent res aliæ, quæ sunt in ipsa. Vnde est anima nostra vera imago illius sapientiæ Dei, et ab ea vere reformatur. Nec solum dicimus, in sapientia Dei omnia relucere, sed et inde habere suum esse, ex inuisibilibus visibilia facta. Dicimus item, eam a Christo sapientiæ lucem, et in angelos, et in animas nostras se diffundentem, velut speculum lucidum, varias nobis et angelis rerum cognitiones dare. Atque ita quicquid angeli vaquam cognouerunt, a Christo acceperunt, sicut et nos. Benedictus ille sit in secula seculorum, qui sapientiam suam infundens, hanc de se nobis cognitionem dedit. Benedicti sint in ipso, qui ipsum vere credent esse filium Dei, ab æterno in Deo relucentem, et in æternum regnantem. Amen. Amen.

M. S. V.
1 5 5 3.

Theodore Beza

Calvin's successor at Geneva was Theodore Beza (1519-1605), a French refugee who had become a Protestant, a pupil and associate of Calvin. He was an eminent preacher, theologian and editor of a Greek New Testament. His position on predestination was extreme (supralapsarian), asserting that man's election or reprobation had been determined *before* the fall of Adam, as a part of the plan of salvation. He justified the execution of Servetus. Religious liberty, he said, is "a most diabolical dogma because it means that everyone should be left to go to hell in his own way" (not consistent, of course, with his own predestinarian views). The fortunes of the Reformed churches were directed by him for some forty years.

77

Monument to the Reformation at Geneva

Erected by international subscription. Begun in 1909 on the occasion of the four-hundredth anniversary of the birth of Calvin and dedicated in 1917.

The Central Panel of the Monument to the Reformation at Geneva

Left to right: Farel, Calvin, Beza, Knox.

The Mennonites

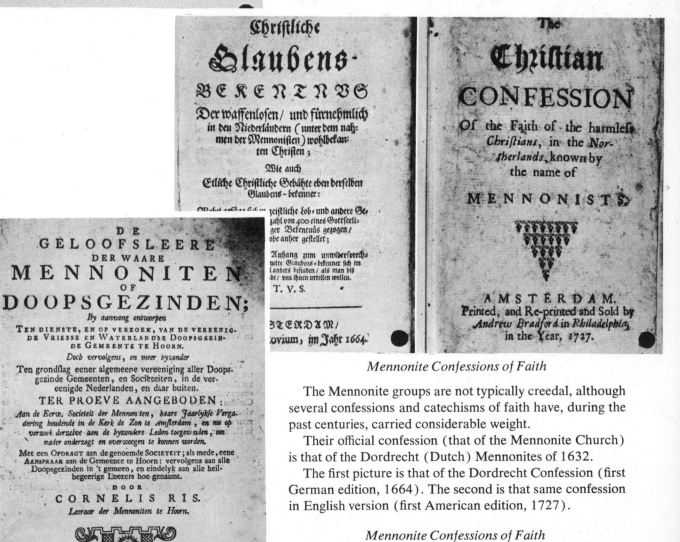

EUROPEAN MENNONITES

Mennonite Confessions of Faith

The Mennonites are of two independent origins, Swiss and Dutch. The Swiss group, at first called "Brethren," were nicknamed Anabaptists.

In 1525 the Swiss Mennonites were founded under the leadership of the young Zurich scholar, Conrad Grebel (*ca.* 1498-1526). Grebel was first a follower of Zwingli, but then broke with him, feeling that the Reformation was proceeding too mildly. Grebel insisted on separation of church and state, the abolition of infant baptism and an ethics of absolute love and thus opposition to militarism. The majority of this group of Mennonites live in the United States, east of the Mississippi and in Ontario, Canada.

The accompanying picture is that of the First Anabaptist Confession, the *Schleitheim Articles,* the creed of the "Brethren" (1527, edition of *ca.* 1560).

Mennonite Confessions of Faith

The Mennonite groups are not typically creedal, although several confessions and catechisms of faith have, during the past centuries, carried considerable weight.

Their official confession (that of the Mennonite Church) is that of the Dordrecht (Dutch) Mennonites of 1632.

The first picture is that of the Dordrecht Confession (first German edition, 1664). The second is that same confession in English version (first American edition, 1727).

Mennonite Confessions of Faith

The confession of the General Conference Mennonite Church was originally written by Cornelis Ris of Hoorn, Holland, in 1766.

"Zur Eintracht" House, Zurich, Switzerland, Home of Conrad Grebel, 1508-14 and 1520-25

Conrad Grebel (*ca.* 1498-1526) was one of the leading figures of the "Brethren." A follower of Zwingli, he withdrew in protest against the policy of the union of church and state.

Balthaser Hübmaier, Anabaptist Reformer (1480-1528)

A reformer in north Switzerland, influenced by the writings of Luther. He doubted infant baptism since it was not explicitly Scriptural, organized a large Anabaptist community, suffered persecution and fled to Moravia, where his movement met with great success.

Langnau Emmental

Langnau Emmental in Switzerland is probably the oldest congregation in the world. The Mennonites had their beginning in Switzerland in 1525. This structure dates from 1888.

Rathaus, Zurich, Switzerland, Where the Anabaptist-Zwinglian Debates of 1525 Were Held

Zurich, Switzerland

Scene of the first Mennonite martyrdom. Felix Manz was condemned to death in the fish market, the building that extends into the Limmat River on the left near the Gross Munster, Zwingli's church. He was then drowned in the river in the immediate foreground.

Passau Castle, Germany

Where the Anabaptist prisoners composed one part of the *Ausbund* (*ca.* 1535), the first Mennonite hymnal, still in use by the Old Order Amish.

AMERICAN MENNONITES

The Christian Herr House

The Christian Herr House (built in 1719), which is still standing, is the first building to have been used as a Mennonite meeting house in Lancaster County, Pennsylvania, the largest center of Mennonites in America.

Mennonite Meeting House, Germantown, Pennsylvania

The first Mennonite settlement in America was at Germantown, Pennsylvania. The picture is of the church (meeting house) built in this settlement (1770).

An Original European Edition of the Ausbund, *the Swiss Brethren Hymn Book of 1564*

Ephrata, Pennsylvania, Cloister Press, Where the
First American Edition of Martyrs' Mirror
Was Printed in 1748-1749
(Sketch by O. W. Schenk)

Conestoga, Pennsylvania, Pioneer Wagons,
Used in Westward Migrations
(Sketch by O. W. Schenk)

Martyrs' Mirror is one of the most famous Mennonite
books. It is a martyrology.

Immigrant House Interior Near Newton, Kansas. Russian Mennonites Arriving in 1874
(From Frank Leslie's Illustrated Newspaper, *New York, March 20, 1875)*

82

MENNONITE ART THEMES

Menno Simons *by Arend Hendricks (1948)*

Menno Simons *by C. van Sichem (1605)*

Menno Simons (1496-1561), a Roman Catholic priest, in 1536 united with the Obbenites (Dutch Mennonite brotherhood, founded by Obbe Philips in the years 1533-1534), and the Dutch group adopted the name "Mennist" or "Mennonist" in recognition of his leadership. The church took its name from this source.

Hans de Ries *by M. J. van Mierevelt (ca. 1630)*

The Arrest of the Martyr Anneken Jans, *from the Dutch* Martyrs' Mirror *(1685)*

The Martyrs David and Levina *by Jan Luiken, from the Dutch* Martyrs' Mirror *(1685)*

A Martyr Scene *by Jan Luiken, from the Dutch* Martyrs' Mirror *(1685)*

The Mennonite Church was born in martyrdom.

Famine in Russia *by J. P. Klassen (U.S.A., 1888———)*

Amish Family *by Arthur Sprunger (U.S.A., 1897———)*

Extreme traditionalists among the Mennonites, the Old Order Amish arose in Switzerland in 1693 under the leadership of Elder Jacob Ammann. This group began the practice of shunning (*Meidung*). Until the middle of the nineteenth century the Amish of America were basically one group. Thereafter progressives and conservatives each went their own way, the latter attempting to remain close to the manner of living and dress of 1700.

MENNONITE COSTUMES

Hutterite Family and House
(From C. Erhard's Historia, Munich, 1588)

The Hutterian Brethren or Hutterites were followers of Jacob Huter (d. 1536), Swiss Brethren minister. Strict disciplinarians and sharers of community goods, the Hutterites flourished in Moravia and, under steady persecution, fled to Rumania and Russia. Many Hutterites in America (settling in South Dakota) fled to Canada to avoid conscription in the World War.

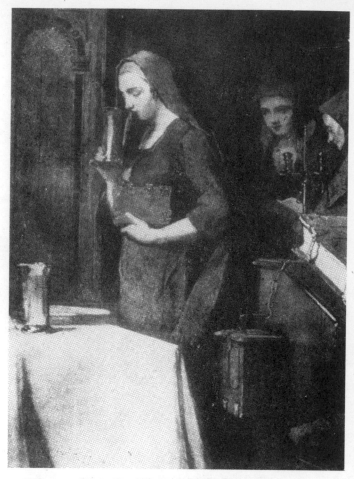

Woman of Friesland Taking Communion (ca. *1700*)

Anabaptist Preacher, Switzerland (ca. 1750)

Alsatian Amish Couple (ca. 1815) by Lewicki

Woman of Aalsmeer, Netherlands (ca. *1880*)

Lancaster Mennonite Woman (ca. *1830*)
by *Jacob Eichholtz (1776-1842)*

Two Amish Men (ca. 1950)

Several Types of Bonnets and Prayer Veilings

Lutheranism in Sweden, Norway, Denmark and Finland

The Church in Sweden separated from Rome in 1523 — before England had made the break and before the power of Calvinism had begun to be felt.

Olaus Petri (1493-1552) was the spiritual leader of the Reformation in Sweden. He trained at Leipzig and in Wittenberg at the time Luther began his protests. Along with Laurentius Andrae (*ca.* 1470-1552 — influential chancellor of Gustavus Vasa who helped to make royal power independent of papal power and superior to the power of the nobles), he introduced reforms in the Swedish Church and state. Petri was a literary figure whose work consisted of Bible translations, a Swedish hymn book, devotional literature and historical works.

A younger brother of Olavus, Laurentius Petri (1499-1573) became the first Lutheran archbishop of Sweden in 1531. He, too, was a literary figure.

The development of the Swedish Church followed the pattern of the Petris for generations. In 1593 it formally declared itself Lutheran.

In Denmark the Reformation was introduced as early as 1522. After a political struggle the Lutheran Church was established in 1536. Legislation on church matters became a matter of parliamentary action and royal approval. Denmark has other Protestant groups, although they are in a minority.

Norway, overwhelmingly Lutheran, was declared Protestant by the decree of a Danish-Norwegian king soon after the Reformation in Germany. From 1380 to 1814 Norway was joined to Denmark, and from 1814 to 1905 to Sweden. Björnson was the hero in its advance to independence. Church legislation remained in the hands of Parliament. Free churches, however, are permitted.

SWEDEN

Sigtuna

The quaint little village of Sigtuna, on an arm of Lake Mälaren (between Uppsala and Stockholm), is the oldest surviving town in Sweden, founded early in the eleventh century. It rose to become the foremost town in the land. Its ruined churches (Sweden's first cathedral being one of them) date from the eleventh century.

It is noted for its educational institutions. The Sigtuna Foundation (1917) is an Evangelical College, including a people's college, internationally known. The Scandinavian Ecumenical Institute is located here, in contact with the Protestant world movement.

Pictured here is the Rose Garden of the Sigtuna Foundation.

St. Per Ruins, Sigtuna, Sweden

The ruins of Sweden's first cathedral, built for defense.

Ruins of St. Lars, Sigtuna

These ruins attest to the former greatness of Sigtuna.

Town Hall, Sigtuna

On the picturesque little square stands the Town Hall, small and quaint, dating from the mid-eighteenth century.

Visby

Gotland is an island about seventy-five miles long and thirty-five miles wide. It is a county of Sweden, with Visby the seat of the county government.

When the Hanseatic League was organized under the leadership of Lübeck in the middle of the fourteenth century, Visby became the center of one of the three main divisions of the League. Visby was thus once a city of wealth and power. The shift of trade routes caused its sharp decline. The island became a football of contention among the great powers.

In 1524 Gustavus I of Sweden conquered the rural areas. A year later the city was taken.

Visby is an archaeologist's paradise. It has treasures of ancient and medieval times still buried and still being uncovered.

The churches now standing date from the thirteenth and fourteenth centuries. The architecture is most pleasing to the eye. The "impregnable" walls around the city, though in partial ruins, still stand to remind visitors of the power and self-sufficiency of this ancient stronghold of the North.

Pictured here is a section of those historic walls.

Dalhem Church, Gotland

Out in the countryside of the island of Gotland stands this present-day Lutheran church, typical of Scandinavian church architecture: high and narrow.

Built in 1225, it originally had no graves or doors on the north side, so that bad spirits could not enter. The windows and paintings are from comparatively recent times.

The benches on one side are lower, and reserved for women, with men sitting on the other side on benches at a higher level. The pulpit is from 1741. The bishop's chair is set apart in an enclosure on the right. Wedding chairs on each side of the altar (1708) are where the bride and groom must sit.

Crosses along the roadside were erected to keep away evil spirits from those killed in accidents or war.

Kruttornet, Visby

This is the oldest tower of the wall of Visby, facing the Baltic Sea. It is the most ancient fortification of the city, built in the twelfth century, originally surrounded by water on three sides, an impregnable fortress. Inner rooms were connected with movable ladders. "Kruttornet" means the Powder Tower.

Gustavus Vasa

The patriot who roused the Swedes to fight for independence from the Danes. He was King of Sweden, 1523-1560.

90

The Castle, Uppsala

It was here, on the crest of the ridge, that King Gustaf Vasa began to build his castle in the 1540's, with a tower for defense. The castle, facing the town, was completed in 1611, when Gustavus Adolphus ascended the throne. In the State Hall Gustavus was crowned in 1617 and in 1654 took place the abdication ceremony of the famous Queen Christina, his daughter.

Now the castle houses the provincial governor, government offices, etc., and a public state hall.

Pictured here is the "Walpurgis Night" on Castle Hill (castle in the background), which occurs annually on April 30 as a welcome to spring, when university students congregate and ceremoniously replace their winter hats with "student caps."

Uppsala Cathedral

The largest in Scandinavia. Its measurements: exterior length, 118.7 meters; interior length, 107 meters; interior width, 45 meters; height of nave, 27.3 meters. The height of the towers is the same as the length of the cathedral, 118.7 meters.

The cathedral dates back to the year contributions were first solicited, 1257. It was not consecrated, however, until 1435. It was completed in 1440. It was restored between 1885 and 1893. Behind the high altar is the silver shrine of St. Eric, containing the relics of that king (a martyr in 1160).

The cathedral is the third in the archiepiscopal diocese (Uppsala was earlier called East Aros). The first was St. Peter's in Sigtuna, of which only ruins remain; the second, St. Laurentius (1156) at Old Uppsala, built on the site of a famous pre-Christian temple, later a Roman cathedral.

Skyline View of the Castle and Cathedral, Uppsala

The University of Uppsala spreads out on the hill between the castle and the cathedral. In 1477 Sweden's first university was founded here.

Interior of the Uppsala Cathedral

One of the Many Chapels of Uppsala Cathedral

The chapels were built into the original design of the church and intended as special places of worship. At different periods they have been consecrated to the glory of different saints by means of pious foundations.

After the Reformation the crypts of these chapels were used as tomb-chambers for high-born families and the chapels were named after them.

The Lady Chapel with the Tomb of Gustavus Vasa, Uppsala Cathedral

King Gustavus Vasa selected the Lady Chapel as a burial place for himself and his two consorts. When the King died in 1560, his remains and those of his queens were brought from Stockholm with great honors.

The altar, the largest of the chapels behind the altar of the cathedral, was consecrated in 1311, and several archbishops were previously buried in this chapel.

Many Swedish notables are buried in the cathedral: Emanuel Swedenborg (d. 1772), Johann Banér (d. 1600, father of the famous general of Gustavus Adolphus), Linnaeus (Swedish botanist), and Laurentius Petri (the first Lutheran Archbishop of Sweden).

University at Uppsala

Top: The University building (1887), one among many. The statue of Erik Gustav Geijer (celebrated professor of history at the University, 1817-1846) is in the foreground.

Bottom: The Gustavianum — site of the old University destroyed by fire in 1702 — named after Gustavus Adolphus, a medieval bishop's palace rebuilt in 1622-1624, restored in 1744-1757. The cupola was added as an anatomical theater in 1663, where Olof Rudbeck (1630-1702) gave his celebrated lectures in anatomy — now a museum.

Students automatically belong to one of thirteen "nations" (the eleven provinces of Sweden and the cities of Stockholm and Göteborg).

The High Altar, Uppsala Cathedral

This picture shows the high altar decorated for the fifth centenary, Whitsuntide, 1935.

Near these steps lie buried Archbishop Nathan Söderblom (1866-1931) and his wife Anna (1870-1955). The Archbishop is internationally famous for his leadership in the early years of the ecumenical movement in contemporary Protestantism.

The following words are inscribed upon the marker of his grave:

> När I Hafven Gjort Allt,
> Som Har Blifvit Eder Befalldt,
> Då Skolen I Säga: Vi Äro
> Odugliga Tjänare,
> Vi Hafva Allenast Gjort
> Det Som Vi Vovo Pliktiga Att Göra.
> Luke 17:10

Argenteus or "Silver Bible," which is the only extant source of the ancient Gothic language (related to English and other Germanic languages). The "Silver Bible" originally comprised the Four Gospels as translated by Bishop Wultila (Ulfilas) in the fourth century. The manuscript (only part of it is preserved) was executed two hundred years after Ulfilas' time in northern Italy (then the East Gothic Kingdom). It was discovered in the 1550's and brought to Sweden as a war booty following the storming of Prague by the Swedish armies in 1648.

Pictured here is a page from the *Codex Argenteus* (John 7:52 — 8:12-17).

It is lettered in silver and gold on purple parchment. The chased silver covers were made in 1669.

Codex Argenteus, *Uppsala University Library*

The Chased Silver Covers of the Codex Argenteus, *Uppsala University Library*

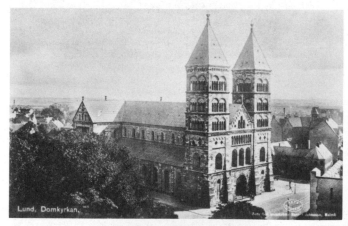

Cathedral at Lund, Sweden

During the campaigns of Gustavus Adolphus (his reign: 1611-1632) in Livonia and Poland and during the Thirty Years' War, the Swedish armies brought back, following the current custom, a vast amount of war booty from the Continent. Such booty consisted of books and seized manuscripts. In this manner Uppsala University came into possession of a large share of rare volumes and precious literary material.

In 1692 it was enacted by law that all Swedish publications printed in the major cities must be represented by copies in this library, and in 1707 this ruling was extended to all matter printed in the kingdom.

King Gustavus Adolphus was the actual founder of the great Uppsala University library. Sweden's principal medieval libraries (Vadstena Abbey, the Franciscan Monastery in Stockholm, the Dominican Monastery in Sigtuna, the library of King John III [1568-1592]) were gathered for preservation in this library.

Among the greatest of its acquisitions was the *Codex*

Lund has a history of about a thousand years as a community. Its greatest days were during the Middle Ages, when the town was known as the "Metropolis Daniae," the capital of Denmark.

Around 1100 it was the seat of the archbishop, primate over the whole of the North. The Cathedral's history dates back to the 1080's. The towers were built *ca.* 1200. It has undergone a series of restorations.

It is a cultural center of Sweden, near the University of Lund (1608) in southern Sweden.

Entrance to Lund Cathedral

Interior, Lund Cathedral

TOP: Interior, showing many steps to high altar. Ceremony of a doctor's graduation.

BOTTOM: The crypt, showing column into which is hewn the "Giant Finn."

Esaias Tegnér in the Circle of Friends in Lund

A professor in the University of Lund (1813-1826) and a Lutheran bishop (1824-1846), Tegnér is one of Sweden's great literary figures. He was born in Värmland in 1782 (the province of the celebrated novelist, Selma Lagerlöf). His epic *Frithjofs Saga* is internationally known and was written during his professorship.

The Famous Medieval Clock in Lund Cathedral

An astronomical clock which shows, among other things, the date and exact time and the course of the sun and the moon.

It is surmounted by two horsemen in armor. When the clock strikes twelve, these two figures strike each other twelve times, whereupon the Wise Men from the East call on the Holy Virgin, while two trumpeters blow the medieval hymn, *"In dulci jubilo."*

Tegnér's Study in His Home in Lund

One of Sweden's literary shrines is the modest one-storied Tegnér house in Lund. This is now a museum containing souvenirs of the Lutheran minister-poet. He counted his best days those spent over many years in Lund.

Tegnér's Saga

Pictured here is the copy of *Frithjofs Saga* in Norwegian translation which Roald Amundsen took with him to the South Pole.

Storkyrkan, "The Great Church" and the Royal Palace, Stockholm

The oldest parish church in Stockholm and the royal church of Sweden, in which many coronations of Swedish monarchs have taken place. It is the seat of the Bishop of Stockholm.

Originally erected *ca.* 1260, rebuilt in the late fifteenth century and greatly altered externally in 1736-1742, restored in 1882 and again in 1906-1908.

The above picture reveals the church almost hidden away (to the left). It is hemmed in by buildings in the part of town now called "Old Stockholm," but its tower is conspicuous in the many-towered skyline of the city.

Olaus Petri, the Reformer, was a rector of this parish.

The German St. Gertrud's Church, Stockholm

This photograph shows the elaborate royal box in this German church situated in the heart of Old Stockholm.

The church dates back beyond the seventeenth century.

Interior of Storkyrkan, Stockholm

Beneath the pulpit lies the worn gravestone of Olaus Petri (the stone discovered in 1907 in the vicinity of its present position).

A memorial tablet of the Ecumenical Meeting in Stockholm in 1925 is set in the wall.

Immediately opposite the pulpit are the celebrated royal pews (1684-1686).

In the north inner aisle (to the left and not visible in this picture) is the celebrated late Gothic sculptured group of St. George, the Dragon and the Princess which was dedicated to the adornment of the church in 1489 — one of the greatest sculptural monuments from the late Middle Ages in the whole of Northern Europe.

The German St. Gertrud's Church, Stockholm

Pictured here is the elaborate pulpit, a typical seventeenth century work of art.

Högalid Lutheran Church in Stockholm

A new and very large edifice with two immensely high towers, one capped with a rooster, the other with a cross. A small tower is capped with a star.

Engelbrekts Church, Stockholm

Interior, Engelbrekts Church, Stockholm

An imposing edifice located on a hill in Stockholm, this is one of the city's newest and most popular Lutheran churches. The building was constructed in 1914. It is "Nordic" in its style.

The name "Engelbrekt" is an honored name in Swedish history. Engelbrekt Engelbrektsson led a peasant revolt which spread rapidly, leading to his election as Regent at Arboga. This was the first Swedish *Riksdag* (1435) and the beginning of a modern democratic state in Sweden. Engelbrekt was murdered the following year and though opposed by bishops of Roman Catholicism, his revolt helped establish Protestantism as the Swedish state religion.

Leksand Lutheran Church, Dalarna, Sweden

Rättvik Lutheran Church

The Dalarna is the charming section around Lake Siljan in the heart of Sweden where the old bright Swedish costumes are still worn by the natives, particularly at church and on solemn religious and festive occasions. It is the most colorful area of Swedish Sweden. Leksand is located at the south of the lake.

Pictured here is the lovely church built on a site of a pre-Christian temple. The exterior architecture strongly suggests Russia (reconstruction done by men who, under Charles XII, had been soldier-captives in Russia); the interior is decorated in blue and white, characteristic colors of Dalarna. The picturesque belfry (not shown) is separate from the church. A quaint cemetery surrounds the church.

On the eastern shore of Lake Siljan in the heart of the Dalarna, this picturesque church, surrounded by a beautifully kept cemetery, dates back to 1300 A.D. A series of restorations has occurred.

On a mound south of the church is a monument to Gustavus Vasa, who, in 1520, here called the Dalecarlians to arms against Danish oppression. Twelve stones surrounding the principal one were set up to honor the twelve Dalecarlians who were Vasa's chief helpers.

In the foreground of the picture appear the wooden stables once used for horses of churchgoers.

Interior, Rättvik Lutheran Church

The pulpit of this beautiful country church dates back to 1636. Four sandglasses stand on the pulpit — to remind the preacher of the length of the service (particularly the sermon). The pulpit Bible carries the signatures of the King and Queen.

Magister Olof Jansson Kumblaeus

Minister of the Rättvik Lutheran parish, 1729-1737. This portrait made when he was sixty-six shows a countenance "clear, wise and strong."

Iron Candle Holder, Rättvik Lutheran Church

Lighting of the interior medieval church began very simply. Pictured here is an iron candle holder as then used.

Swedish Communion Cups, Rättvik Lutheran Church

On the left: from the sixteenth century; in the middle: from the seventeenth and eighteenth centuries; on the right: from the twentieth century.

Wedding Crown, Rättvik Lutheran Church

The wedding crown was worn as a symbol of innocence and a reward for purity.

Church Boats, Dalarna

The church boats — reminiscent of their ancestors, the Viking ships — were a familiar custom in the Dalarna, carrying people to the Sunday services.

At the Midsummer Festival, the church boats are still a conspicuous feature.

Church Bells of Rättvik Lutheran Church

From the beginning of the Christian faith in Sweden church bells have called the folk to worship, meditation, prayer and to special observances.

Pictured here are the oldest trio of bells in the Dalarna, dating from 1593, 1622 and 1628.

Church Boats, Lake Siljan, Dalarna

The wreath for the maypole arrives.

The high tide of the year in the Dalarna is Midsummer Night, June 23. This is a pre-Christian festival, when fires are lit to the Vikings' Balder, Lord of Life, adapted as a Christian festival dedicated to St. John.

Maypole dancing, costumed fiddlers, all-night carnival, birch branches (symbol of fecundity), and on June 24 the costumed procession to the churches with boatloads of worshipers — especially at Leksand and Rättvik.

The Vasa Painting, Mora, Dalarna

Gustav Vasa, fleeing from the Danes on his trail in the Dalarna, hid in the cellar of a home of a peasant. The peasant woman covered the hole in the floor with her washtub and pleaded innocence when the intruders searched the small house. This famous incident is a part of the folklore of Sweden.

An elaborate monument is a national shrine near Mora, the northern city of the Dalarna which lies on the shore of Lake Siljan. Tourists may now descend into the cellar hole in their historical pilgrimage.

The Vasa painting by J. F. Höckert (1859) is a valuable treasure for the possession of which a museum of art in the United States once made an offer of five million dollars.

Observe the feet of the peasant woman. They turn with the perspective of the viewer.

Church and Bell Tower, Mora, Sweden

A painting by the internationally famous Swedish artist, Anders Zorn (born in Mora, 1806; died, 1920).

This picture shows the church and bell tower of his native city (in the north Dalarna). Bell towers are common in Sweden.

Zorn's museum in Mora houses many of his paintings. He was famous for his predilection for nude portraits.

Erik Axel Karlfeldt

One of the greatest modern Swedish poets, Karlfeldt (1864-1931) lived on a beautiful small estate not far from Tallberg, Dalarna. He was secretary of the Swedish Academy, close friend of the literary figures of his day. Pictured here is the poet in his exquisite garden of rare flowers and herbs, situated on the shore of a beautiful lake.

Study of Erik Axel Karlfeldt

Karlfeldt was awarded the Nobel Prize in literature posthumously. His study was a cabin built near his gardens away from the big house.

Vireda Church, Småland, Sweden

A typical country parish church in the south-middle section of Sweden called Småland. Built in 1300, it and its cemetery are nestled alone on a little hill overlooking the countryside, near the hamlet of Släthult.

Swedish Lutheran churches are noted for the care with which the records of their membership are kept. The clergy are officers of the empire in this function — required to deposit in the state archives for safekeeping all records older than a hundred years.

The author of this book found, in glad surprise, in this church, by courtesy of the parish minister, carefully written records of his maternal ancestry with many factual details of their lives and relationships.

Emanuel Swedenborg

Swedish scientist, philosopher and religious inspirer of the Swedenborgian Church or the Churches of the New Jerusalem.

Born in 1688, Swedenborg published *Arcana Coelestia* (1749, 1756), *The Apocalypse Revealed* and *The True Christian Religion* (1771), his works not attracting attention until 1783, eleven years after his death. The "New Church" was organized in London in 1787, in America in 1792.

He claimed a series of revelations, with a special understanding of the Scriptures. He repudiated the doctrines of the Trinity and Atonement. On death one enters the realm of spirits, good or bad. The Second Coming, he claimed, occurred in 1757.

He died in 1772 and is buried in Uppsala Cathedral.

Interior, Vireda Church, Småland

In 1938 the interior walls and ceiling of this church were washed. Uncovered there stood forth paintings looking fresh and colorful from the period *ca.* 1755. The baptismal font dates from 1112, the crucifix on the altar from 1212, and the pulpit from 1663. The organ (rear gallery) was the gift of the Brahes in 1755 and is still in use.

Boxed pews with doors are visible in the photograph. The minister's sacristy (to the left of the altar) is cellar-like, resembling a little fortress, with weapons available.

Henric Schartau

Schartau (1757-1825) was an influential Swedish Lutheran clergyman, his ministry spent in Lund, southwest Sweden. He combined orthodoxy and pietism, authored sermons which were widely read both in his own country and among Swedish clergy in America.

Johan Olof Wallin

Wallin (1779-1839) was Sweden's greatest hymn writer. He gave himself to the revision of the Swedish Lutheran Church hymn book, issued in 1819. In 1837 he became archbishop in the state church.

Carl Olof Rosenius

Swedish lay preacher (1816-1868), Rosenius' name is associated with a lay revival of religion not only in Sweden, but among Swedish immigrants in America. Loyal to the state Lutheran Church, he kindled an independent religious pietistic fervor.

Selma Lagerlöf

Selma Lagerlöf (1858-1940) is Sweden's celebrated contemporary novelist. She lived in a charming mansion called "Marbacka," ancestral home in Vårmland where most of her literary work was produced. In 1909 she was awarded the Nobel Prize for literature. She was the first woman to be honored with membership in the Swedish Academy.

She is buried in the churchyard of "Östra Ämtervik," not far from her home. In her family circle were many Lutheran clergymen.

Mårbacka — Literary Shrine

The Library and Writing Table of Selma Lagerlöf at Mårbacka

The Lom Stave Church, Norway

The Lom Church is representative of the Norwegian stave churches. A stave church is a typical relic of the past. Most of such churches in Norway were built in the twelfth and thirteenth centuries — there being at one time some seven or eight hundred of them. There are now relatively few remaining — except for their restorations in such historic outdoor collections of Norwegian culture as those found at Maihaugen, Lillehammer, and at Bergen and Oslo.

One notices today such churches adorned with both pre-Christian and Christian symbols (dragons and crosses). Vertical planks are stacked up and pointed at both ends and set into frames, without nails. The roof is laid upon another, gable topping gable, and a cupola surmounts the whole. The stave church is dark and windowless, with only slits of light. Near the entrance is the usual weapon room.

The Lom Stave Church is a survival, situated not far from the exotic Gudbrands da Pen, made famous by Sigrid Undset in her novel. It is now, of course, Lutheran. It dates from 1200, perhaps 1150. There are distinct witnesses to the Viking era.

With the coming of the Reformation, the old style and splendor which distinguished the services ceased. The Lom Church was repaired and beautified in the seventeenth century, with paintings, a pulpit and an appropriate altar.

The Lom Church is picturesquely situated, under the lofty Lomseggen Mountain and by a mirror lake in the heart of Norway, a few hours' drive from Otta.

Interior of the Lom Stave Church, Norway

There were, of course, no pews, no candelabras, pulpit nor altar, as shown, in the pre-Christian stave church.

A Close-up of the Lom Stave Church, Norway

The Choir, Interior as Seen Eastward, of Cathedral Nidaros

The Cathedral of Nidaros, Trondheim, Norway

This church was the meeting place for pilgrims from all Scandinavian countries and the center of the worship of St. Olav, renowned national saint. His bones rest in his shrine on the high altar, after having been moved from place to place. Within the walls of this church kings were crowned.

In 995 the young hero King Olav Tryggvason came home from England to claim his rulership of Norway. He brought with him the Christian faith and desired to make Norway Christian by law and with sword.

He founded the town at the mouth of the River Nid and erected a royal castle and a church. His successor, Olav Haraldsson, came to the throne and became known as "Olav, the Saint" through his sacrificial death for the Christian faith. Miracle lore sprang up about his name.

After a succession of kings (under Danish dominance) the first Olav's church was completed in 1050. This building stood until fire destroyed it in 1531, but the foundation walls are still visible.

The worship of Olav, the Saint, grew around his shrine. A church of stone was erected, which lasted five hundred years. Papal permission was secured for a metropolitan archbishopric. Gifts poured into the church coffers. A succession of fires ensued.

When the Reformation was introduced in 1537, all the treasures were robbed from the cathedral. In 1564 the Swedes plundered the church. Another fire. Then began the rebuilding in its present form. By 1872 the essential reconstruction was under way. At the present time reconstruction is still going on, with a fifty-year goal set for final completion.

The cathedral stands today silhouetted against the Norwegian sky, an imposing structure in its exterior, but more so in its interior. It is one of the most impressive cathedrals of Northern Europe, and the center of Norway's Lutheranism.

*Interior from the Nave, as seen from the South Aisle,
Cathedral of Nidaros*

*Procession of Bishops from the Chapter House — the
St. Olav Jubilee in 1930*

Carrying the cross is Archbishop Nathan Söderblom of
Uppsala, Sweden. Third from the left is the Bishop of
Guildford. The occasion is the consecration of the re-
stored nave.

The Haugeans

Hans Nielsen Hauge (1771-1824) was a lay preacher
who organized in his native Norway societies resembling
those of the Wesleys in England and in a spirit of revival.
His formal education was limited, but skill at organization spelled success. Followers were called *Vakte* or
"Awakened."

Hauge was not a separatist. The state Lutheran Church,
however, persecuted him, imprisoning and fining him.

In America, the pioneer American Norwegian Lutheran synod, organized in 1846 under Elling Eielsen (a
follower of Hauge), was named after him.

BJØRNSTJERNE BJØRNSON

The man and his work.

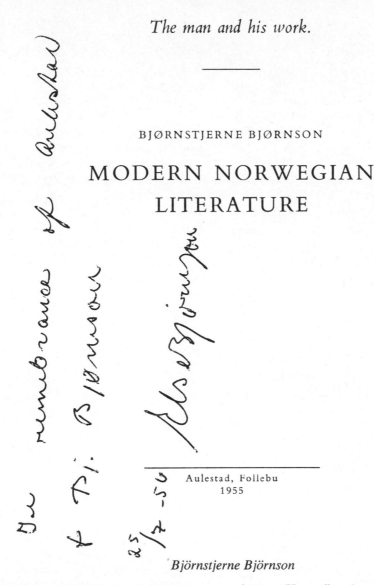

BJØRNSTJERNE BJØRNSON

MODERN NORWEGIAN LITERATURE

Aulestad, Follebu
1955

Björnstjerne Björnson

Novelist, poet, dramatist, nationalist, and a vigorous leader in social legislation, Björnson (1832-1910) wrote the Norwegian national anthem ("Norway, Thine Is Our Devotion") and was the recipient of the Nobel Prize in literature in 1903. He followed Ibsen in Bergen as director in the first effort to found a "National Stage."

He was the leader in the movement which culminated in the peaceful separation in 1905 (in Karlstad) of Norway and Sweden. He has been called "Norway's uncrowned king." At seventy-one he met the crowned king, Oscar II, to negotiate a dissolution dating from 1814. His influence on contemporary Europe was great. Both at home and abroad he had shaken the common masses out of long-accepted ideas in religious, political and educational opinion. He was a practical idealist, despising utopias "beyond our strength."

A clergyman's son, he was a loyal family man. Politics, he held, should have a moral purpose. In America (1880-1881) he was regarded as a controversial figure in his championship of the cause of religious freedom from dogma. He suffered opposition but his aim was steady. The celebrated national Norwegian holiday—May 17—he himself inaugurated in 1871.

His poems became household words and were set to music. "Norwegian literature begins with this book," said a Danish critic, referring to Björnson's *Synnöve Sólbakken* (1857). He wrote historical dramas for the theater, the medium, he thought, of the best communication.

A fond traveler, he stayed frequently in Copenhagen, Munich, Rome and Paris. His farm at Aulestad (not far from Lillehammer) was his great love, and is now a national shrine. His last years were devoted intensely to the cause of pacifism.

Pictured here is an autographed copy of a pamphlet given to this writer and his wife on their pilgrimage to the shrine of Aulestad, July 25, 1956, by the granddaughter, Else Björnson, who, as personal guide, related to us her incarceration at Aulestad during the Nazi occupation and her successful persuasion to allow the shrine to be preserved.

The Danish Reformation

The Reformation in Denmark was not an easy transformation. At the dawn of the Reformation the king upon the Danish throne was Christian II (1513-1523), an enlightened despot of Renaissance sympathies. The chief evils in his kingdom he saw to be the power of the nobles and churchmen. To limit the power of bishops he introduced the Lutheran movement by securing a Lutheran preacher, Martin Reinhard, in 1520.

He was also determined to make himself supreme in Sweden. In 1520 occurred "the blood bath of Stockholm," in which opposing leaders, promised amnesty, were invited to a banquet and then hastily tried and executed. This "blood bath" occasioned such intense fury and resentment that it cost Christian II control of all of Sweden when Gustav Vasa led the masses to rebellion.

Christian was driven from his throne and his Uncle Frederick I (1523-1533) succeeded him. Under Frederick Lutheranism penetrated the land. In Hans Tausen (1494-1561), a former monk and Wittenberg student, Lutheranism was expressed in powerful preaching from 1524 on. In 1523 a Danish New Testament was published. In 1526 King Frederick made Tausen his chaplain and took over the power of the appointment of his own bishops. A law in 1527 permitted Lutherans toleration and gave priests permission to marry.

Christian III (1536-1559) was a Lutheran and with the help of Bugenhagen, Luther's associate, the Danish Church began to organize in Lutheran commitment.

Viborg

Tausen, "the Luther of Denmark," was here held prisoner but succeeded in communicating his heretical Reformation ideas through the bars of his cell window. Released, he began again his public preaching, and Viborg churches welcomed him.

Viborg is called "the city with a past." A thousand years ago it was the greatest and richest in Denmark.

A Danish Château

The Marble Church, Copenhagen

Denmark is a city of churches. Church spires are conspicuous by their number. Pictured here is the Marble Church, begun in 1749, finished in 1874, a gift of Carl Frederick Tietgen (d. 1901), "the J. Pierpont Morgan of the North."

Copenhagen in an Earlier Day

Bertel Thorvaldsen

Bertel Thorvaldsen is the greatest sculptor Northern Europe has produced. He was born in Copenhagen in 1770, son of an Icelander wood carver. Prize after prize he won. For many years he lived in Rome.

He was hailed by the Danish people in his day. The Thorvaldsen Museum almost bursts with his extraordinarily large number of works of art. His grave is in an inner courtyard of the museum. He died in 1844.

In Continental Europe his work abounds. The most familiar of his products is the world-famous "Lion of Lucerne" in Switzerland, commemorating the killing of the Swiss Guards in the Tuileries at the time of the French Revolution. Thorvaldsen did many religious subjects. Pictured here is his statue of St. Matthew.

His last work was a bust of Martin Luther, unfinished, and now exhibited, "even to the lump of clay he had in his hand when he stopped work and stuck on Luther's breast."

Nicolai Frederick Severin Grundtvig

The most prominent figure in the Danish Church in the nineteenth century, Grundtvig (1783-1872) founded the National High School movement and fostered education in general.

He organized free people's congregations in the national churches. He was also the leading Danish religious philosopher at the close of the last century. A patriot, hymn writer and social leader.

Sören Kierkegaard

Kierkegaard (1813-1855), a Dane, has only in this generation come into a place of prominence in religious thought. He has been hailed by his admirers as a keen student of human nature, which underlay his theology of melancholy and pessimism and despair. A vast literature about him has accumulated in recent years and his many works have been translated into English.

The Great Church, Helsinki, Finland

On the north side of the Senate Square — laid out during the first half of the nineteenth century and designed by the architects Johan Albert Ehrenström and Carl Ludvig Engel — stands in majestic pre-eminence the Great Church, dominating the city, the harbor and the near-by university and government buildings.

The town of Helsinki was founded in 1550 by King Gustavus Vasa. After a fire in 1808 a large-scale re-planning and reconstruction began, resulting in one of the most beautiful modern cities in Northern Europe. Helsinki became the seat of the Finnish government in 1812.

Many new, imposing church buildings have been erected in greater Helsinki, witnesses to modern architects' experimentation in design.

The Great Church is Lutheran and its services are conducted in Swedish. Lutheranism prevails in Finland, having long been an outpost of Sweden.

Within this cathedral stand three immense statues facing the pulpit: Luther, Melanchthon and Martin Agricola (the latter the first great Finnish reformer and inspirer of Finnish culture).

Baptism in a Lutheran Parsonage, Finland

Finnish Bride and Groom (Nineteenth Century)

Examination for Confirmation in a Peasant Home, Finland

The Reformation in England

The English Reformation had, of course, its background in the revival of learning in the fifteenth century. Many colleges dedicated to religion and education were founded between 1382 and 1525. The fifteenth century was the supreme period of the Renaissance. The first printed Bible appeared in 1458. In 1477 Caxton was working a printing press in one of the chapels at Westminster Abbey and Aldus was producing exquisite printings of the classics before the end of the century. During Henry VII's reign, cardinals, archbishops and chancellors patronized the humanist movement and promoted scholarship. Clergy were being increasingly educated in colleges rather than in monasteries.

Many factors contributed to the separation of the English from the Roman Church: corrupt practices, nationalism, the revival of learning, persecutions and so on. English separation was not due to differences in belief — at first. The spark that ignited the schismatic flame was a quarrel between the Pope and Henry VIII (1491-1547). Refusal of papal sanction for a divorce from Catherine of Aragon caused Henry to declare the separation from papal authority and his own assumption of the headship of the church as well as of the realm. Henry had earlier (in 1523) been given the title of *"Fidei Defensor"* ("Defender of the Faith") by Pope Leo X in recognition of a work on the sacraments in opposition to Luther. Now Henry acted on his own. He swept away the monasteries; taxes were no longer paid to the papacy; the Bible in English translation was to be placed in every parish church in England. Doctrines remained intact.

Under Edward VI (1547-1552) Protestant reformers gained control. Two editions of the English Prayer Book appeared.

During the reign of Mary Tudor (1552-1558) Roman Catholicism was revived in England, with allegiance once again asserted to the papacy. The Latin Mass was restored and Thomas Cranmer and Bishops Ridley and Latimer (Protestants) were burnt at the stake.

When Queen Elizabeth acceded to the throne in 1558, conditions were complex: the majority of Englishmen still remained Catholic in sentiment, although they disliked both the authority of the papacy and Catholic Spain (with which England had been allied in the reign of Mary). There was a threat of attack by Philip of Spain, champion of Catholicism.

Queen Elizabeth was obliged to establish a church in a form suitable to the majority. "The Elizabethan Settlement" was the solution arrived at, in which the English Church took on a form that was neither the old Roman Catholic Church nor the kind of Protestant Church many Protestants desired. Much of tradition was maintained: the rule of the church by bishops (the episcopacy); the English Bible was to be publicly read and distributed; the queen was declared not supreme head but Supreme Governor of the Church of England "in so far as the laws of Christ allow." An Act of Uniformity declared this compromise binding on all Englishmen, requiring church attendance (with penalty of payment of fines).

The Church of England thus consciously preserved Catholicism to a great extent. Elizabethan Puritans hoped for more nonconformity but many remained faithful to the order. Some nonconformists left the church (the Brownists, for example). The classic literary expression of the point of view of the Church of England in the days of the English Reformation was the work entitled *Laws of Ecclesiastical Polity* (1594-1597) by Richard Hooker (1554?-1600). Both theology and church government were dealt with, and a mediating position taken between Calvinism and Romanism.

The quarrels between the Puritans and the Anglican Church increased in intensity with the years. During the reign of Charles I a civil war broke out, a struggle between king and Parliament. In general, Anglicans sided with the king and the Puritans with Parliament.

For a brief period Puritanism gained power under Oliver Cromwell (1599-1658). He was an Independent. During his Protectorate (1653-1658) he granted toleration to all except the Roman Catholics, Anglicans and extreme sects. He hoped to establish a church which would embrace Presbyterians, Independents and Baptists, with Calvinism as a theological base.

After Cromwell's brief reign the Anglican Church was restored to its old position under Charles II. The prayer book was brought again into use and a new Act of Uniformity was passed by Parliament. This act included a promise demanded of the clergy not to attempt any changes. Thus began a separation of many clergy from the established church, those who could not subscribe to the new order. These Dissenters were cruelly persecuted. John Bunyan, author of *The Pilgrim's Progress,* was such a one. He was imprisoned in Bedford for having preached without a proper license.

In 1688 occurred what is called the "Glorious Revolution" in which contending parties joined to oppose an attempted restoration (by James II) of an absolute monarchy and Roman Catholicism. In the Toleration Act of 1689 Protestant Dissenters were granted freedom of worship and in 1828 they were given political rights.

Edward IV Visiting Caxton's Printing Press at Westminster Abbey

Henry VIII, King of England

Freedom of the Church of England from the control of the papacy was attained under Henry VIII.

Sir Thomas More

Lord Chancellor of England, author of the *Utopia*. He gave himself energetically to the cause of church reform, was a friend of Erasmus, opposed Henry VIII's assumption of supremacy over the church and was beheaded in 1535.

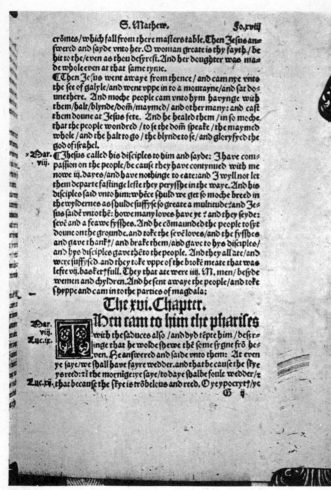

Tyndale's New Testament, the First English Translation to Be Printed (1525-1526)

In 1450 Johann Gutenberg perfected the art of printing by the use of movable type. In Mainz, Germany, he set up his first printing press. The Gutenberg or Mazarin Bible in Latin was the first book publication from this press. In 1516 Erasmus' edition of the New Testament in Greek appeared, with a new translation into Latin.

William Tyndale (1495?-1536) issued the first English translation (directly from the Greek) in 1526. This became the foundation on which all the later translators built. It was in "racy English." In his day it was held dangerous by churchmen for the common person to read the Bible without the benefit of clergy and so Tyndale had difficulty in securing a printer. The leaders in the English Church violently opposed such an effort. Tyndale went to Germany, to Hamburg, Cologne and later to Worms. In this latter city the first printing in English of the New Testament was completed. This edition had to be smuggled into England.

In 1536 Tyndale suffered a martyr's death in exile.

Another translation into English (before Tyndale's death) was that of Myles Coverdale in 1535, a complete Bible in English.

Pictured here is the strangling (and later burning) of Tyndale whose last words were, "Lord, open the King of England's eyes."

"There is no grander life in the whole annals of the Reformation," it has been said, "than that of William Tyndale."

Burning Tyndale's Testaments at St. Paul's, London

Vigorous measures were taken to stamp out the influx of Tyndale's Testament into England. In the city of London thousands of copies discovered in various hiding places were burned with solemn ceremony. This was called "A burnt offering most pleasing to Almighty God." The printing presses kept printing more and more!

Tyndale's Martyrdom

117

The Title Page of the Great Bible (1539)

The first English version to be definitely authorized for use in public worship. Produced by Myles Coverdale.

King Edward VI

A boy king who wore the crown for a few brief years in difficult times. During his reign grammar schools were multiplied in England, as well as institutions of mercy and the English Prayer Book.

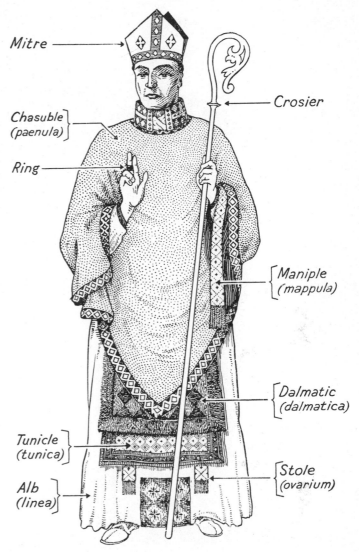

Mitre

Chasuble
(paenula)

Ring

Crosier

Maniple
(mappula)

Dalmatic
(dalmatica)

Tunicle
(tunica)

Alb
(linea)

Stole
(ovarium)

English Robes and Vestments

The Church of England, along with many ritualistic Protestant churches, in its liturgical forms continued the Catholic custom of appropriate costumes for its clergy in the performance of altar services.

The eucharistic vestments in the Anglican Church were prescribed in the First Book of Prayer of Edward VI (1549) and restored to practice in the Prayer Book of Elizabeth. Some of these vestments date far back in Christian forms of worship.

Chief of the eucharistic vestments are the *alb, amice* and *girdle,* in addition to a *chausible, stole* and *maniple.* On special occasions the deacon wears a *dalmatic,* the subdeacon a *tunicle* in place of the *chausible* worn by the celebrant (three ministers officiating).

Pictured here is a medieval bishop wearing the *"linea-tunica-paenula"* combination.

119

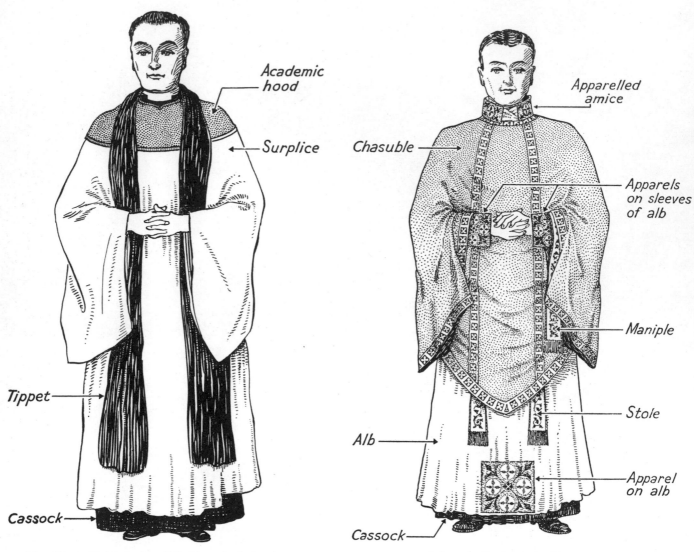

The Choir Habit in English Liturgical Services

Academic hood

Surplice

Tippet

Cassock

Apparelled amice

Chasuble

Apparels on sleeves of alb

Maniple

Stole

Alb

Apparel on alb

Cassock

Priest in Eucharistic Vestments

In the Anglican Church the choir habit is worn by the priest at Matins and Evensong, called "choir" because the robes were worn in earlier days when services were said or sung in the choir of the church.

The choir habit consists of *cassock, surplice, hood* and *scarf* or *tippet.* The hood is the symbol of a university degree. The *cotta,* worn in some churches, is an abbreviated garment like a surplice, only shorter. Pictured here is a priest in choir habit.

Back view to
show hood

Morse

Orphreys

Cope

Priest Wearing a Cope

Mary Tudor, Queen of England

Her supreme duty, she thought, was to return England to the Roman Catholic Church.

Views of the Town of London

The famous Tower of London, full of the memory of the martyrdom of saints and sinners, of enemies and defenders of faith and crown, of heretics — symbol of man's inhumanity toward humanity.

Instruments of Torture from the Tower of London

Thomas Hawkes

Hawkes became involved with the Church when he refused to permit the baptism of his son. The issue of religious liberty had become dominant in English thought. During Hawkes' imprisonment various devices were made to impel his subjection. To all he replied, "I am no changeling." He was finally summoned before a bishop to recant and to these summonses Hawkes boldly affirmed his preference to die rather than renounce his own faith.

He was led to the place of execution and as the fire burned him he held his hands high above his head to tell friends (by a prearranged signal) that a martyr's death was bearable, to urge others to bravery.

*The Martyrdom of Bishops Hugh Latimer of Worcester
and Nicholas Ridley of London*

Latimer (*ca.* 1490-1555), educated at Cambridge University, came into contact with influential Reformers. He threw himself into the cause. He became a preacher at Wiltshire where his Reformation views were expounded, causing the bishops in London to summon him to trial. He was ordered to sign a document declaring his belief in the forms of worship and practices of the Roman Church. He refused his signature. Under pressure he continued to refuse. The bishops were halted by Latimer's unexpected appointment to the important bishopric of Worcester. He became an eloquent preacher, establishing Reformation principles in the minds of the people. Because of his courage in speaking against injustices he was hurled into the Tower (without trial) for a six years' confinement. Under Edward VI he was released. He refused his former bishopric, helping instead the unfortunate of his country. Under Mary he was sentenced

to the Tower, from which he was removed to Oxford.

Nicholas Ridley (1500-1555) was put in prison about the same time as Latimer. A master at Cambridge, he was chaplain to Henry VIII. He became a convert to Reformed principles.

Both these bishops were brought to trial at Oxford in 1555. Accused of heresy, both were sentenced to death after refusing to recant. The place of public burning was in the town of Oxford.

Said Ridley: "So long as the breath is in my body I will never deny the Lord and His known truth. . . . I commit our cause to Almighty God, who shall impartially judge all."

Said Latimer: "Be of good courage, brother **Ridley**, and play the man. For we shall this day light such a candle by God's grace in England, as I trust shall never be put out."

Queen Elizabeth

For forty-five years (1558-1603) she directed the destinies of England — "a statesman" of the first order in difficult times.

Bishop Thomas Cranmer

Archbishop of Canterbury, his elevation in the church was bestowed after his aid to Henry VIII in the quarrel over the King's first divorce. He promoted the circulation of the English Bible and he directed in the reformation of both creed and liturgy in the English Church.

Cranmer (1489-1586) was the chief author and inspirer of the Church of England's prayer book — *The Book of Common Prayer*. Under Queen Mary he was martyred by burning at the stake.

The Signature of Queen Elizabeth

King James I and the Authorized Version of the Bible

During King James I's reign (1603-1625) (James VI of Scotland) the big issue was the rivalry between "the established church" and the Puritans. Both parties sought his favor, since he came from Presbyterian Scotland. Early in his reign the issue of Sabbath observance came to a head, along with an expressed desire to promote a revised translation of the Bible. Many petty differences were made large issues.

At the Hampton Court Conference in 1604, over which the King presided, and with the insistence of the Puritan leadership, he appointed a committee for a retranslation of the Bible composed of "the best learned." The outcome was a revision of the Bishop's Bible (of 1568). For three centuries and more it has been the most popular and revered version of the Scriptures. It is known as "the Authorized Version" (1611). Over forty revisers were engaged in this "holy task." It has been called "the greatest literary monument of the English language."

Pictured here is the presentation to James I by the translators.

Guy Fawkes and the Chief Conspirators
(From a contemporary print)

Guy Fawkes was the leader of an effort by the supporters of the Roman Catholic Church to overthrow the government in England and to secure a government more favorable to Catholic subjects.

The Gunpowder Plot of 1605 was devised to destroy the House of Lords. When the plot was uncovered, strong waves of anti-Catholic sentiment spread throughout England.

The Book of Sports

In 1618 King James I published a *Book of Sports* "to encourage recreation and sports on the Lord's Day."

Since Constantine it had been the practice to honor the first day of the week as a rest from work and as an observed Sabbath. Luther had opposed the idea of the observance as binding. Puritans, however, resenting the frivolity of the times, sought to promote a stricter life, especially reverence for Sunday. No work, no sports.

Charles I (1625-1649), successor to James I, reissued the "Declaration of Sports," which permitted dancing, archery, leaping, May games and the like as lawful where worship was not interfered with. Bishop Laud ordered the declaration to be read in the churches. All this aroused the ire of the Puritans.

Pictured here, in a contemporary print, is the burning of the *Book of Sports* by a common hangman in 1643.

Puritan fever ran high.

Bishop William Laud

Laud (1573-1645) was Archbishop of Canterbury in troubled times in England. He stood with Charles I against the Puritans, and sought to impose by force the Catholicism of the Church of England. He was executed by the "Long Parliament."

The Execution of Charles I
(A contemporary print)

Four years after Laud's death, Charles I was beheaded (1649). It was an era of intense civil war. Charles had been obsessed with the concept of the divine right of kings, arbitrary in his actions, and with little capacity to understand the drift of public opinion.

Oliver Cromwell

Richard Baxter
(From a portrait taken in 1677)

During the Puritan Revolution, Richard Baxter (1615-1691) became a power in Puritan affairs. In 1662 he became a nonconformist, striving, however, to secure a comprehension of the Presbyterians in the Anglican Church.

His *A Christian Directory* contains the best summary of Puritan ethics. He declined a bishopric.

John Milton

Milton (1608-1674), English poet, educated at Christ's College, Cambridge, was an Anglican of moderate Puritan leanings, became a Presbyterian, and later a radical Independent. Regarded in his day as a heretic. His *Paradise Lost* (1667), written during his blind years, is his major work. He also wrote brilliant pamphlets advocating church reform.

He is pictured here dictating *Samson Agonistes* (1671), a biblical story told as Greek tragedy.

Commonly known as S.P.C.K., this Society was founded in 1699 under the leadership of four laymen and the Rev. Thomas Bray (1656-1730). (Bray also founded the Society for the Propagation of the Gospel in Foreign Parts in 1701, known as the S.P.G., the latter founding and nursing the American Episcopal Church.)

Religious education was the main business of the original S.P.C.K., which enormously promoted the cause of the Church of England all over the world (as did the S.P.G.). It engaged in printing and circulating Christian literature.

One of its very first objectives was to convert the Quakers, "to redeem that misguided people to the knowledge and belief of Christ," by issuing an edition of *A Discourse upon the Baptismall Covenant* by the Rev. Mr. Bray.

Besides books on various topics (catechisms, Christian behavior, etc.) the Society issued Bibles and editions of the *Book of Common Prayer* "at ye easiest Rates."

Pictured here are a few early reproductions of its publications.

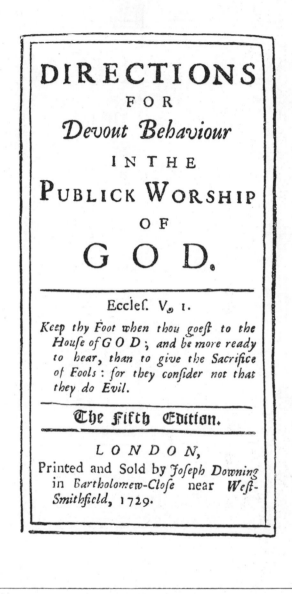

S.P.C.K. Directions for Behavior in Worship

S.P.C.K.

A Discourse on Regeneration.

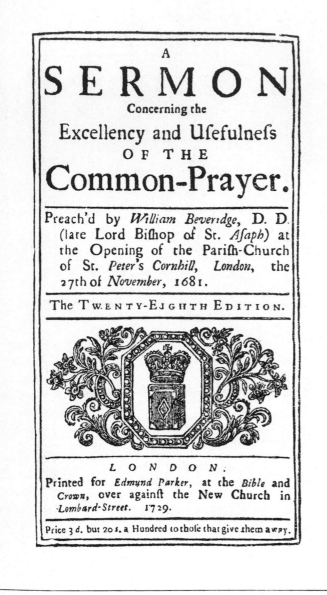

<table>
<tr><td>

A

SERMON

Concerning the

Excellency and Usefulness

OF THE

Common-Prayer.

Preach'd by *William Beveridge*, D. D.
(late Lord Bishop of St. *Asaph*) at
the Opening of the Parish-Church
of St. *Peter's Cornhill, London*, the
27th of *November*, 1681.

The TWENTY-EIGHTH EDITION.

LONDON:
Printed for *Edmund Parker*, at the *Bible* and
Crown, over against the New Church in
Lombard-Street. 1729.

Price 3 d. but 20 s. a Hundred to those that give them away.

</td><td>

FOUR

SERMONS,

UPON THE

Great and Indispensible DUTY

Of all CHRISTIAN

MASTERS and MISTRESSES

To bring up their

NEGRO SLAVES

IN THE

Knowledge and Fear of GOD

PREACHED AT THE

Parish Church of St *Peter* in *Talbot* County,
in the Province of MARYLAND.

By the Rev. *THOMAS BACON*,
Rector of the said Parish.

Then *Jacob* said unto his Houshold, and to all that
were with him, Put away the strange Gods that are
among you, and be clean. GEN. XXXV. 2.
But as for me and my House, we will serve the LORD.
JOSH. XXIV. 15.
Well done!—thou hast been faithful over a few Things,
I will make thee Ruler over many Things: enter
thou into the Joy of thy LORD. MAT. XXV. 21.

LONDON:
Printed by J. OLIVER, in *Bartholomew-Close*,
near *West-Smithfield*. M.DCC.L.

</td></tr>
</table>

An S.P.C.K. Sermon on the Common Prayer   *S.P.C.K. Sermons on Duties toward Slaves*

St. Paul's Cathedral, London

Old St. Paul's had been a great Gothic church with a tapering spire. Sir Christopher Wren was engaged in carrying on the work of restoration when it fell in ruin in the great fire of London in 1666. Wren envisioned a great dome conspicuous throughout the new city of London he planned.

The dome was built in the reconstruction, to the delight of Wren. But the church never became a great center with a plaza, as he envisioned. Its dedication was a day of national festivity. The Freemasons gave their support to the rebuilding. As time passed, the building fell into sad neglect.

The early leaders of the Oxford Movement (a revival of liturgical and ceremonial usages), the Tractarians (*ca.* 1833-1841), reawakened this church from neglect to "splendor of worship." A succession of notable clergy brought the cathedral into eminence, and it became a growing center of Anglican religious life. In the present generation, W. R. Inge, well known as a brilliant scholar and prolific writer, was for many years dean of the cathedral.

St. Martin-in-the-Fields, London

In the eighteenth century this church was known as His Majesty's Parochial Church. It is very well known in our time, due to the present-day miracle of broadcasting and to the popular ministry of the Rev. H. R. L. Sheppard. It

Westminster Abbey, London

One of the most famous churches in the world. It was once a great convent, made up of chapels, prisons, bell towers, gatehouses and domestic quarters. The Abbey possessed, at one time, besides an expansive immediate surrounding, 97 towns and villages, 17 hamlets and 216 manors.

The dean, as successor to the Westminster abbots, "yields precedence in his own church to no ecclesiastic, not even the Archbishop of Canterbury." The Abbey still remains exempt from episcopal jurisdiction.

Here lie buried most of England's Kings (from Henry VII to George II), Queens Mary and Elizabeth, poets, religious leaders, the Unknown Soldier and many others. "English history is indeed written in every stone of the Abbey."

The date of its founding is not known. It was long dedicated to St. Peter. It was rebuilt by Edward the Confessor, and again by Henry III, whose Chapel is now famous. The western towers are the seventeenth-century additions of Sir Christopher Wren.

In the Jerusalem Chamber of the Abbey the first meeting of the Westminster Assembly was held on July 1, 1643. The last session was held there on February 22, 1649. Hence, it is also a Presbyterian shrine.

is an active church, appealing to the normally non-church-going crowd, and is open day and night.

The old church dates back to Henry VIII. George III, it is said, had the habit of "slamming" the sash windows of the royal box, "if he was bored with the sermon."

131

John Knox and the Beginnings of the Scottish Reformation

PRESBYTERIANISM

The distinctive feature of Presbyterianism is its polity, from which the name is taken. An elder, or *presbuteros* (a New Testament word), is the elected representative who, with other elders as a "session," governs the church. A group of churches and clergy compose the presbytery. Presbyteries form a synod and synods an assembly. Ministers and laymen are equally representative in church courts, and ministers all stand on the same level.

Presbyterianism stems from the Reformed wing of the Protestant Reformation (1529). John Calvin (1509-1564) was the father of this Reformed faith. Calvin's theory of polity prepared the way for the separation of church and state (although this was not achieved in the church-state in his own Geneva). The Huguenots of France gave impetus to Presbyterian polity. Protestantism in Holland was, and continues to be, chiefly Presbyterian. The Dutch Reformed Church of our own day is Presbyterian.

It was in Scotland that Presbyterianism became focalized. The great leader there was John Knox (1505-1572). (See the section on the United Presbyterian Church.) From 1690 the Presbyterian Church of Scotland has continued without interruption.

The purifying group in England — called the Puritans — began in the Church of England during Queen Elizabeth's reign. Many of these Puritans were partial to the Presbyterian polity. (The Separatists — the Pilgrims — followed the Congregational form.)

JOHN KNOX

Great Scottish reformer, Knox (1505-1572) was a convert from Roman Catholicism. He was early associated with George Wishart, the evangelist, and his type of Protestantism began in the Zwinglian stream.

He was brought up in the neighborhood of Haddington and went to school there. He learned Latin and French. University trained and a tutor, he came under the spell of Wishart, a preacher of the Reformation and a martyr. Knox, as his friend, was in danger of his life and took refuge in the castle of St. Andrews, where his preaching began. He was shipped to France. A galley slave for two years, chained with others to a bench, he sailed the seas as a French outcast. In 1549 he found haven in England, still an exile from his native Scotland. He continued to preach, and married an Englishwoman. Newcastle was the scene of his early ministry.

With a new monarch, Mary Tudor, on the throne in

John Knox

1554, England became anti-Protestant. Knox sought refuge in Geneva. Here he learned Calvinism first-hand, from Calvin himself. At Frankfort-on-the-Main he ministered to a church of exiles. Knox here began to defend a Puritan way of life in the disputes that went on. He returned to Geneva and was chosen minister to English exiles there. With a new monarch favorable to Protestantism in England (Queen Elizabeth), he set himself to return to his homeland in 1559. The Queen, however, disliked his brand of Protestantism and forbade his entry. So he bided his time by preaching at Dieppe, in northern France.

In 1559 he arrived in Edinburgh, to find dissension between the crown and the Protestants. Knox entered the fray of a civil war, which finally established the Protestant Church in Scotland. He stood out for a national Protestant Church. In 1560 a Parliament consummated the union of church and state, a victory for Knox and his cohorts. He became minister of the church of St. Giles, and helped draw up a Confession of Faith and a *First Book of Discipline*.

When Mary returned from France to reign as Queen of Scots in 1561, there was fear of a return to Catholicism since she had been reared a Catholic. Knox and young Mary quarreled, both with suspicions of the powers the other held. Then Mary became embroiled in affairs of marriage which shocked public opinion. She was dethroned and her son James VI was crowned King of the Scots. This established Protestantism once more in Scotland.

Knox's last days saw a struggle between two parties, the one for Mary (now a prisoner in England) and the other for James and Protestantism. In Edinburgh Knox was no longer safe. He sought refuge in St. Andrews. After a truce he returned once more to St. Giles, where, broken in health, he died in 1572.

His work was national in scope. His is a commanding figure in the struggle of early Reformation history.

The Castle of St. Andrews

A French Galley

The House of John Knox in Edinburgh

George Wishart

George Wishart (1513?-1546), a contemporary of Luther, Zwingli and Calvin, was a preacher of power who, when he visited Scotland to carry on the cause of the Reformation, came to know and to leave the mark of his influence on John Knox. His sermons irked Cardinal Beaton. Having taught doctrines contrary to Roman Catholicism, he was taken prisoner, strangled at the stake and burned before the castle of St. Andrews — to strike terror into the minds of other Reformatory heretics. His views followed those of Zwingli.

Knox's Modest Study Room

133

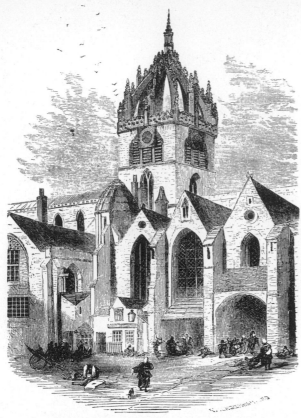

*John Knox
Preaching in St. Giles
in Edinburgh*

Knox's Pulpit in St. Giles

Old St. Giles Church, Edinburgh

Knox Preaching to the Lords of Scotland

Pictorial Scene of the Irish Massacre of 1641, When Upward of 40,000 Protestants Were Murdered

Presbyterians came to Ireland in 1608. The religious wars between Roman Catholics and Protestants ended in the suppression of the great Roman Catholic Rebellion in 1641 and the settlement of Scottish soldiers in the country. Protestant mass murders, in the judgment of history, are to be balanced with Catholic mass murders.

Statue of Knox in Edinburgh, Erected by Grateful Scotsmen

The Massacre of Protestants at the Bridge over the Baen in Ireland

The Swearing and Subscribing of the National Covenant in Greyfriars' Churchyard, Edinburgh, 1638

An effort by the Scottish Protestants to preserve a Presbyterian form of government and to oppose the re- establishment of the episcopacy.

The Huguenots of France—The Inquisition— Spanish Martyrdom

THE HUGUENOTS OF FRANCE

For centuries France had been a battleground of the Roman Church and the sects opposing it. The Albigenses and Waldenses suffered in the struggle, and only scattered remnants remained after their persecution.

In 1530 French Protestantism seemed likely to prevail, even at the court of King Francis I, influenced by Luther's tracts and by the preaching of German, Swiss and English Reformers. Calvin, a native of northern France, had given his support to the stirrings, but he fled along with the others under the growing persecutions.

In 1555 the first French Huguenot church was established in Paris. Other Protestant congregations sprang up. The Huguenots became an important political force which attracted nobles and lords with political motives. Religion and politics became inextricably woven, even among Protestants.

Between 1562 and 1598 a most significant chapter in political philosophy was written. The French monarchy was threatened — especially by the Huguenots, who stood for local autonomy. A plot to seize the king resulted in the persecution of thousands of innocent Huguenots. Under the rule of Catherine de Médici, the renewed persecution of Protestants was pressed and there raged a ferocious series of religious wars. Massacres and assassinations were frequent.

When Catherine could not succeed one way, she tried others to curb the Huguenots. She gave out pretenses of religious freedom and even arranged marriages between people of different religious loyalties. The marriage of the King's sister to Henry of Navarre, a commander in the Huguenot army, was a plot to draw to Paris thousands of Huguenots. The conspiracy was mass murder. When they came, she claimed their intent to overthrow the government.

The unsuspecting Protestants were attacked on August 24, 1572 on the eve of the church feast of St. Bartholomew and the event has come to be known as "the Massacre of St. Bartholomew."

Catherine de Médici

The Execution of Anne du Bourg

The so-called Inquisition, a medieval ecclesiastical tribunal for the preservation of the Faith — to combat heresy — was instituted by Gregory IX (1227-1241). It meant punishment, torture, exhortation to repentance and even death to the guilty.

It was revived in the sixteenth century. Even the Protestant Reformers, including Luther, Calvin and Zwingli, believed in the death penalty for heresy (Luther called heresy "blasphemy").

Here is pictured the execution by hanging and burning of Anne du Bourg. The French monarch, Francis II, sought to stamp out Protestant heresy. The *"Parlement"* (court) at Paris arrested suspects and hundreds of public executions took place. Anne du Bourg boldly defended Lutheranism and defied papal authority. The special French tribunal came to be called *"La Chambre Ardente"* (the burning chamber). The King delighted in witnessing such executions.

Sixty Huguenots Slain in a Church at Vassy (March, 1562)

Vassy, in northern France, was a town in which a great many Huguenots lived. Religious services were held in a church and the number of converts increased rapidly.

The Duke of Guise with two hundred soldiers passed through Vassy, and hearing the bell of the church inquired, "Why does that bell ring so loud?" Learning that Protestants were many in this town and attended the church, he cried out, "Back — we shall take them in the act!" Leonard Morel, the minister, was preaching when the soldiers rushed the sanctuary. "Death to the Huguenots!" they cried. Arms and hands and heads were cut off the victims. The minister was cruelly tormented and imprisoned. The trumpet sounded and the army moved on.

*The Massacre of Huguenots in Paris on the Eve of
St. Bartholomew, 1572*

The "Wars of Religion," Huguenots against Catholics in France, lasted three decades. Thirty thousand Protestants lost their lives in the Massacre of St. Bartholomew, which lasted a whole week. Leaders on the Catholic side were Catherine de Médici (1519-1589) and the Guises; on the Protestant side, Coligny, Condé and Henry of Navarre.

In the Edict of Nantes, 1598, Navarre, as King Henry IV, guaranteed Huguenots a measure of freedom. After his death further cruel war broke out, culminating in the Revocation of the Edict of Nantes in 1689, as a result of which several thousand Huguenots, some of them the best intellects and skilled artisans of France, were forced into exile.

Protestants did not really enjoy religious toleration until 1787.

Gaspard de Coligny, Admiral of France and a Beloved Leader of the Huguenots

Of noble birth and large family influence, Gaspard, Count of Coligny, was born in 1518. He was at one time a favorite of King Henry II. A governor of the Isle of France and captain of a hundred men-at-arms, he was made a prisoner in 1557. Through his brother, Andelot, he became a convert to the Reformation. He studied the Scriptures and received letters and encouragement from Calvin. Gaspard became the idol of the Reformed party, a fearless leader, hated by Catherine.

Coligny was signaled out for murder on St. Bartholomew's Eve. An assassin came upon him and plunged a sword into his body, which was then thrown out of a window, and finally, to make his death certain, he was decapitated.

Tortures of the Inquisition — the Rack

A Spanish Prisoner of the Inquisition Strangled in Prison

A Spaniard named Juliano traveled into Germany and became a convert to the Reformation. Upon his return he took with him to Seville a number of Bibles to distribute among his countrymen. He was betrayed to the powers of the Inquisition.

Juliano and twenty others were burned at the stake. Other possessors of Scripture were publicly whipped, imprisoned or sent to the galleys.

The Auto-da-fé — Public Burning of Martyrs in Spain

From the Portuguese, the term means "act of faith." It was applied to a public ceremony accompanying the official final sentence of the Inquisition. During the sixteenth century the ceremony in Spain consisted of a procession to the place of condemnation, a sermon, a reconciliation or a condemnation and a turning over to the civil power those who were found guilty of heresy. All this preceded the burning.

Pictured here are the condemned going to the stake.

English Separatists, Independents and Congregationalists

CONGREGATIONALISM

The distinctive historic character of Congregationalism is its polity. Each congregation sets its own creed and requirements. Thus, Congregationalism has taken on a variety of theological tenets. Ministers are subject to local societies. Synodical groups have been advisory. Churches should co-operate in simple friendship rather than by organizations, according to Robert Browne (1550?-1633), architect of a church independent of the Church of England because of its union with the state.

There was no confession of faith recognized by *all* Congregational churches in the seventeenth century. The Amsterdam exiles formulated one in 1596. In 1658 the Savoy Confession was drawn up in London, patterned after the Westminster Confession, substituting the Congregational form of polity for the Presbyterian.

English Congregationalism suffered persecution and was checked in its development. In America the church struck deeper roots, particularly in New England.

In 1691 Congregationalists and Presbyterians — bitter competitors in England — came to agreement on certain principles, called "Heads of Agreement." In 1696 Congregationalists, Presbyterians and Baptists joined in a political compact against the Quakers.

Congregationalists were among the Puritans who migrated to Massachusetts to escape the despotism of Charles I and Archbishop Laud. These people were Presbyterian in polity and came under the influence of the more independent Pilgrims. John Endicott (Puritan) and Samuel Fuller (deacon of Plymouth) met and from this meeting issued the Salem Church in the Massachusetts Bay Colony which adopted the "Congregational Way" of the independent Pilgrims.

After a controversy, "the New England Way" was adopted as a compromise, each church remaining independent but neighboring churches advising and approving the ordination and installation of ministers and teachers. "Congregationalism" was the name applied to "the New England Way," and was definitely employed by John Cotton in 1648.

After this period American Congregationalism became dominant in the New England colonies and states, up to the nineteenth century. Then it joined with New York and New Jersey Presbyterians in a plan of federated churches for extending churches to the West. This turned out to be a disadvantage as far as Congregationalism itself was concerned.

Calvinism was the predominant theology of American Congregationalism — there being, however, disputes on account of the autonomous character of Congregational churches. Liberals emerged gradually to spheres of influence, many ministers supporting institutions of higher learning.

John Cotton

John Cotton (1584-1652) was an English-born colonial minister in Boston, a strong defender of the freedom of the American churches.

In 1648 Cotton published *The Way of the Congregational Churches Cleared,* in which the term "Congregational" seemed to convey a distinct title for the churches of "the New England Way."

THE ENGLISH SEPARATISTS BECOME
THE PILGRIM FATHERS

The Leyden Separatists group under John Robinson found life hard, customs strange and foreign in Holland. They longed to live again under English law, but they remembered their persecutions in the mother country. Appealing to the London-Virginia Company for the right to settle somewhere in Virginia, they made rash promises to the throne in return.

A small band returned to England and in the fall of 1620 set forth in the *Mayflower* for the new world, their minister remaining behind.

Two months later they anchored off Cape Cod. They drew up the Mayflower Compact, by which they covenanted before God and each other a civil body. This was Congregational in polity, though civil rather than religious.

This Plymouth Colony, the Pilgrims, barely survived the first New England winter. Our Thanksgiving Day, of course, is a reminder of their first thanksgiving on American soil.

*The John Robinson Memorial Tablet, St. Peter's Church,
Leyden, Holland*

This inscription reads:
The Mayflower, 1620
In Memory of
Rev. John Robinson, M.A.
Pastor of the English Church worshiping over
against this spot, A.D. 1609-1625, whence
at his prompting went forth
The Pilgrim Fathers
To settle in New England
in 1620
Buried under this house of worship
4 March, 1625
AET XLIX Years
In memoria aeterna erit justus
Erected by the National Council of the Congregational
Churches of the United States of America,
A.D. 1891

Scrooby

Early in the seventeenth century an English Separatist group, under persecution, divided in holding assemblies, one meeting in Gainsborough with John Smyth as its minister (migrating later to Amsterdam), the other becoming the historic church at Scrooby, meeting in the house of William Brewster (1560?-1644). This manor house has been called "the beginning of New England." This group also removed to Amsterdam under Richard Clifton and John Robinson (1575?-1625) and from there to Leyden, Holland.

Pictured here is Scrooby Manor House.

The Departure of the Pilgrims from Delfthaven, July, 1620
(From a contemporary Dutch painting)

The Embarkation at Delfthaven

The Compact in the Cabin of the Mayflower

The Pilgrims Make a Safe Landing in the New World

Plymouth Rock

Sabbath in the Common House at Plymouth

Burial Hill, Plymouth

John Endicott

"The First Meeting House of the First Protestant Church Organized in America," Salem, Massachusetts

Under the leadership of John Endicott, a colony of Puritan Separatists had come to Salem late in 1628 (during the time of the Pilgrims at Plymouth). The meeting house pictured was built in 1634.

John Winthrop

The year 1630 saw the arrival in America of many immigrants under the leadership of John Winthrop (1588-1649). The Boston Colony was founded, which was Calvinist in theocracy (union of church and state).

First Church, Hartford, Connecticut

One of the most remarkable men in seventeenth-century New England was the Rev. Thomas Hooker. It was he who grasped the significance of the idea of the separation of church and state. In the little meeting house of the First Church of Hartford in Connecticut there took place, under his guidance, the first and original "declaration of independence" signed in America. To worship God in accordance with the dictates of their own consciences and to enjoy freedom from governmental control inspired the early refugees from England who, dissatisfied with the situation in Massachusetts, after a hard journey by foot settled at Hartford. In 1638 the church was founded by Hooker, who declared, "The foundation of authority is laid first by the free consent of the people" — the cornerstone of Congregational polity and of the later political constitution of a united commonwealth.

The edifice shown here was erected in 1807. The influence of this congregation reached far beyond its immediate parish.

150

John Eliot

Pictured here is John Eliot, the apostle to the New England Indians, preaching to his flock. His first sermon was preached in a hut on the Charles River, near Watertown, on October 28, 1646. At the close of this service he served apples to the children and tobacco to the Indians.

He completed a translation of the Bible into the Indian language, published in 1663. He also prepared a catechism and a paraphrase of the Psalms in the native tongue.

An example of the Indian vocabulary: "Our lusts" in their language was *"nummatchechodtantamoonganunnoash."*

The Old South Church, Boston, Massachusetts

Within the walls of the Old South Meeting House were spoken some of the boldest utterances of patriotism and the strongest appeals for freedom against British tyranny. In the early Massachusetts Colony church and state were one. In Old South Church began the struggle to separate them. The church came into existence in 1669.

It was after a meeting held there on December 14, 1773, that many of the Boston citizenry dressed themselves as Indians and took part in the famous tea party in Boston Harbor. During British occupation this church was used as a riding school for the Queen's Light Dragoons.

The name "Old South" was given to the church from the fact that a new church, built near the old structure in 1817, was called "New South Church."

John Davenport

John Davenport (1597-1670), an early leader in asserting the Bible as the sole law of church organization — toward the Congregational model.

Memorial Hall, Harvard University, Cambridge, Mass.
(Nineteenth-century picture)

Harvard was founded by the Puritan Massachusetts Bay Colony for the training of ministers in 1636. The colony taxed itself heavily, year after year, for the support of the college. The Rev. John Harvard (Cambridge University) left a sizable library (for that day) to the college, and in gratitude the school took his name.

Unitarian beliefs among Congregational ministers developed during the eighteenth century. Jonathan Mayhew (1720-1766) was among the first publicly to oppose the Trinity doctrine. Harvard became "infected" with anti-Trinitarian views. When, in 1805, Henry Ware (1764-1845) was appointed Hollis Professor at Harvard—along with four others—Harvard became "exceedingly and dangerously liberal." It departed from Congregationalistic Calvinism and conservatives withdrew their support of the institution.

Center Church, New Haven, Connecticut

Central of three churches on the spacious New Haven green stands Center Church. Within its walls for a century were held the graduation festivities of Yale University. In its basement is still to be seen the graveyard wherein lie many of the city's pioneers. The present structure dates from 1814, the fourth in succession of much less pretentious houses of worship.

This church commemorates the pioneer preacher, John Davenport, who conducted services under the shade of immense oak trees, in the spirit of religious freedom. New England Congregationalism was largely the product of the clergy, among whom was the notable Davenport. To secure membership in this church, the early requirement was a simple acknowledgment of belief in Christianity. One of the earlier structures served as both a house of worship and a courthouse. The beating of a drum signaled the hour of worship in the days of threatened Indian attacks.

Cotton Mather

Jonathan Edwards

Called the "prodigious" Cotton Mather (1663-1728), his writings, it is said, included some four hundred books, large and small. His *Magnalia Christi Americana,* in two volumes, published in 1702, treated of the founding of the New England colonies, their early leaders and the founding of Harvard College — a monumental literary effort of colonial times.

His father was Increase Mather and his mother a daughter of John Cotton.

Edwards (1703-1758), a Yale graduate, is best known for his ministry in Northampton, Massachusetts (1727-1750), for his philosophical speculations and his part in the "Great Awakening" in New England. His Enfield sermon, of July 8, 1741, is still a classic in the area of the preaching of fear in the minds of men. He held to Calvinism with full acceptance of determinism (opposing Arminianism). God chooses for salvation and damns according to His own sovereign will. Edwards died as he was beginning the presidency of the College of New Jersey (Princeton).

Yale University
(Nineteenth-century picture)

As early as 1654 there was an attempt to found a college in New Haven, which resulted in the establishment of the Hopkins Grammar School. Again in 1700 steps were taken at a meeting of the clergy, first in New Haven and later in Branford. Loss of control of Harvard by conservatives in Boston and elsewhere underscored the hope of a college of sound doctrine and polity in the New Haven Colony. Five Connecticut ministers drafted a charter in 1701, among them Abraham Pierson, who became the first president of the college.

Elihu Yale was a benefactor. Cotton Mather suggested his name for the new institution.

Beginnings were at Saybrook. The ten ministerial trustees took leadership over church and state. There was an effort to consolidate Congregationalists into a more confessional position and a closer fraternity with the Presbyterians. The Divinity School as a distinctive department came in 1822, with the Rev. Nathaniel W. Taylor as its head.

Timothy Dwight

Dwight (1752-1817) was a Congregationalist minister, president of Yale College and professor of theology. Under his powerful preaching a "Second Great Awakening" in America was sparked. He favored a return to Old Calvinism.

Charles G. Finney

A revivalist of the pre-Civil War days, Finney (1792-1875) became the first minister of Broadway Tabernacle in New York and the first professor of theology at Oberlin College, later its president. George Williams, organizer of the Y.M.C.A., was influenced by reading Finney's *Lectures on Revivals of Religion* (1834).

Lyman Beecher

Beecher (1775-1863) served both Congregationalists and Presbyterians and led a religious revival in his day. He opposed the Unitarians of his time, and was particularly anti-Catholic. He became president of Lane Seminary in Cincinnati. His son was Henry Ward Beecher.

Oberlin Theological Seminary, Oberlin, Ohio

Oberlin was founded by a Pilgrim colony as was Plymouth, Massachusetts. By a covenant the settlement began in 1833. Two pioneers were the Rev. John J. Shipherd and a missionary to the Choctaw Indians in Mississippi. The first college building was erected in 1833, and it was the first college to give women equal educational advantages with men. The First Congregational Church of Oberlin was organized in 1834.

Oberlin became known widely as a place "where peculiar and pronounced views" were held concerning religion, theology, politics and social life.

Mary Lyon

A leader in advocating education for women, Mary Lyon was born in 1797. After some years of teaching she began working on a plan for a seminary for girls. In 1837 Mount Holyoke was opened, on the basis of her solicitation of friends and funds. She died in 1849, leaving a widening influence in her field of special labors.

Leonard Bacon

A foremost leader in Congregational history. In 1846 Bacon published a volume on *Slavery Discussed,* to which Abraham Lincoln paid tribute years later as a book having led him to some clear convictions on the subject.

For fifty-seven years, from 1825 until his death in 1881, Bacon was minister of the First Church in New Haven. From 1866 on he was a teacher in the Yale Divinity School.

Mount Holyoke College, South Hadley, Massachusetts

Henry Ward Beecher

Congregational minister, Beecher (1813-1887) is known as the "eminent pulpit and platform orator" of his day. In 1847 he settled at Plymouth (Congregational) Church in Brooklyn, serving the remainder of his somewhat stormy life there. In 1874 he was the main figure in a famous adultery trial which ended in a stalemate, an ecclesiastical council later acquitting him.

A leader in the antislavery movement, supporter of the Union, advocate of theological modernism and the doctrine of evolution, propagandizer in politics, author of many books—his life was full to the brim.

Beecher in His Prime in His Pulpit

Plymouth Congregational Church, Brooklyn, New York

Beecher's Literary Workshop

Beecher's Home in Brooklyn

He also maintained a country home at Peekskill, New York.

An Appeal for Liberty

"My anti-slavery sentiments began to be well known in New York [1847-1849]. Upon the establishment of the *Independent* I was invited . . . to furnish 'Star Papers' for the paper. And in those I avowed such anti-slavery sentiments as made it a little uncertain whether the three adjunct editors . . . could sustain me. It was a time of very great caution and prudence, but I stuck right at it!"

— HENRY WARD BEECHER

Quelling the Tumult at Manchester, England

In 1863 Beecher visited Great Britain and the Continent. He was asked to speak in Manchester, Glasgow, Liverpool and London.

"Southern agents," aided by their English friends, organized gangs of roughs to attend and break up the meetings. He was greeted with hisses. Suggesting "fair play," he soon gained a hearing. His wit and eloquence brought cheers. Here he was known as "Ward Beecher, a brother of Mrs. Beecher Stowe." Now he became "Henry Ward Beecher" in his own right. He hurled himself against the slave traffic.

Beecher on Trial

On November 2, 1873 *Woodhull & Claflin's Weekly* charged Beecher and Mrs. Tilton with adultery. The paper was suppressed and the editors imprisoned for a time. Tilton was an assistant to Beecher as editor of the *Independent* and a member of Plymouth Church. The pros and cons of the case consumed six months, with Brooklyn society divided.

Plymouth Church "Silver Wedding" Celebration,
October 10, 1872

A Group of Negroes Just Landed from Surinam to Be
Sold as Slaves
(*An artist's conception, ca. 1796*)

Harriet Beecher Stowe

Henry Ward Beecher, foremost among orators, was the target of abuse from proslavery journals. No epithet was too low, no name too mean, no characterization too offensive to be applied to him. The name "Beecher" became a hissing and a by-word.

It was circulated about that he was the inspirer or even the author of Mrs. Stowe's *Uncle Tom's Cabin*. To the contrary, he knew nothing about it until the serial appeared in a Washington journal.

In June, 1851, the famous story began to be serialized in *The National Era*. Harriet had learned from her father, Lyman Beecher, as had all the children, to despise slavery. She was married to a Biblical scholar, a professor at Lane Seminary in Cincinnati. There was little time for careful writing, with six children on her hands. Across the Ohio River she had seen slavery in operation and she yearned to do something about it. When the Stowes moved to Brunswick in Maine (her husband becoming a teacher at Bowdoin College), she envisioned the story while in church on a Sunday. At home she sat down and began her potential novel.

As a book *Uncle Tom's Cabin* was rejected by one publisher and accepted doubtfully by another. "I hope," she said, "it will make enough so that I may have a new silk dress." The first week it was published (March, 1852, in Boston) the whole edition of 5,000 copies was sold out. Before the summer's end her royalties amounted to more than a silk dress — the sum of $10,000. Three hundred thousand copies went through the market during the first year.

The effect of the novel was "amazing, instantaneous and universal."

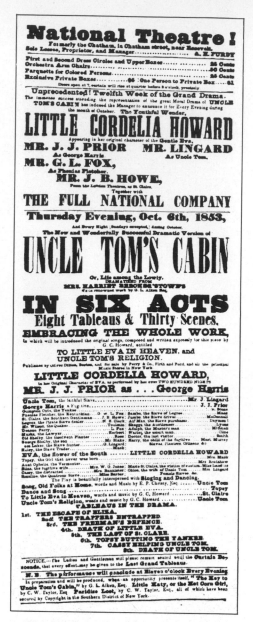

Uncle Tom's Cabin *on the Stage*

Uncle Tom's Cabin appears in *The National Era,*
June 2, 1851

The Escape of Eliza and Her Child across the Ohio
(From Uncle Tom's Cabin*)*

In her preface to *Uncle Tom's Cabin* Harriet Beecher Stowe wrote: "The object of these sketches is to awaken sympathy and feeling for the African race, as they exist among us; to show their wrongs and sorrows, under a system so necessarily cruel and unjust as to defeat and do away with the good effects of all that can be attempted for them by their best friends."

This little book lighted "a million campfires in front of the embattled hosts of slavery" (Frederick Douglass).

A dramatization of the book opened in Troy, New York in the fall of 1852. Pictured here is the notice by the National Theatre of New York City of its performance.

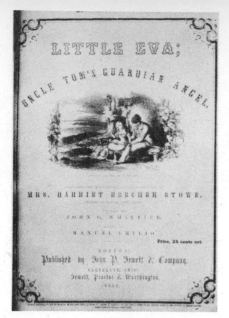

A Song, "Little Eva," by John Greenleaf Whittier

Mary E. Webb, a Free Colored Woman, Reading from Uncle Tom's Cabin *at the Home of the Duchess of Sutherland in London, 1856*

Uncle Tom's Cabin was quickly translated into many languages. Its circulation was forbidden in the South.

Negro Churches Following the Civil War

The Negro churches, after the Civil War, grew by leaps and bounds, with the new freedom. They were used for meetings concerning civil rights and new political problems.

Pictured here is a colored convention in Washington, D. C., in 1869.

161

John G. Fee

The Fisk Jubilee Singers

A missionary clergyman, son of a slaveholder, who crusaded against slavery in the state of Kentucky, Fee began an interracial school at Berea, was driven away by the community and succeeded in re-establishing his school, now Berea College (1858).

After the Civil War Berea College benefited from funds collected by Congregationalists and others. Its history is part of the story of the American Missionary Association (organized in 1846), an offspring of Oberlin College.

This famous choir of nine toured America and Europe to raise funds for Fisk School, established by the American Missionary Association at Nashville (1866).

Dressed in ordinary clothes, the choir met with increasing success as the tour progressed. They stirred the Oberlin campus with their spirituals, and impressed Henry Ward Beecher's church, the White House and finally Europe. Their campaign netted $150,000 for Fisk and for themselves the honor of being "the first group of Negro musicians to win international acclaim."

Berea College

Jubilee Hall, Fisk University, Nashville, Tennessee

Incorporated as a university in 1867, it was sparked by old slave songs and spirituals into one of America's best-known Negro colleges. The first year's enrollment (before incorporation) numbered 1,200 students.

Negro Prayer Meeting after Liberation

Lyman Abbott

Lyman Abbott (1835-1922) was successor to Henry Ward Beecher as minister of Plymouth Church in Brooklyn. His thought was with the liberals. He tried to reconcile the physical sciences and religion and stressed the progressive character of revelation. The doctrine of a depraved human nature he emphatically opposed. The immanence of God, rather than transcendence, was a doctrine which he stressed. His work entitled *The Theology of an Evolutionist* (1897) suggests his point of view.

Horace Bushnell

Minister of the North Church in Hartford, Horace Bushnell (1802-1876) was a graduate of Yale College and Divinity School. He helped to dethrone Calvinism in the New England churches by teaching the doctrine of normal religious growth (as against a marked conversion experience), by his conception of miracles as other than the abrogation of natural laws, and by a less arbitrary conception of the atonement doctrine. His *Christian Nurture* (1846) marked a new development in the ideas of Christian education.

His own church stood with him against the attempts of Congregational clergy and churches to disavow him.

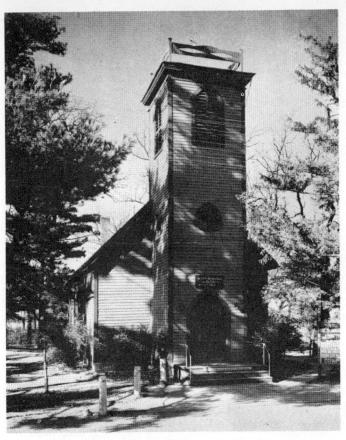

The Little Brown Church in the Vale

This church, located near Nashua in northeast Iowa, in "a pleasant woodsy spot," was made famous in the song, "The Church in the Wildwood" (written a hundred years ago by Dr. William S. Pitts).

This rural Congregational church was founded in 1855 by the Rev. Ozias Littlefield and five members. Until 1859 it was a modest log house. The new church was painted brown because at the time this was the cheapest color.

A favorite place today for weddings and an attraction for tourists.

Mark Hopkins

From the beginning of the settlement of New England, Congregationalists were deeply interested in maintaining an educated ministry. For that purpose Harvard College was founded. Yale College was also begun by ministers for ministers.

The name of Mark Hopkins (1802-1887) was associated for more than fifty years with Williams College, as preacher, teacher and philosopher. (Williams was incorporated in 1793 and a Congregational minister became its first president.)

President Garfield, a student at Williams, later made this famous remark about President Hopkins: "A log cabin in Ohio, with a wooden bench in it, and Mark Hopkins on one end of it and I on the other, would be college enough for me."

George Angier Gordon

For over forty years, Scottish born George Gordon (1853-1929) was minister in the Old South Church in Boston. His viewpoint was strongly liberal and his sermons and essays were widely read. His preaching was attractive to Harvard students and faculty. He taught the doctrine of universalism.

Francis E. Clark

Congregational minister in New England, Francis E Clark (1852-1927) is best known as a founder of the "Christian Endeavor" (Young People's Society). He was nicknamed "Father Endeavor" (from his first two initials). In 1895 the World's Christian Endeavor Union was organized. The societies were interdenominational, seeking to promote Christian living and activity *within* the church.

German Mysticism

Jakob Böhme

Böhme (1575-1624) was a plain Saxon shoemaker who, indignant at the religious controversies of his day, came to look afresh within himself. He held that the inspiration behind the Bible is little different from that available to any good person. Revelations come to anyone. He claimed to possess such revelations, about which he wrote poetically and symbolically.

Böhme's *Aurora* was his chief work. His influence was exceedingly great: upon German pietism, Quakerism and even philosophers such as Hegel, Schelling and Schopenhauer.

Johann Arndt

Arndt (1555-1621) is known especially for his *True Christianity*. He attempted to turn the attention of the whole church of Germany away from the sorry disputes of his time. This work had a wide circulation and a great influence. It came to America along with the German Bible in the early German immigration.

The Reformed Church in America

About halfway between the English settlements in Virginia and what came to be New England, a small craft called the *Halve Maen,* under a Dutch flag, sailed up a broad estuary in 1609, seeking a passage to the Orient. This was Henry Hudson's discovery of the river now bearing his name.

The Reformed Church in America looks back to this beginning. The new territory was claimed by the United Provinces of the Netherlands. Trading posts followed. Since the majority of Hollanders belonged to the "Church of Jesus Christ Reformed According to the Word of God," it is claimed that Reformed people settled in the Hudson Valley after 1614. Thus the Dutch Liturgy and Catechism were used in the New World before the Pilgrims' landing at Plymouth.

New Amsterdam (New York), the island that guarded Hudson's entrance to the river, and Fort Orange (Albany) at the head were the first villages of permanence. Two laymen were sent to minister to these settlers in 1623. In 1628 Michaelius arrived in New Amsterdam as the first Reformed minister. He organized a first congregation. The lineal descendant of this congregation of fifty members is the present Collegiate Church of New York.

The Reformed Church can claim to be the oldest Protestant Church in the New World with a continuous ministry. Megapolensis, the first minister in Albany, mastered the Mohawk language that he might preach to the Indians.

In 1664 there were thirteen organized churches. The colony, however, was taken over by England in 1664, and Dutch colonization gave way to English. There were disputes, of course. In 1696 King William III granted a royal charter to the Church in New York.

The Dutch divided in the eighteenth century on issues of relationship with Holland. One group in the New York area wished to maintain close contact with the mother country. The second, under Frelinghuysen in New Jersey, sought an Americanization of the church. The latter won out, establishing in New Brunswick Queen's College, now Rutgers (opened in 1770).

After the Revolution a new order began. New Brunswick became the seat of a seminary in 1784. A second wave of immigration, beginning in 1847, concentrated on the Middle West. Hope College and Western Seminary, Holland, Michigan; Central College, Pella, Iowa; and Northwestern Junior College in Orange City, Iowa — all are the result of this immigration.

In 1956 the Reformed Church in America claimed 211,000 members. The church is liturgical, Presbyterian in polity — a national body meeting annually. The Heidelberg Catechism is held with reverence.

The Treaty Between Governor Minuit and "the Aborigines"
for the Sale of Manhattan Island in 1626

The first director-general of the Dutch colony was Peter Minuit. In 1626, after his arrival, a regular purchase of Manhattan Island from "the Aborigines" was made. In Brodhead's *History of the State of New York* we read:

"As soon as Minuit was established in his government, he opened negotiations with the savages, and a mutually satisfactory treaty was promptly concluded, by which the entire Island of Manhattan, then estimated to contain about twenty-two thousand acres of land, was ceded by the native proprietors to the Dutch West-India Company for the value of sixty guilders, or about twenty-four dollars of our present currency."

The Synod of Dort

The Walloons

The Dutch Church in the New World was bound to the churches in Holland by the formulas of unity, viz., the Belgic Confession, the Heidelberg Catechism and the Canons of Dort.

The Synod of Dort (1618-1619) was convened to settle doctrinal disputes between Arminians and extreme Calvinists. To it came theologians from England, Scotland, Germany, Switzerland and the Netherlands. Politics, as usual, were involved.

The Heidelberg Catechism (1562) was composed by Kaspar Olevianus (1536-1587) and Zacharias Ursinus (1534-1583). Both it and the Belgic Confession were adopted as the orthodox teaching of Dutch Calvinism — a disavowal of Arminianism.

Pictured here is the Synod of Dort, from an original painting in Stadhuis, Dordrecht, Holland.

Among the small number of the first settlers in the New Netherland were the Huguenot-Walloons, who, during persecution in the seventeenth century, had fled from the French Belgic provinces to Holland.

The first-born white child was the daughter of George Janse D' Rapalie, a Walloon settler on Long Island at a place called Walleboght (Walloon Cove). Peter Minuit was a Walloon.

In 1924 the tercentenary was marked by a special commission for the commemoration of the French and Belgian-Huguenot (or Walloon) settling in New Netherland. A commemorative volume was issued.

Pictured here is the ship, *New Netherland.*

Ursinus and Olevianus

The Landing of the Walloons at Albany

Authors of the Heidelberg Catechism, a popular manual of instruction in the Reformed faith.

Unveiling the Walloon Monument in New York, May 18, 1924

A View of New Amsterdam in 1656

The Dutch Reformed Church was built in the fort (now the Battery) in 1642. Dimensions: 70 by 52 feet; built of stone. It was occupied until 1693 and then relinquished to the British government. It was burnt down in 1741.

In 1790 when the foundations of the fort were dug to make way for the government house, a stone marker was uncovered, dated 1642, designating *"dese tempel."*

The Old South Church in Garden Street, New York Built in 1693

A Print of the Old Middle Dutch Church, as First Built, Executed in 1731

Inscribed: "To the Honorable Rip Van Dam, Esquire, President of His Majesty's Council for the Province of New York."

168

North Reformed Dutch Church, corner of William and Fulton Streets, New York. Dedicated May 25, 1769

The Dutch Reformed Church, Fort Herkimer, New York

The Fort Herkimer Church is the only church still in use for worship of those old stone churches in New York state erected on the banks of the Mohawk through the mediation of Queen Anne. Its walls are three feet thick, for protection against the Indians. The pulpit is drum-shaped, set high on a pedestal. It was the scene of many an Indian attack in both the Indian Wars and the Revolution.

The Marble Collegiate Church of New York

This church recently celebrated its centennial.

New Brunswick Theological Seminary, New Brunswick, New Jersey

The first theological seminary of the Reformed Church in America, founded in 1784.

*The Middle Dutch Church on LaFayette Place, New York.
Dedicated May 9, 1839*

Chapel at Hope College, Holland, Michigan

The Baptists

Baptists claim no single leader, no distinctive creed, nor a single primitive or all-inclusive body. They disagree on origins. The Anabaptists, known today as Mennonites, were of the left wing of the Reformation and are perhaps closest to the original ancestors of the Baptists.

Many Baptists argue that their denominational history began with the English Separatists in Amsterdam, Holland. John Smyth, an Anglican priest who became a Puritan and Independent, led a group there in 1609 and is sometimes referred to as an originator of the Baptists since he accepted the principle that baptism belonged to believers and not to infants. He baptized himself and administered baptism to forty others. A part of this group returned to England under the leadership of Thomas Helwys. This is the source of the so-called General Baptists (Arminian in theology).

Another stream of Baptists reverts back to John Spilsburg, a former Congregationalist, in 1638. This group became Particular or Calvinistic Baptists, teaching predestination. In 1641 this group restored the practice of immersion, which eventually came to be a practice generally accepted by Baptists.

Not until 1891 was there a merger of Baptists, occurring in Great Britain and Ireland. As a larger group, this union became influential.

A Baptist church was established in Providence, Rhode Island in 1639 by Roger Williams, a Separatist minister who had initiated a colony to promote religious liberty (after being driven out of the Massachusetts Bay Colony). The claim of the Providence church for a "first" among Baptist churches of America is disputed by the Newport church founded by John Clarke in the same colony.

In the freedom of the Pennsylvania Colony, there was organized in 1707 the first association of Baptist churches in America, the Philadelphia Baptist Association. It took to itself a Calvinistic Confession.

During the Great Awakening of the eighteenth century Baptists became, along with other Protestants, evangelists.

Some encouraged emotionalism in religion — the New Lights or Separates, who developed antiorganization tendencies. This group developed in New England and the South. The other group, Old Lights or Regulars, were conservative in such matters as revivals.

In 1814 the General Missionary Convention was organized and this helped to solidify American Baptists. The American Baptist Publication Society (organized in 1824 as a General Tract Society) and the American Baptist Home Mission Society (organized in 1832) were national groupings and helped to make the denomination self-conscious.

The Northern Baptist Convention (now the American Baptist Convention), organized in 1907, became a corporation with restricted powers. The Southern Baptist Convention dates back to 1845 and a schism with the General Missionary Convention (Triennial Convention). Its growth was phenomenal, winning the allegiance of masses of people in the Southern area.

Both Southern and Northern Baptists held basic principles in common, the former being more aloof from interdenominational movements and more revivalistic in emphasis.

The Baptist World Alliance (organized in 1905) is an advisory but strong alliance.

There are some seven million Negro Baptists in America, organized into two main groups, the National Baptist Convention of the U. S. A., Inc., and the National Baptist Convention of America.

There are also a number of smaller Baptist bodies, some Arminian in theology and others extremely Calvinistic.

The local church as the unit of organization is basic to Baptist polity. Strongly democratic in spirit, holding the view that church and state are separate loyalties, Baptists have had a strong influence in American history in standing for the rights of the common man.

Roger Williams' Banishment

Founder of Rhode Island and great apostle of civil and religious freedom, Roger Williams was born in 1599 of Welsh parentage. He was a student at Cambridge University, where he took his Bachelor's degree. He became a student of law and then of theology, becoming a priest of the Anglican Church.

He disagreed with some of the high-churchism of his group, and in 1631 he came to America. He was then a Separatist and an advocate of the Baptist view of religious freedom as against state compulsion. At Salem, Massachusetts, he became, in 1631, a minister of the church, but for a brief time only. At Plymouth, beyond the jurisdiction of the Massachusetts Bay Colony, he found a more congenial place of work. Always he proclaimed church-state separation, arousing antagonism of non-Baptist Separatists. At Salem once again, he became a popular preacher.

A controversy began to rage with the clergy and the Massachusetts Bay court, which ended in Williams' banishment from the colony. When he left, many loyal sympathizers went with him.

Pictured here is a facsimile from the original records of the order for his banishment. The sentence was passed on October 9, 1635. He was to be arrested and sent to England, but he had already fled as an exile.

The colony of Rhode Island and Providence Plantations was the result of this flight, with a liberal charter granted by King Charles II. Thus a new kind of America was being born.

In 1639 he was publicly immersed. He did not remain loyal to the society which administered this baptism, but became a "Seeker." He died in 1683.

Facsimile of a Portion of a Letter of Roger Williams to John Winthrop, Jr. (1648)

Order Banishing the Founders of the First Baptist Church in Boston

John Bunyan

English preacher, famous for his *Pilgrim's Progress* (Part I, 1678; Part II, 1684), Bunyan (1628-1688) suffered twelve years' imprisonment for his activities as a Nonconformist leader. Some sixty books and tracts on religious subjects are credited to him.

Pictured here is Bunyan in Bedford Jail in 1667. His blind child is leaving him for the night. He was pardoned in 1672, becoming the most popular preacher in the England of his day.

Early in his preaching he denounced the desecration of the Lord's day by labor, sports or otherwise. Baptists remind us that in 1655 he was "immersed" upon his conversion.

Isaac Backus

A Congregationalist, Separatist, Baptist minister and historian. Born at Norwich, Connecticut, 1724, Backus was converted in the Great Awakening in 1741 and began preaching at first without license. He came out for the view that baptism must be accompanied by a profession of faith. He did not at first consider himself a Baptist, but continued as an evangelist. He was for many years a trustee of Brown University and became an ordained Baptist minister.

He is known for his labors for the separation of church and state. In 1774 he was sent to Philadelphia as a representative of Baptist churches to enlist the sympathies of the Continental Congress for oppressed Baptists. He was an inveterate traveler and a compiler of historical data. He died in 1806.

John Gano

Of a Presbyterian family, Gano (1727-1804) became a convert to Baptist views. In 1762 he became minister of the First Baptist Church of New York, where he remained for more than a quarter of a century.

His name is associated with the Revolutionary struggle. He was an army chaplain in General Clinton's New York Brigade, shunning no dangers. From General Washington he and chaplains like him received tribute and special commendation. He participated in furthering Baptist interests, particularly at Brown University.

Isaac Eaton's Academy

In 1756 the Rev. Isaac Eaton of Hopewell, New Jersey, opened "the first Baptist Seminary in this country" for the education of young men for the ministry. It was supported by the Philadelphia and Charleston Baptist Associations.

Brown University

The First Negro Baptist Church, Savannah, Georgia

In Savannah, George Liele founded a Baptist church for Negroes in 1779. A slave, Andrew Bryan, became minister of the First Baptist Church for colored worshipers, built in 1796. Although its members were whipped by the whites, the church continued.

The Rev. James Manning was commissioned to interest Baptists in establishing an educational institution for an educated ministry. He was sent to Newport to stir up interest.

In 1765 he was elected president of "Rhode Island College." In 1770 the college was removed to Providence. The trustees were designated by the charter to be twenty-two Baptists (forever), five Friends or Quakers, four Congregationalists and five Episcopalians. The president must be a Baptist. "Into this liberal and catholic institution shall never be admitted any religious tests."

The name "Brown" was given in 1804 in honor of Nicholas Brown, a benefactor.

The Rev. Andrew Bryan, Baptist Preacher in Georgia

William Carey

An English Baptist minister who was largely responsible for the earliest English foreign missionary society, in 1792.

Born in Purey, Northamptonshire, England, in 1761, he arrived in India as a missionary in 1794, remaining there until his death in 1834.

His salary as minister of the parish of Moulton was $75 per year. He had great facility in the use of foreign languages, and was the author of several grammars and lexicons.

Regent's Park College, London

Home of the Baptist theological seminary, formerly known as Stepney College, founded in 1810. It began at Regent's Park in 1856. Affiliated with the University of London.

Colby University

Incorporated in 1813, located in Waterville, Maine, Colby University took the name of Waterville College in 1820. It got its name from Gardner Colby, Esq., of Boston, a generous patron. A Baptist-sponsored school in its inception, theological training was included in its early curriculum.

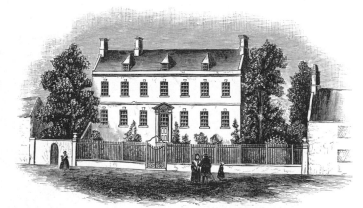

The House in Kettering, England, in Which the Baptist Missionary Society Was Formed

William Carey was the moving spirit in this society, founded in 1792. Said Carey: (1) Expect great things from God. (2) Attempt great things for God. Carey offered himself as a missionary, ready to embark for any part "of the heathen world."

Newton Theological Seminary, Newton Center, Massachusetts

Began its existence in 1825 under the sponsorship of New England Baptists.

First Infant Sunday School, First Baptist Church, Boston

From Reformation days, the schools of Luther were held seven days a week. John Knox introduced into Scotland a system of Sunday schools. New England early had its religious instruction of children. The German Seventh-Day Baptists established a school at Ephrata, Pennsylvania. Robert Raikes (1780-1785) and William Fox, London Baptist, established systematic training in religious instruction. These schools early used paid instructors. In 1791 the Philadelphia Society instituted support of First Day or Sunday schools.

Infants were included around 1829, a beginning being made in Boston by the use of marching, pictures and ensemble learning.

Here shown is an early engraving of such a school.

Tremont Temple, Boston

Formerly Tremont Theatre, this building was purchased in 1843 by the Tremont Street Baptist Church for a place of worship where seats would be free of rental.

It was destroyed by fire in 1852, and a new building erected in 1853. The Evangelical Baptist Benevolent and Missionary Society took over the edifice in 1858. Another fire occurred in 1879 and again the temple was reconstructed. It was at one time one of the largest congregations in the United States, and headquarters for New England Baptists.

Denison University

Located in Granville, Ohio, this school was founded by the Ohio Baptist Education Society in 1831. Its name is in honor of one of its benefactors. First intended as a manual-labor school, it is now a liberal arts college.

Baylor University

This college, located in Independence, Texas, was chartered in 1845. The Texas Baptist State Convention has appointed five of its trustees annually and received its yearly report.

Rochester Theological Seminary — Trevor Hall

Founded by Baptists in 1850. In 1854 a German Department of the Seminary was instituted to serve the needs of German Baptist churches.

One of its most distinguished professors was Walter Rauschenbusch (1861-1918), who, German trained and a graduate of the University of Rochester and Rochester Theological Seminary, and minister of a German Baptist church in New York City, was professor of church history in the seminary, 1903-1919. His name is associated with the emphasis on Christianity as a "social gospel."

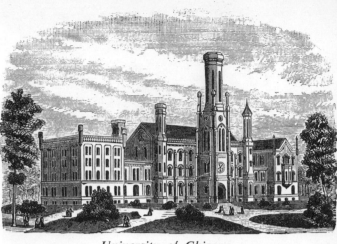

University of Chicago

Senator Stephen A. Douglas made proposals about the year 1856 to donate the site for a university upon land owned by him in Cottage Grove, south of the southern limits of Chicago. The Baptists seized the opportunity and acquired the site for the purpose of education. Ten acres near the lake were deeded over to them. The agreement was for a university of general education under Baptist supervision, its president and majority of trustees to be Baptists, but with no sectarian requirements for faculty and students. The Rev. J. C. Burroughs negotiated for this gift, resigning his pastorate to set out to raise funds. Mr. Burroughs became the first president of the institution (1858-1873). The cornerstone of the building was laid on July 4, 1857.

Spurgeon's Tabernacle, London

Raised as an Independent, converted in a Primitive Methodist chapel in Colchester, Charles Haddon Spurgeon (1834-1892) was baptized in the Baptist communion in 1851. His was a metropolitan ministry of large proportions. All London was talking about his preaching. In 1856 he began his work in the Music Hall, a building seating 7,000, where people flocked to hear and study this "pulpit phenomenon." The Metropolitan Tabernacle was founded in 1859, seating 5,500.

His sermons were published and distributed widely. He edited his own magazine, the *Sword and Trowel,* organized a Book Fund, developed a Pastors' College and engaged in philanthropic work of large proportions. In 1887 he withdrew from the Baptist Union.

Vassar College

An institution for the liberal education of young women, located in Poughkeepsie, New York, Vassar College was founded and endowed by Matthew Vassar with a benefaction of more than $700,000. Mr. Vassar was a Baptist. "The president and a majority of the board of trustees of the college" were Baptists. It is in no measure sectarian. Founded in 1861.

Crozer Theological Seminary

Located in Chester, Pennsylvania, south of Philadelphia, this seminary under the patronage of Baptist churches was incorporated in 1867. Mr. J. P. Crozer, founder of the borough of Upland, had given financial support in its early beginnings and the family continued to add benefactions. The first class graduated in 1870. Until very recent years, it has been favorably known as a stronghold of liberal theology and exerted a nationwide influence through its *Crozer Quarterly,* so well edited and conducted by Professor Morton Enslin.

Douglas Clyde Macintosh

One of the most distinguished philosophical theologians of the twentieth century. He was born in Breadalbane, Ontario, in 1877. A graduate of McMaster University, Toronto, and the University of Chicago (Ph.D.).

From 1897 to 1899 he was minister of the Baptist Church of Marthaville, Ontario and from 1903 to 1904 he taught philosophy at McMaster. He came to Yale in 1909 and was Dwight Professor of Theology and Philosophy of Religion, 1916 to 1942.

In World War I he served overseas first as chaplain with the Canadian Expeditionary Force and then as a secretary for the Y. M. C. A. with the American Expeditionary Force.

His many books on religion, philosophy and theology brought him to an enviable prominence as a systematic religious thinker and as an influence upon a generation seeking a reasonable faith. He died in 1948.

His name became widely known in what has been called "the celebrated Macintosh case." In the October Term, 1930, the Supreme Court of the United States handed down a split decision (5 to 4) — Chief Justice Hughes among the dissenters — denying him (and Miss Marie Averill Brand) American citizenship, for having affirmed scruples against promising to bear arms in defense of this country unless he believed a given war to be morally justified. Considerable discussion occupied the pages of the press on this decision of the Supreme Court.

The Thirty Years' War

Gustavus Adolphus and the Thirty Years' War

Gustavus at Lützen

Roman Catholicism girded itself against Protestants divided in loyalties. No longer could the combat be confined to pamphlets, councils and universities. It was now a question of political power. The soldier is the ambassador of theology and the symbol of political opportunity.

The Thirty Years' War began in 1618 and closed in 1648 (at the Peace of Westphalia). The issue between the two camps flared up in Bohemia.

Gustavus Adolphus, King of Sweden, led the Protestant forces. His cause, he thought, was a holy war. His soldiers marched singing *"Ein feste Burg ist unser Gott."* In the hour of victory he died on the battlefield in 1632.

A war of extermination, both sides claimed victory. The South, in general, remained Catholic, the North Protestant.

Albert von Wallenstein

The great general who led the Catholic forces against the Protestants. At Lützen Gustavus Adolphus' army defeated Wallenstein's powerful forces.

The Society of Friends (Quakers)

George Fox (1624-1691) is the founder of Quakerism. He and his early followers proclaimed their views and manners as those in accord with primitive Christianity.

The movement arose in reaction to the dead formalism of the church and looks back to medieval mystics as Christians of a sounder approach. Fox drew smaller sects and so-called "Seekers" to his cause. The inner voice is the source of its positive beliefs — bringing reformation to traditional doctrines. Man himself personally may appropriate the will of God. He needs to be bound by no creed. The Scriptures were not neglected; they are the instruments for an inner experience and a personal witness. God is in the soul of everyone. Simplicity of life and commitment to truth as one sees it — these are the characteristic tenets of the Quakers.

Persecuted, the Friends carried on. In the American colonies, notably William Penn's "Holy Experiment" in Pennsylvania, the Friends expanded in numbers and organizations.

Robert Barclay (1648-1690), converted to Quakerism in 1666, gave theological expression to the Friends' viewpoint in his *Apology for the True Christian Divinity,* wherein he appealed to the Scriptures, reason and the testimony of others.

John Woolman (1720-1772) exemplified the Quietist temper of life and dedication to the Spirit.

At the end of the eighteenth century, under the influence of the Wesleyan revivals, the Quakers took on certain characteristics of the Protestant revival, e.g., the emphasis on Scriptural authority. A schism developed. Elias Hicks reaffirmed the doctrine of the Inner Light. The Orthodox controverted with the Hicksites, the former being more hospitable to the ways of the Protestant churches.

Joseph John Gurney (1788-1846) attempted to bring the Hicksites into a more sympathetic relationship with the Orthodox (although not finally with success), and as a theologian he directed the Orthodox into a more definite Biblical theology and even to the practice of the sacraments. John Wilbur (1774-1856) renewed the Inner Light emphasis. All these emphases caused a diversification into special organized groups.

Today the Friends divide into groups: the General Conference (established in 1892), a fellowship of six Hicksite Yearly Meetings; the Wilburites or Conservatives; the Orthodox (Philadelphia Yearly Meeting); and other Independent Meetings. The "Five Years Meeting" is a large association composed of eleven Yearly Meetings with headquarters in Richmond, Indiana.

George Fox

Born in 1624, Fox early turned against the insincerities of current religious practices and social behavior. He experienced a conversion, an "opening," in 1646. He suffered ridicule and persecution for his preaching, and was accused of blasphemy and disturbance of the peace. He was imprisoned eight times. He married Margaret Fell. His mysticism was influenced by the Böhmists and others. Evangelistic in temper, he boldly espoused his convictions. He died in 1691. An apostle of "the Inner Light."

Chastising a Quaker at Paul's Cross, Cheapside, in the Time of Cromwell

A Public Whipping in the London Sessions House Yard
(*From the* Malefactor's Register, *1745*)

Punishment by flogging was not only directed to vagrants and rogues, male and female, but in time of persecution against heretics and obstinate dissenters. Quakers, in their initial efforts, suffered public whipping.

Order of the Lord Mayor of London Not to Require Oaths of Quaker Constables, 1687

King James II excused Quaker constables from swearing oaths in 1687 or from the fines imposed for such refusal.

The Quakers refused to fight for the state, take oath and give "hat honour," the first two on the authority of Scripture, the latter on their own belief that the uncovering of the head is an honor reserved for God alone.

Sample of George Fox's Handwriting

George Fox's note to Ann and Thomas Curtis in Reading Prison. Quakers looked after their fellow Friends in prison, keeping account of their names and collecting funds for their relief.

A William Burtt Addressing the Monthly Meeting of South-West Division in Lincolnshire, 1692, Held in His House at Welbourn North End

George Whitehead Opening the Yearly Meeting of the Quakers, 1696

Seventeenth-Century Quaker Costume

Every article from head to foot should exhibit plainness. This early Quaker rule covered beasts as well as man. No hat bands, needless buttons, no buckles, no fine bridles.

A Certificate of Release (by Sarah Roberts) from a Marriage Engagement, 1710

A Quaker couple intending to marry should first consult privately some of the older Friends. Their proposal might afterward be announced at a public Quaker meeting. The marriage ceremony was a signed, dated certificate of all the Friends present (at least twelve) where a testimony had been given on behalf of the couple. No agent performed the ceremony. Said George Fox, "We marry none, but are witnesses of it."

William Penn

(This picture is regarded as the most authentic of William Penn, made while in Ireland — aged 22 years. Original at Pennsylvania Historical Society, Philadelphia)

Friends' Meeting House Built in 1688 and Penn's Grave at Jordans, Buckinghamshire, England

(Reproduced from a painting by Hazlehurst. Original at Germantown Friends School, Philadelphia)

Penn was born in London in 1644. A student at Oxford, he developed a taste for wide reading. A nonconformist, he was banished from school. At a Huguenot college in France, he studied early Church history, then entered a law school in England. He went to Ireland in his early twenties to manage a large estate. At a Quaker meeting he was converted and immediately took a place of leadership, suffering ostracism, persecution and imprisonment — even in the Tower of London.

He wrote many books, some of them in prison. He envisioned an assembly of nations, with political justice and religious freedom. With a good financial heritage and a land grant in America from the crown, a charter was granted him in 1681, making him proper owner and governor of the Province of Pennsylvania (named in honor of his father by the King).

"The Holy Experiment" was Penn's name for his undertaking in America. He envisioned a colony where religious freedom and equality should obtain. He had in mind the persecuted of his own faith, although Quakers were not to obtain undue favors. He drew up a "Frame of Government" guaranteeing religious toleration and the power of revision of the constitution. Prisoners were to have the right to be heard. In 1682, with a hundred immigrants, Penn set sail for his province. He played fair with the Indians. The colony grew rapidly, with immigrants of various backgrounds. There were many discouragements, however, before he died in 1718.

A London Quaker
(From a Print of 1711)

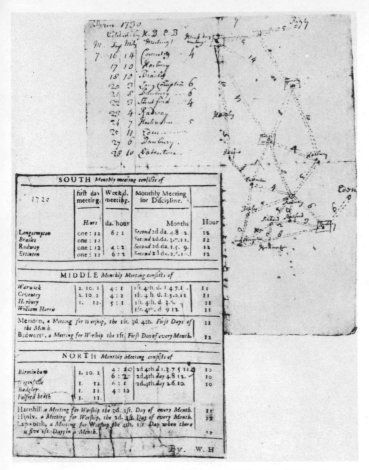

Sketch Map and Monthly Meeting Guide Used by Henry and Elizabeth Bradford During Their Ministerial Visits, 1730

In 1730 Henry and Elizabeth Bradford rode eighty-six miles to visit eleven meetings in eleven days. Ministers traveled usually in pairs. Sketch maps of ministerial journeys were made by such ministers, showing the meetings and riding distances and printed lists of First Day, weekday and Monthly Meetings were available at certain centers.

A Table of Heads

No			No		
1	Appeals	1	28	Parliament	147
2	Arbitrations	5	29	Persecution	149
3	Books	13	30	Plainness	153
4	Certificates	17	31	Poor	161
5	Children	19	32	Preachers	171
6	Conversation	30	33	Prisoners	181
7	Correspondents	38	34	Questions	185
8	Covetousness	43	35	Records	191
9	Days	47	36	Removals & Settlements	197
10	Defamation	49	37	Representatives	205
11	Discipline	52	38	Salutations	211
12	Disputes	62	39	Schools	
13	Epistles	66	40	Scriptures	219
14	Families	69	41	Servants	
15	Fighting	73	42	Singing	225
16	Kings & Governours	77	43	Steeple-house Rates	239
17	Law	85	44	Stock National	243
18	Love	89	45	Sufferings	
19	Marriages	91	46	Talebearing &c	257
20	Meeting houses	103	47	Tombstones	
21	Meetings for Discipline	105	48	Tithes	
22	Meetings for Worship	110	49	Trading	288
23	Morning Meeting	127	50	Wills	302
24	Mourning	128	51	Yearly Meeting	308
25	Negroes	131			
26	Oaths	139			
27	Orphans	143			

A Table of Heads, Christian and Brotherly Advices (1738)

Manuscript copies of *Christian and Brotherly Advices* were distributed to local meetings. In 1738 each meeting for church affairs could secure, for fifty shillings, a copy of these *Advices* from the Yearly Meetings in London, alphabetically digested under proper heads. The picture is of a table of contents.

Colthouse Meeting House, Lancashire

William Wordsworth occasionally attended meetings for worship here when at school at Hawkshead.

The Devonshire House (Now Demolished), the Former London Headquarters of the Society of Friends
(*From an old print*)

An Eighteenth-Century Friends Meeting

The Third Haven Meeting House, Easton, Maryland

Generally regarded as the oldest Quaker meeting house still standing in America. Built in 1684.

The Quaker Meeting House, Flushing, Long Island

First meeting in private homes, the New York Quakers in 1692 began to solicit funds for the building of a meeting house in Flushing, Long Island. A plain structure, lacking heating facilities and even floors, was their first building venture. In a remodeled building in 1716 was held the first public meeting in New York to agitate for the freedom of the slaves. In fact, the first antislavery publication is associated with this church, in which discussions were held. The British used the building during the Revolution as a hospital, prison and warehouse. Since 1783 this Friends meeting house has served its prime function.

Meeting House at Merion, Pennsylvania

Built in 1695, this is also one of the oldest of the American Quaker meeting houses. It is still in use.

Meeting House at Fourth and Arch Streets, Philadelphia

Built in 1804 on ground given to Friends by William Penn. The annual sessions of the Philadelphia Yearly Meeting are still held in this building.

Elias Hicks, Central Figure in the Hicksite Quaker Controversy of 1827-1828

Quaker and Quakeress of the Early Nineteenth Century

Said George Fox: "When the Lord sent me forth into the world . . . I was required to Thee and Thou all men and women without any respect to rich or poor, great or small."

In Fox's day one said "thou" to servants, employers and children and "you" to one's "betters." Now this was done away with by those who bowed to God alone. For Quakers there are no "betters" among men, hence "thou" and "thee" to all.

*A Quaker Meeting for Worship — the Arch Street,
Philadelphia, Meeting, May 19, 1900*
(One of the few photographs in existence, taken by Walter Jacob)

John Greenleaf Whittier, Well-known Quaker Poet

He has been called "the bard of freedom."

Founders Hall, Haverford College

Under the leadership of the Orthodox Philadelphia Quakers, the Society of Friends founded Haverford College in 1833. (In the late 1830's the Indiana and Ohio Friends began a program of higher education at Richmond, Indiana, which today is Earlham College.)

Rufus Jones

Rufus Jones (1863-1950) is considered the leading American Quaker of the twentieth century. A philosopher in his own right, he taught for many years at Haverford College. Born in a small Quaker community in Maine, he rose to eminence as a public lecturer and author of more than a score of books dealing with history, biography, philosophy and religion.

German Pietism

Philipp Jacob Spener

Spener was born in Alsace in 1635. A preacher in Strasbourg, he denounced the spiritual decline of the Church and eloquently called his people back to the religious life of the early Reformation. In 1666 he moved to Frankfort, becoming minister of an old influential church. He organized his *Collegia Pietatis* (meetings for Bible study and religious inspiration) and published, in 1675, his *Pia Desideria (Pious Desires),* which had an enormous influence for Christian commitments.

Around him the Pietist movement centered. He was a Lutheran and held that there should be reform *within* the church. He died in Berlin in 1705.

August Hermann Francke

The Pietist movement in Germany resulted in the founding of Halle University. The teachers there were in the spirit of Spener.

Francke (1663-1727) became the central figure at Halle, a teacher, minister, founder of philanthropic enterprises (notably an orphanage), missionary and a person of vital faith. From Halle radiated intense missionary influences. It became a celebrated Protestant center.

Presbyterianism in the U.S.A.

The largest and main Presbyterian group in this country is "The Presbyterian Church, U.S.A.," with more than two and a half million members.

Presbyterians began in America with some English Puritans and, of course, the Scotch-Irish. In 1611 Alexander Whitaker organized a church of "congregational presbytery." In Maryland (as early as 1657) and in New England (before 1640), Presbyterian polity was observed in some local churches in spite of the dominant majority of Congregationalists. At Southold, Long Island, in 1640 a Presbyterian church was founded. The oldest church with a continuous Presbyterian history is that at Jamaica, Long Island (1672).

The middle colonies — New Jersey, Maryland, Pennsylvania — became the center of Presbyterianism even before the advent of the Scotch-Irish.

The Rev. Francis Makemie (*ca.* 1658-1708) is known as the "father" of organized American Presbyterianism. He came from north Ireland in 1683 to Rehoboth, Maryland. He was a leader in the organization of the first presbytery — 1705 or 1706 — and its first moderator.

(See the section on the United Presbyterian Church, with which the Presbyterian Church, U.S.A., is merging.)

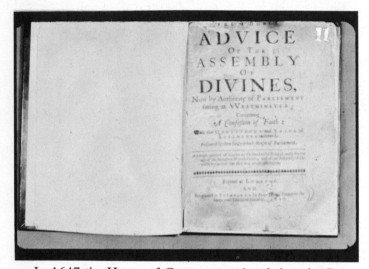

In 1647 the House of Commons ordered that the Presbyterian form of government should be tried for a year, but Oliver Cromwell later forbade the use of it. In America, however, in 1729, the synod adopted this Confession of Faith as containing the essential doctrines of the Presbyterian Church in America.

A Monument Erected to Francis Makemie by the Presbyterian Historical Society in Accomac County, Virginia, on the Site of Makemie's Home and Adjoining His Grave.

Rehoboth Church

Rehoboth Presbyterian Church in Maryland claims to have been founded by Makemie in 1683. The original building is still in use.

Lord Cornbury, Governor of New York, arrested Francis Makemie for preaching without a special license, because he was a dissenter from the Church of England. But Makemie argued: "My license which I got in England as a dissenter is good in all Her Majesty's dominions . . . including New York." He managed to win his case and thus helped to establish religious freedom in New York.

"Old Buttonwood"

Presbyterians seeking religious freedom organized the first Presbyterian church in Philadelphia in 1698 and built their first building, fondly called "Old Buttonwood," six years later. In this building they held the first presbytery followed by the first synod.

Presbyterian Minutes

These time-worn minutes show that seven ministers formed the first presbytery in Philadelphia in 1706 for mutual help and encouragement in the American wilderness.

Norriton Church

So many ministers and churches, like this Norriton Church, joined within eleven years that the presbytery expanded into a synod and three presbyteries.

Colonial Church

This picture is typical of the colonial church services. The people sat in square box-pews which were enclosed to prevent drafts along the floor. There was no heating system and the lighting was generally poor.

The Scotch and Scotch-Irish who fled to America in the eighteenth century were accustomed to having their ministers catechize them in this informal manner.

Communion Tokens

The churches in Britain and the colonies of America used little lead discs called "communion tokens." The minister gave the token to each member at the preparatory service after he had been catechized. He had to present it later to be admitted to holy communion.

William Tennent opened his school for the training of a Presbyterian ministry in a log cabin on the banks of the Neshaminy in Bucks County (north of Philadelphia) about 1735. This is the famous Log College, some of the alumni of which founded the College of New Jersey (now Princeton).

Charles Beatty (a student with William Tennent at the Log College) traveled with the Rev. George Duffield over the Appalachian Mountains in order to preach to the Indians, in 1766.

Princeton University

The history of early Presbyterian education is substantially the history of Princeton College. When, in 1745, Tennent died, his school was closed. Then followed an attempt to continue his work with a school located at different places, first at Elizabethtown, New Jersey, then in Newark (under the care of Aaron Burr).

The inhabitants of Princeton, New Jersey, offered two hundred acres of land and a sum of money for the location of the school. In 1753 this offer was accepted.

In honor of William, Prince of Orange and Nassau, the first building was called Nassau Hall. Jonathan Edwards became the successor of Aaron Burr. Not until 1869 did the faculty exceed eight professors.

Pictured here is "Princeton College," late in the nineteenth century.

Chaplain Caldwell, minister of the church at Elizabethtown, New Jersey, was among the many Presbyterians who served in the American Revolution. When soldiers lacked wadding for their rifles at the Battle of Springfield, Caldwell ran into the church, gathered up an armful of Watts' Metrical Psalms or hymnals and distributing them to the men, shouted: "Give 'em Watts, boys!"

195

As a member of the Continental Congress, John Witherspoon (1722-1794) was the only minister to sign the Declaration of Independence. His strong leadership caused Walpole to say, "Cousin America has run off with a Presbyterian parson." He was president of the College of New Jersey at Princeton and the organizing moderator of the First General Assembly in 1789.

The John Witherspoon Clock

When he came from Scotland, Witherspoon brought with him this grandfather's clock.

George Duffield was a chaplain of the Continental Congress. One Sunday from the pulpit of the Pine Street Church, he said, "There are too many men in this congregation. . . . Next Sunday there'll be one less!" And off he went to serve as chaplain. After the Revolution Duffield became the first stated clerk of the General Assembly.

Old Pine Street Church

The only colonial Presbyterian church still standing in Philadelphia.

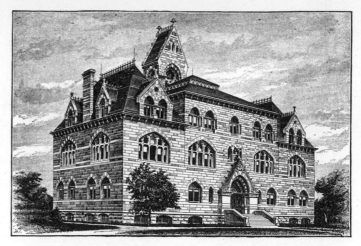

Princeton Theological Seminary

The General Assembly determined, in 1812, to establish a school for Presbyterian ministers. After hesitation as to place, the location was settled as Princeton. The institution was opened in 1812 with three students. The cornerstone of its building was laid in 1815.

Pictured here is Stuart Hall, Princeton Theological Seminary (late nineteenth century).

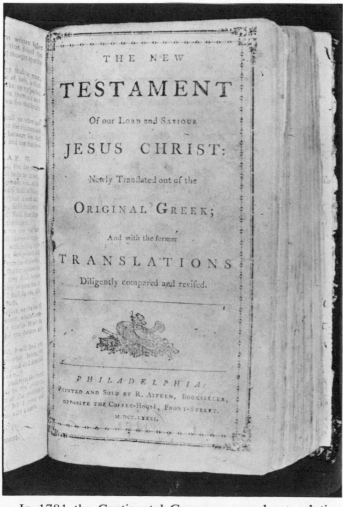

In 1781 the Continental Congress passed a resolution approving the publication of a Bible because the British blockade prevented importations. Robert Aitken, a Presbyterian elder, printed this first Bible in America.

Archibald Alexander

Archibald Alexander became the first professor in Princeton Theological Seminary when it was formed in 1812. Alexander and Samuel Miller, the church historian, began what is known as "the Princeton theology." The three-volume *Systematic Theology* of Charles Hodge (1797-1878) is regarded as the culmination of this line, of theological thought.

Many local women's missionary societies, like this one, promoted work for the spiritual welfare of Indians and others.

Indian Peace Pipe

Dr. Marcus Whitman, a physician and Presbyterian elder at Wheeler, New York, learned that the Indians of Oregon needed medical care and the Gospel. Against enormous obstacles he drove a wagon across the Rockies in 1836. His wife and Mrs. Henry Spalding were the first white women to cross the Rockies. In 1843 Dr. Whitman led a thousand settlers over the Oregon Trail. During a measles epidemic the Indians murdered both Dr. and Mrs. Whitman.

This peace pipe was presented by Chief Nacheninga of the Iowa Indians to the moderator of the General Assembly in Cincinnati in 1845 as an expression of the appreciation of his tribe for missionary work.

"White Fathers teach Great Spirit love Ioways. Teach Ioways make food come from ground. Good."

Dozens of missionaries preached, taught school and encouraged better agriculture in Indian villages like this.

Sheldon Jackson found numerous raw settlements in the Rockies after the Civil War and he planted churches in them. He traveled one million miles in missionary service. He organized the public school system for the United States in Alaska and he introduced reindeer from Siberia for food for the starving Eskimos.

Auburn Theological Seminary, Auburn, New York

Chartered in 1820 and offering its first classes the following year, Auburn represented a liberal theology. Soon after 1937 this seminary was absorbed by the Union Theological Seminary in New York.

McCormick Theological Seminary, Chicago, Illinois

In 1859 accepting a proposal and gift of $100,000 from the Hon. C. H. McCormick of Chicago for the location of a seminary in that city, and an offer of twenty-five acres added by others for a site, the General Assembly joined two smaller institutions into one. In 1886 "The Theological Seminary of the Northwest" became "McCormick Theological Seminary."

In the field of education there are over forty Presbyterian colleges. The first picture is of Kauke Hall (classrooms) on the campus of the College of Wooster, Ohio. The second is of Lafayette College, Easton, Pennsylvania.

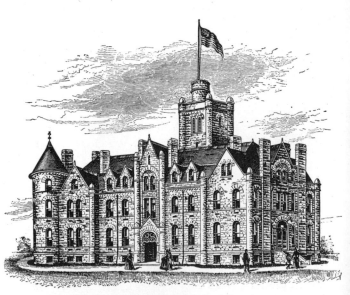

San Francisco Theological Seminary

Projected by the Synod of the Pacific in 1871. Now at San Anselmo, California.

University of Wooster

Founded in 1866, Wooster had, for a time, "an effective medical department at Cleveland."

Here pictured is the main building as it appeared before its destruction by fire in 1901.

Parsons College, Fairfield, Iowa

Founded in 1875.

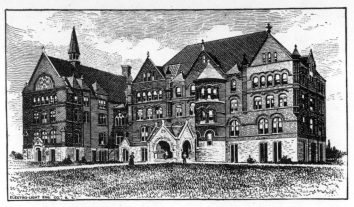

Macalaster College, St. Paul, Minnesota

Founded in 1885.

Charles H. Parkhurst

Parkhurst (b. 1842), a Congregationalist, is known for his down-to-earth preaching and for his courageous attacks upon the Tammany political machine and on crime of any type. For thirty-eight years (1880-1918) he served the Madison Square Presbyterian Church in New York City.

One of his bits of wisdom is this: "When we return to the original simplicity of the Church we shall in several respects modify existing forms and methods. For example, we shall then lay more stress upon truth and less upon the forms of truth." Denominationalism, he held, is "unapostolic." "The church is as large as the sky and wants to be open, with no customhouse port of entry to tax spiritual commodities that are in *transitu.*"

Charles Augustus Briggs

Briggs (1841-1913), a professor in Union Theological Seminary, New York, was suspended from the Presbyterian ministry by the General Assembly in 1893 for his liberal views on the Scriptures. (He became a priest in the Protestant Episcopal Church in 1899.)

The Briggs case was a factor in dividing Presbyterians into conservative and liberal groups, bringing about the withdrawal of Union Seminary from affiliation with the General Assembly. The revision of the Westminster Confession was a question involved.

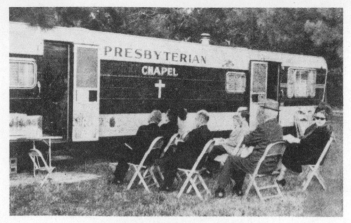

Chapel Trailer in South Carolina

Columbia Theological Seminary, Columbia, South Carolina

This seminary served the Southern Church.

"The Presbyterian Church in the United States"

Westminster College, Fulton, Missouri

This college has been sustained by the Synod of Missouri Presbyterians.

This is the so-called Southern Presbyterian Church. The Presbyterian churches in America divided, in 1837, into "Old School" and "New School" over the question of the "Plan of Union" with the Congregationalists. The Old School accused the New of being too liberal. Many of the New School favored abolition of slavery. In 1857 the New School Assembly took action which condemned the holding of slaves by church members. A result was the formation of an independently organized United Synod of the Presbyterian Church in 1858. In 1861 the Old School Assembly divided, one becoming the Presbyterian Church in the Confederate States of America. In 1864 the United Synod and the Confederate Church joined under the name of the latter. After the Civil War the name "The Presbyterian Church in the United States" was taken.

The church has traditionally been conservative in theology.

Pictured here is an early leader, the Rev. James H. Thornwell, in the formation of the Confederate Presbyterian Church.

Southwestern Presbyterian University, Clarksville, Tennessee

This college is now located in Memphis, engaged in an expansive program. It formerly had a theological department.

The Church of the Brethren

Schwarzenau in Wittgenstein, a county of Westphalia, was a gathering place for all kinds of religious dissenters. To this place in 1700 came Alexander Mack (1679-1735), who with seven others initiated the Brethren as a church in 1708. By lot the first baptizer was chosen and all were immersed three times, according to their conviction of conformity to New Testament primitive practice. The Schwarzenau congregation became the largest center in Europe for this church group. Under persecution they migrated to Holland in 1720 and nine years later moved as a body to Pennsylvania. Peter Becker in 1719 came to Germantown with a Brethren following.

The Church of the Brethren thinks of its origin in terms of "Biblical Pietistic mystics" and "imitators of primitive Christianity." In Germany the church was known as "Die Brüder Gemeinde," in America as "The German Baptist Brethren," and since 1908 under the present title.

Branches are: Brethren Church (Ashland), 1882; Brethren Church (Winona), *ca.* 1939; Old German Baptist Brethren, 1881.

The Brethren practiced nonconformity. This covered the whole of life: buildings, amusements, expenditures, furniture and even costumes. Like the Quakers and Mennonites, for them a person's garb was a witness of whether or not he was dedicated to luxury and worldly indulgences. In Dunker tradition colors were somber. A plain man wore his hair in simplicity. His speech, too, should be a witness of plainness.

In Pennsylvania they were called Dunkards, Tunkers or Dumplers.

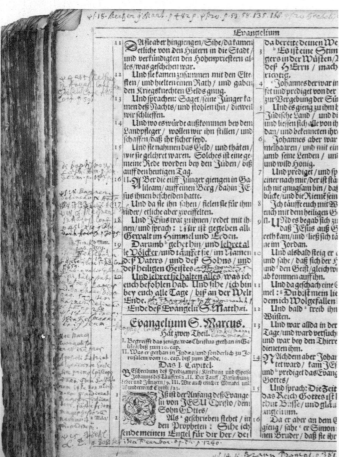

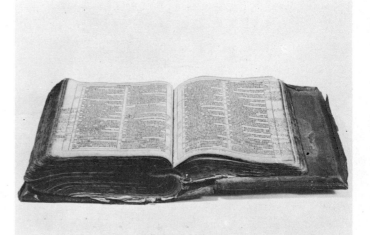

An Old German Bible Printed in 1664

Found in Hüttental above Schwarzenau and probably used by Alexander Mack. It is opened at the eighteenth chapter of Matthew and many notes are along the margins.

German Bible of 1664 Found in Hüttental by M. R. Zigler

Interesting notes along the margin of Matthew 28:16-20. The Great Commission and the basis of trine immersion.

The Brethren from 1708 to 1770 worshiped in homes and barns. Their first church building was erected in 1770 in Germantown. Alexander Mack was buried in the rear churchyard.

The Eder Bridge

Site of the first baptism of the Brethren group.

Hüttental

A suburb village of Schwarzenau, high above the Eder. Alexander Mack's home in center. Here is the place where the decision to initiate the church occurred in 1708.

Ship Allen *Bringing Alexander Mack and Members of the Brethren Group to America*

The entire shipload were Brethren. This is a symbolical painting. An earlier immigration of Brethren under the leadership of Peter Becker had come to Germantown, Pennsylvania, in 1719.

Panel of the Mural History of the Church

It portrays (1) the eight "founders" in prayer, (2) their first baptism, and (3) the two embarkations for America in 1719 and 1729. Practically all the Brethren in Europe came in these two ships.

The National Association of Free Will Baptists

The Free Will Baptists look back as far as the early seventeenth century for their origins. An entire church came from Wales and settled on the Delaware River. They were Arminian in doctrine. Paul Palmer was the first organizer of a Free Will Baptist church in Perquimans County, North Carolina, in 1727.

The National Association of Free Will Baptists is today "the largest group of Arminian Baptists in the world." Among its distinctive doctrines are: the human will is free to yield to or resist the truth and the Spirit; a saved individual may suffer "the shipwreck of faith" and become lost; baptism by immersion, the Lord's Supper and the Washing of the Saints' Feet are the "three Gospel ordinances"; tithing. The polity is Baptist, each church "the voice of authority." Their headquarters is at Nashville, Tennessee.

The name "Free Will" was taken to distinguish this body from the "fatalistic predestination known as Calvinism."

The Rev. Benjamin N. Randall (1749-1808) was the founder of the Free Will Baptist Church in the New England states. He organized the first church in New Durham, New Hampshire, in 1780.

The Gum Swamp Free Will Baptist Church

Located near Greenville, North Carolina, this is the oldest church of the Free Will Baptists in America. It was organized between 1725 and 1750. The present building was completed in 1948.

Methodism

John Wesley

Charles Wesley, the First "Methodist"

Charles Wesley (1707-1788), the first leader of the Holy Club which was the original Methodist fraternity. His fame — beyond his connection with his brother John — is associated with hymn writing, with some 6,500 lyrics to his credit. Among them: "Jesus, Lover of My Soul," "Come, Thou Almighty King," "Hark, the Herald Angels Sing," "Love Divine, All Loves Excelling."

John Wesley (1703-1791) was born in the village of Epworth of a Church of England family, his father a minister in the church. He himself became an Anglican priest in 1728.

His fame and that of his younger brother Charles are interwoven with the early development of Methodism. The two (and later, George Whitefield) and others made up a religious fraternity dedicated to a commitment of holiness. They were singled out as peculiar, receiving such nicknames as "Holy Club," "Bible Moths" and "Methodists."

In 1735 the brothers left for foreign missionary service to the redskins of Georgia in America. On shipboard a meeting with simple and dedicated Moravians left a lasting impression. On his return to England, John Wesley sought out a Moravian leader, Peter Böhler (Lutheran by training). It was while attending a Moravian service in Aldersgate Street, London, and hearing the reading of Luther's *Preface to the Romans* that he felt himself "strangely warmed." His conversion occurred, he said, about 8:45 P.M. on May 24, 1738. This occasion is known as "the Aldersgate Awakening."

A visit with Zinzendorf failed to draw him into that company. The Moravians seemed too aloof to Wesley, while his own Anglican Church seemed cold and formal.

Whitefield, meanwhile, had become a street preacher with evangelistic fervor. During his absence John Wesley took over the preaching among the neglected at Bristol, making his decision by lot. Thus began the Wesleyan revival, of which he was the outstanding champion. On horseback he traveled through the cities and villages of England, Scotland and Ireland, appealing for changed lives. Regeneration was his emphasis.

He was loyal to the Church of England, but the Church was unsympathetic to his manner of appeal. He went on his own way, with hundreds of clergy following in his path. He inspired some eight thousand societies in England and Wales, and bequeathed an organized Methodist Episcopal Church in America.

Illustrated here is John Wesley in his early twenties.

The Birthplace of John Wesley

Susanna Wesley, Mother of the Wesley Brothers

There were eighteen or nineteen children born to Susanna Wesley, of whom only ten survived their infancy. She greatly influenced her sons.

Samuel Wesley

A man of learning, student at Exeter College, Oxford, and the father of the Wesley brothers. A dissenting minister, he disapproved of the beheading of Charles I and returned to the established Church of England. Minister at Epworth, near Oxford.

The Sleeping Congregation

The picture of "The Sleeping Congregation" (by Hogarth, 1736) is somewhat suggestive of the times. The controversies of yesterday within the church had turned many away from religion, in reaction against both Puritanism and Roman tendencies. For many there was no longer any spark to religion. As one writer put it, "The Church was alive, but it was living on its capital."

Christ Church College, Oxford

In 1720 John Wesley, a youth of seventeen, was admitted to this college, to which brother Charles came six years later. He had entered the most aristocratic of all the Oxford colleges and he soon excelled in the classics and in logical skill. Here he saw among his young contemporaries drinking and gambling as a matter of accepted practice and for a brief period he entered into the campus spirit. His poverty, however, was his protection.

Chapel of Lincoln College, Oxford

The Holy Club

In 1726 John Wesley was awarded a fellowship in Lincoln College, one of the smallest and poorest of Oxford's nineteen colleges. In 1727 he took his Master's degree and a year later became ordained by the Bishop of Oxford. For a brief period he served as a curate to his father.

John's brother Charles, a student at Christ Church College, pored over his books and developed a strong feeling of piety. Urging two or three companions to join a systematic attempt to achieve holiness, these young men adopted rules for holy living, with emphasis on devotions. They even fasted.

"The Holy Club" added John (and others), the elder brother becoming the leader after his return from service under his father.

"Methodism" means "exact method," but John later defined the word to mean "the method laid down in the Holy Scriptures."

The Holy Club was not given to a withdrawal from the world. It set out to visit the destitute and minister to the wretched. The Bocardo Prison in Oxford offered ready opportunity. (It was from this prison that Archbishop Cranmer had been taken to suffer martyrdom.)

The Holy Club

George Whitefield in His Twenties

The Broad Walk, Oxford

The Holy Club increased in membership, including a "poor Miss Potter," who also departed from the dignities of the rituals of the Established Church. Ridiculed as fanatics, some of its members left the fraternity. The club was in its decline when George Whitefield (1714-1770) joined it.

Whitefield became the powerhouse preacher of early Methodism. He was born in Gloucester, England. At Oxford he was admitted to Pembroke College. Already of a similar spirit, he found the Wesley group to his liking. In his enthusiasm he became a near fanatic. He found his conversion after a tumultuous experience in 1735. Regeneration was to him an experience, not a doctrine. He is known as an evangelist par excellence.

Tormented in soul, George Whitefield sought the will of God for him. "I went out into Christ Church Walk, near our college, and continued in silent prayer under one of the trees for near two hours. The night being stormy, it gave me awful thoughts of the day of judgment. The next night I repeated the same exercise at the same place."

Benjamin Franklin

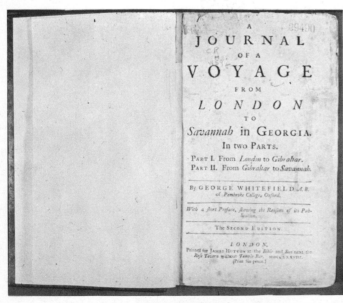

George Whitefield's Journal

George Whitefield kept a careful record of his travels in his journal. He came to America in 1739.

Listening to Whitefield preaching, Franklin (1706-1790) was heard to say: "I perceived he intended to finish with a collection and I silently resolved he should get nothing from me. I had in my pocket a handful of copper money; three or four silver dollars and five pistoles in gold. As he proceeded, I began to soften . . . and . . . concluded to give the coppers. Another stroke of his oratory made me ashamed of that . . . and determined me to give the silver. But he finished so admirably that I emptied my pocket wholly into the collection, gold and all."

John Wesley, Missionary to the Wilds of North America

Commenting on his decision to become a missionary to the Georgian Indians, John Wesley said: "My chief motive is the hope of saving my own soul. I hope to learn the true sense of the Gospel by preaching it to the heathen. They have no comments to construe away the text, no vain philosophy to corrupt it, no luxurious, sensual, covetous, ambitious expounders to soften its unpleasant truths. They have no party, no interest to serve, and are, therefore, fit to receive the Gospel in its simplicity. They are as little children, humble, willing to learn, and eager to do the will of God."

His idealism was blasted by cruel disillusionment in his experiences with the Georgian Indians.

John Wesley and Count Zinzendorf

John Wesley, now a real convert, conferred with the Lutheran Zinzendorf at Herrnhut.

Peter Böhler

Peter Böhler (1712-1775), a Moravian Pietist with Lutheran training, counseled with John Wesley when the latter returned from his American sojourn a dejected man. Salvation is by faith alone, said Peter. This simple counsel moved Wesley to a different level in his preaching. Peter taught him also that a saving faith could come instantaneously. Charles Wesley became a "convert" on May 3. John followed in the same month, on the twenty-fourth. The two, it is said, sang together Charles' new hymn, "Where Shall My Wondering Soul Begin?" — the famous "Birth Song" of the Methodist Revival.

Methodism Rose from Moravianism

Pictured here is the interior of Fetter Lane Chapel (1867), built after Wesley had left.

On January 1, 1739 Whitefield and the brothers Wesley and some sixty others were at Fetter Lane Chapel (organized in 1738 in London by Peter Böhler as the Fetter Lane Society of which John Wesley was a charter member). At 3:00 A.M. they experienced "a new high" in religious fervor, feeling the inner assurance of a special mission. In a few days a conference was held by the Big Three and others which was to lead to a separation from the Moravian group. Whitefield especially had felt the sting of the Established Church and was ready to break all barriers. His street and out-of-door preaching was attracting thousands. Fetter Lane was too quietistic and suspicious of good works to continue to hold exponents of a more masculine expression of religious devotion.

John Wesley Preaching in Matthew Bagshaw's House

Crowds came to hear the preaching of John Wesley. Some of the Anglican clergy approved the unconventional manner of Wesley, but it was difficult to secure Anglican churches. From St. Mary Church in Islington (where he was serving as curate) the Methodist preacher was ejected. Small societies began to be formed with meetings in homes. Modest were the beginnings of organized Methodism.

John Wesley as a Preacher in Newgate Prison, London

"In a prison ministry," the Wesleys frequently visited the cells of men about to die.

Music of Charles Wesley

In 1739 *Hymns and Sacred Poems* was published in three volumes, marking a new era in the history of church music.

John Wesley Preaching on His Father's Tomb

In 1742 John Wesley visited Epworth after seven years' absence. Only his father's tomb remained — the family was gone. Not permitted by the curate to preach in his father's church, he stood on the tombstone and preached to "such a congregation as, I believe, Epworth never saw before." "Nearly forty years did my father labor here — he saw little fruit of his labor; but now the fruit appeared," he exclaimed a week later to a vast multitude gathered at the same place.

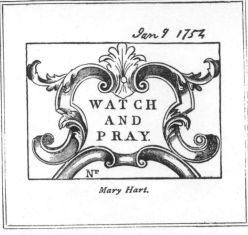

Love Feast Ticket

Methodism began to develop, under a leader, what was called "the class," which had weekly testimony meetings and received contributions. It had "bands" of smaller groups. Class tickets were honored as admission. Wesley, to separate the wheat from the tares, conversed in person with members of societies, giving a ticket to those he found acceptable. These tickets were renewable as letters of recommendation quarterly. Lay leaders were encouraged, and some addressed large congregations.

Whitefield and John Wesley Separate

Whitefield toured America and stirred the Eastern seaboard with his preaching. In Northampton he visited Jonathan Edwards, champion of predestinarian Calvinism. He came eventually to argue for predestation and a school of Calvinistic Methodism developed after him. John Wesley remained an Arminian, that is, he believed that God has elected those who repent, believe and persevere, while reprobation is directed only at those who remain aloof. Thus man has a responsible part in his destiny.

Wesley spoke against Whitefield's views and Whitefield retaliated. The result: Whitefield built his own tabernacle and Methodism divided. Pictured here is that tabernacle.

Satire of Wesley's Method of Preaching
(A contemporary satire by Hogarth, 1762. In the British Museum)

Jacobus Arminius

Methodism has been called Arminian in theology (with the exception of Calvinistic Methodism). Arminius (1560-1609) was educated at the University of Leyden. He is famous for his position on the hotly debated question of the day — predestination. Arminius came to adopt the view that man has freedom as opposed to unconditional election to salvation. In this he took a position against Calvinism.

Selina, the Countess of Huntingdon

Rich and influential, she became the patroness of George Whitefield in the development of Calvinistic Methodism.

John Fletcher

A devoted friend of John Wesley, his right-hand man and an outstanding leader, John Fletcher (1729-1785) was born in Switzerland and became an Anglican priest. He was a superintendent of Trevecca College until Countess Huntingdon's separation from Wesley.

Of him Wesley said: "We were of one heart and one soul. We had no secrets between us." A vicar of Madeley for a time, Fletcher is known also for his religious work, *Appeal to Matter of Fact and Common Sense* (known as "Fletcher's Appeal").

Trevecca College

The Countess of Huntingdon founded chapels. In 1768 she founded a college for preachers at Trevecca. This Calvinistic wing of Methodism drew some of Wesley's preachers, though he himself maintained a relationship with those who differed from him.

The Riot at Wednesbury

John Wesley suffered abuse and assaults. In 1741 he was stoned in London. In 1743 a riot occurred at Wednesbury in which he was struck in the face with a missile, leaving a scar which he carried to his death.

"I look upon all the world as my parish"

The picture of John Wesley's outdoor preaching is suggestive of his famous remark. In Westminster Abbey the Wesley Tablet carries these words.

The First Methodist Conference

On June 25, 1744, at the call of John Wesley, there convened in London the first Methodist Conference, to consolidate the societies.

Methodism affirmed: "In speculative things each can submit only so far as his judgment shall be convinced; in every practical point, so far as we can without wounding our own consciences." Five points of Methodism were emphasized: repentance, faith, justification, sanctification and the witness of the Spirit.

The Countess of Huntingdon entertained this conference in her London house.

John Wesley at Forty Years of Age

City Road Chapel, London

City Road was the headquarters of John Wesley from 1778 until his death there in 1791. It is still in use. Adjacent is the publishing house of British Methodism. The picture shows the monument to Mrs. Susanna Wesley and the John Wesley House.

AN
EXTRACT
OF THE
Rev. Mr. JOHN WESLEY's
JOURNAL

From his Embarking for GEORGIA

To his Return to LONDON.

---

*What shall we say then?——That Israel which follow'd
after the Law of Righteousness, hath not attained to
the Law of Righteousness.—— Wherefore? Because
they sought it not by Faith, but as it were by the Works
of the Law.*   Rom. ix. 30, 31.

BRISTOL:
Printed by S. and F. FARLEY.

And sold at the New School-House in the Horse-Fair:
and by the Booksellers in Town and Country.

Title Page of the First Edition of John Wesley's Journal.

Wesley began composing this *Journal* during his visit to Georgia and continued writing it until his death. He also began a diary in 1725, in shorthand of his own

---

The PREFACE.

1. IT was in Pursuance of an Advice given by Bp. *Taylor*, in his *Rules for Holy Living and Dying*, that about fifteen Years ago, I began to take a more exact Account than I had done before, of the manner wherein I spent my Time, writing down how I had employed every Hour. This I continued to do, wherever I was, till the Time of my leaving *England*. The Variety of Scenes which I then past thro', induced me to transcribe from time to time, the more material Parts of my Diary, adding here and there such little Reflections as occurr'd to my Mind. Of this Journal thus occasionally compiled, the following is a short Extract: It not being my Design to relate all those Particulars, which I wrote for my own Use only; and which would answer no valuable End to others, however important they were to me.

2. Indeed I had no Design or Desire to trouble the World with any of my little Affairs: As can't but appear to every impartial Mind, from my having been so long *as one that heareth not*, notwithstanding the loud and frequent Calls I have had, to answer for myself. Neither shou'd I have

Preface to the Same Edition

invention.

Wesley produced more than three hundred books and pamphlets, cheaply published and widely distributed.

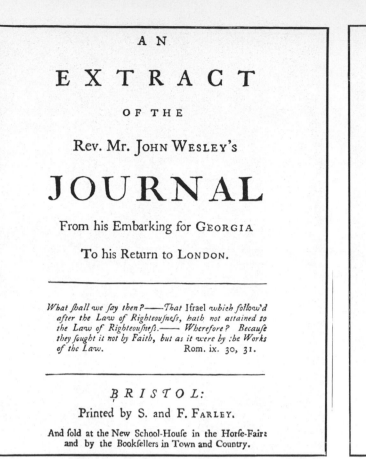

The Deed of Declaration

John Wesley gave legal form to the Methodist movement in Great Britain in 1784. Heretofore he alone had controlled the movement. The Deed of Declaration provided that one hundred preachers in a self-perpetuating body should be vested with legal authority to administer British Methodism (as it has to this day).

Wesley and Wilberforce

William Wilberforce (1759-1833), evangelical layman, fought the slave traffic. A member of Parliament, wealthy and popular, he was "converted" in 1784. He published in 1797 his *Practical View of the Prevailing Religious System of Professed Christians in the Higher and Middle Classes in This Country Contrasted with Real Christianity,* a popular treatise.

John Wesley denounced the slave traffic and urged Wilberforce to continue his condemnation of it. Wesley's last letter was addressed to Wilberforce.

John Wesley on his Deathbed

Pictured writing a letter to Wilberforce.

Robert Strawbridge

Robert Strawbridge came to Maryland in 1759 or 1760, built a log house, preached, formed circuits and inspired other men to preach. He died in 1781.

Philip Embury

Methodism was carried to America by Philip Embury (1728-1773), who began his labors in New York in 1760.

Barbara Heck

Barbara Heck had reformatory zeal. She exhorted against sin. Card playing she considered backsliding. She urged Embury to preach and she led a "class."

The Rigging Loft

A sailmaker's attic at 120 William Street in New York, which early Methodists rented for services in 1767. The first Methodist building was erected on John Street a year later.

John King Preaching the First Methodist Sermon in Baltimore

This occurred in 1770 in front of a blacksmith shop at Front and Center streets.

Francis Asbury

Thomas Coke

In 1771 Wesley sent Francis Asbury (1745-1816) to America in the interests of Methodism. When he arrived, there were but a dozen Methodist preachers in the country. When he died there were nearly seven hundred. He himself ordained four thousand. He was a "General Superintendent of the Methodist Societies in the United States of America."

The first Protestant bishop in America, called the "Foreign Minister of Methodism." An LL.D. of Oxford, Coke (1747-1814) was a scholar and voluminous writer. He and John Wesley ordained Richard Whatcoat and Thomas Vasey as presbyters for American assignments. Coke, a presbyter, was "set apart" as superintendent for the same work. This was a breach with the Church of England. Wesley had tried in vain to secure proper ordinations for his clergy from the Bishop of London. Himself a presbyter, he believed that bishops and presbyters were one order in the ancient church and thus a presbyter might ordain in case of necessity.

Thomas Coke and Francis Asbury were set apart as general superintendents. They called themselves "bishops" over the protest of John Wesley. Thus began the organization of the Methodist Church. In 1784 the famous Christmas Conference met in Lovely Lane Chapel and the societies were given the name "Methodist Episcopal Church."

Interior of Strawberry Alley M. E. Church, Baltimore (1773)

Dickinson College, Carlisle, Pennsylvania

The oldest Methodist college in America, although it is not under the control of Methodism. Founded in 1783, it was named after John Dickinson, a Revolutionary patriot.

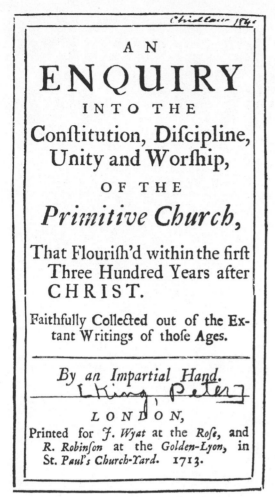

AN ENQUIRY INTO THE Conſtitution, Diſcipline, Unity and Worſhip, OF THE *Primitive Church,*

That Flouriſh'd within the firſt Three Hundred Years after CHRIST.

Faithfully Collected out of the Extant Writings of thoſe Ages.

By an Impartial Hand.

LONDON,

Printed for *J. Wyat* at the *Roſe,* and *R. Robinſon* at the *Golden-Lyon,* in St. *Paul's Church-Yard.* 1713.

Title Page of King's *Enquiry*

Lord Peter King's book on the primitive church convinced John Wesley that he, as a presbyter, had the same right to ordain as a bishop.

Bethel African Methodist Episcopal Church

Founded in Philadelphia in 1794.

A First Camp Meeting in Kentucky, 1799, at Night

First Methodist Meeting House in Ohio and in the Northwest Territory

Erected in 1800 on the Scioto circuit, Brush Creek.

Orange Judd Hall of Natural Science.   Observatory.   Library.   Chapel.   Gymnasium.   South College.   North College.

Wesleyan University, Middletown, Connecticut

This is the oldest surviving educational institution related to American Methodism. It began as an academy in 1825 and became a university in 1831.

African Methodist Episcopal Bishops

The African Methodist Episcopal Church, "oldest and largest religious organization among the Negroes," originated in 1785-1787 as a result of the ill treatment of the Negro members of St. George's Methodist Church in Philadelphia by the white members.

In 1816 an independent organization was founded, sparked by Richard Allen, a wealthy Negro who became bishop.

Pictured here is a group of bishops in the late nineteenth century.

School of Theology, Boston University, Mt. Vernon Street

Pictured here is the old Mt. Vernon Street site. The school is now housed in an elaborate new building with Marsh Chapel in the university area. In 1867 a former school (1841) was affiliated with the university.

Garrett Biblical Institute, Evanston, Illinois

This theological school opened in 1854 with funds provided by Mrs. Eliza Garrett.

Wilberforce University

The original building of Wilberforce University, Ohio, (1856) for the education of Negro youth was supported by the Methodist Church.

The second picture shows Negro children denied entrance to a school.

Chautauqua Institution

In 1864 some Methodist preachers interested in a camp-meeting site found a spot on Chautauqua Lake in southwestern New York. John Vincent (1832-1920), an editor of the Sunday school publications of the Methodist Church until his election as bishop, was a leading founder of the Summer Assembly at Chautauqua, its original purpose being to train Sunday school teachers.

The camp developed into an interdenominational summer resort. In 1878 it began a program of education, a "school out of school" and a liberal arts college course. Through the years it grew into a strong cultural and religious center, patronized by Protestants of various church groups.

Here is an early picture of Chautauqua.

B. F. Randolph

An Oberlin graduate, B. F. Randolph was a Methodist minister in the South, a member of the South Carolina Senate. He was murdered in 1868 while on a lecture tour.

Masked Ku-Kluxers (Klan formed, 1865) persecuted by tarring and feathering, beating and murdering Negroes and keeping the freedmen in the South from exercising the right of suffrage.

The Ocean Grove, New Jersey, Camp Meeting Association

This association was formed in 1869 under the auspices of Methodism. In 1887 this camp attracted more than a million because of its resort facilities and for religious purposes.

Pictured here are services on the beach.

Ocean Grove Auditorium (1800)

It covered nearly half an acre, seating some five thousand.

Edgar Sheffield Brightman

Born on September 20, 1884 in a Methodist parsonage at Holbrook, Massachusetts, he received his higher education at Brown University and at Boston and German universities. He became Methodism's outstanding recent philosopher, teaching in the tradition of Borden P. Bowne from 1919 until his death in 1953. Author of almost a score of books on philosophy and religion and numerous articles, he has exerted an enormous influence in American higher education. The photo was taken in 1947.

Methodist Unification

In 1939 the Methodist Church was formed by the union of three branches of American Methodism.

Pictured here are (center) Bishop Edwin Holt Hughes representing the Methodist Episcopal Church, (left) Bishop James H. Straughn of the Methodist Protestant Church, which in 1830 had formed its own group in opposition to the episcopacy, and (right) Bishop John M. Moore of the Methodist Episcopal Church, South. The Methodist Church is now the largest Protestant body in the United States.

Early Lutheranism in America and the Lutheranism of the Muhlenberg Tradition

Lutherans like to recall that ancestors of their denomination were on the American Continent a year before the arrival of the *Mayflower*. Rasmus Jensen, a Lutheran minister, sailing in the company of Danish seamen, held services on Christmas Day, 1619, on Hudson Bay.

Among the Dutch in New Amsterdam there were many Lutherans. Lutheran refugees from the Palatinate of the Rhine, Germany settled later along the Hudson River as far north as Albany.

The Swedes established their famous colony on the Delaware in 1638, calling it New Sweden. Their churches were ministered to by Swedish-born clergymen of the state church. These people were absorbed by other churches largely because of language and cultural difficulties. (There were as yet no American-trained clergy.)

In 1742 Henry Melchior Muhlenberg arrived on these shores. His firm hand united scattered Lutherans into a strong organization. The Muhlenbergs took an active part in American colonial history. The persecuted Salzburgers settled in Georgia near Savannah.

In 1839 under the leadership of C. F. W. Walther, Saxon immigrants settled in Missouri, developing into the strong and conservative body popularly known as Missouri Lutherans. Other groups were formed in the Midwest, all conservative in theology.

The Scandinavians in larger numbers came later — a Norwegian synod organized in 1853, a Swedish Lutheran church organized at New Sweden, Iowa in 1848 and a Lutheran synod in 1860 (Augustana). The Danes and Finns came still later.

Old Swedes Church, Wilmington, Delaware

First Lutheran pastor in America, Reorus Torkillus, arrived in 1639 at what is now Wilmington, Delaware.

Holy Trinity (Old Swedes) Lutheran Church was dedicated June 4, 1699, and is still standing.

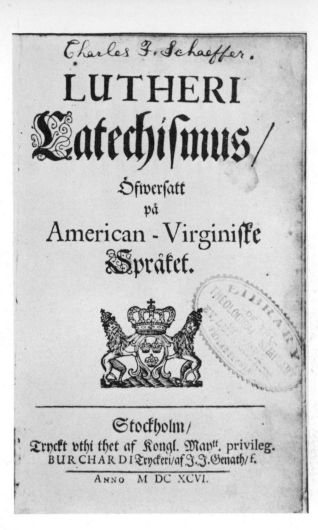

Luther's Small Catechism

Translated into the language of the Delaware Indians, *ca.* 1646, by John Campanius, pastor of the Swedish Lutheran Church in Philadelphia, and first Protestant missionary among North American Indians. This translation was used in manuscript form for many years before its publication in Stockholm in 1696.

The Persecution of the Salzburgers

In the Austrian province of Salzburg, in the Noric Alps, a small body of Protestants had persisted, surrounded by Roman Catholics. Either they must be absorbed by the Catholics or emigrate. They took the covenant of salt and resolved not to surrender.

As exiles from their homes in the Alps, they set on a pilgrimage they knew not where. They wandered northward and finally found a haven in Prussia. Some emigrated to America, settling in Georgia near Savannah (*ca.* 1734) founding a Lutheran colony. Their chief minister there was Bolzius (b. 1703). John Wesley found these people to his liking and received from them their support.

Pictured here is the farewell of the Salzburgers to their homeland.

Henry Melchior Muhlenberg

He is called the "father of the Lutheran Church" in America. In response to requests from America he was sent from the Halle leadership, arriving in 1742. Ordained in Leipzig, 1739, Muhlenberg (1711-1787) was a graduate of the University of Göttingen the previous year. He was minister of the United Congregations, which were St. Michaels and Zions in Philadelphia, Augustus in Trappe and New Hanover in New Hanover. He visited Lutheran churches in New York, New Jersey, Maryland, Virginia, the Carolinas and Georgia.

In 1748 he founded the first Lutheran synod of America, known for many years as the Ministerium of Pennsylvania. His motto, *"Ecclesia plantanda"* ("The church must be planted"), brought fruit. Cordiality with other Protestant groups marked his ministry. He was mildly confessional and strongly Pietistic. He preached in German, English and Dutch and handled Latin fluently.

Augustus Lutheran Church, Trappe, Pennsylvania

Built in 1743 and still standing. One of the United Congregations which called H. M. Muhlenberg, where he was pastor for most of his career and where he and his family are buried.

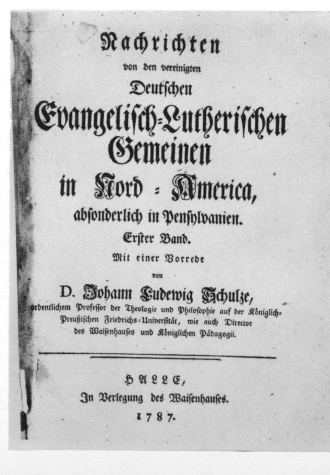

Halle Reports

H. M. Muhlenberg, in some respects a missionary to America responsible to the authorities of the Orphan House and University of Halle, sent them a continuous stream of reports, letters and diary entries about his work; other pastors and teachers emanating from Halle carried on this practice. Excerpts from the reports were published by the Halle authorities from 1744 to 1786; the first collection appeared in 1787. These reports are the primary source of the early history of the Lutheran church of Germanic origin.

[handwritten German journal entries dated 1776, July 2, July 4]

From the Journals of Henry Melchior Muhlenberg

1776 July 4 Today the Continental Congress openly declared the united provinces of North America to be free and independent states. This has caused some thoughtful and far-seeing "melancholici" to be down in the mouth; on the other hand, it has caused some sanguine "miopes" to exult and shout for joy. This remains as a comfort to believers; There is One who sits at the rudder . . . who has never yet made a mistake in his government.

Zion Lutheran Church, Philadelphia

Organized in 1742 by H. M. Muhlenberg.

This drawing shows the official memorial service of Congress for George Washington, December 26, 1799, with General Harry Lee delivering the address which first pronounced Washington "first in war, first in peace, first in the hearts of his countrymen."

Here, also, Congress met for a thanksgiving service after the Battle of Yorktown, and held memorial services for Benjamin Franklin.

John Peter Gabriel Muhlenberg

The patriarch Muhlenberg had three illustrious sons.

Peter (1746-1807) was a major-general under Washington in the American Revolution, U. S. Senator, Lutheran minister (ordained in 1768) and Episcopal minister (ordained by the Bishop of London in 1772). He commanded the Eighth Virginia Regiment, which he organized in 1776. He was vice-president of Pennsylvania, 1785-1788, and served three nonsuccessive terms as U. S. congressman from Pennsylvania. He held other civil positions in Philadelphia. Peter is pictured here.

A second son, Frederick (1750-1801), a Lutheran minister in New York state, was speaker of the first and third Congresses.

Gotthelf Henry Ernst (1753-1815), the third son, was a minister and scientific student of America flora.

Samuel Simon Schmucker

Lutheranism in America, under the professorial leadership of Samuel Simon Schmucker (1799-1873), developed a liberal position. Schmucker was a first theological professor of the Gettysburg Theological Seminary, where his influence was commanding for some twenty-five years. He aided in establishing the General Synod of the Lutheran Church (organized 1820). He founded a classical school, forerunner of Gettysburg College. His published works were many, among which his *Elements of Popular Theology* (1834) was a first English text in Lutheran systematic theology. He published a plan of union of churches, *Appeal to the American Churches* (1838) and many tracts. His was an American type of Lutheranism, pietistic, irenical and broadly tolerant of other Protestant faiths. In his later years his life was cast under a shadow, conservative Lutherans taking command in the new waves of European immigration.

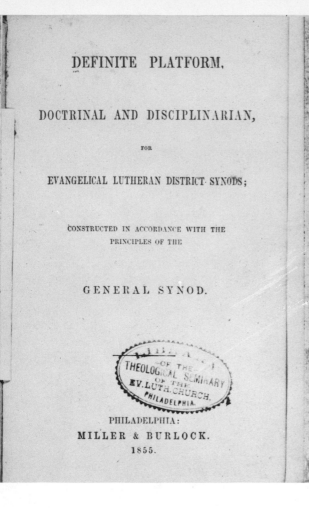

The Definite Synodical Platform

In 1855 this pamphlet was published anonymously, setting forth a modest revision of the Augsburg Confession. It was an attempt by S. S. Schmucker and close friends to stem the tide of conservatism, in favor of a liberal "American Lutheranism." It marked a turning point, a "crisis," in Lutheranism in America — from liberalism to a growing conservatism, which still characterizes the American Lutheran Church. Historic creeds, it was learned, must not be tampered with. *The Definite Synodical Platform* died almost at birth.

Charles Porterfield Krauth

Champion of the conservative Lutheran revolt in America against his old teacher, S. S. Schmucker, and against a liberal "American Lutheranism," Krauth (1823-1883) led the movement in the Eastern states toward a full acknowledgment of the historic Lutheran confessions as the basis for a sound Lutheranism. Mt. Airy Seminary, Philadelphia, became the citadel for this conservative opposition to liberal Gettysburg.

Krauth's chief work was published in 1871, *The Conservative Reformation and Its Theology,* a work which enjoyed the acclaim of conservatives. He was a leading figure in the organization of the General Council (in 1867), which competed with its rival, the General Synod (and was later its president). From 1868 to 1883 he was a professor of moral and intellectual philosophy at the University of Pennsylvania, a vice-provost, editor of Lutheran journals and a member of the American Revision Committee of the Old Testament.

232

*Lutheran Headquarters Building, Located at
231 Madison Avenue, New York City*

The brownstone section of the building to the right was the J. P. Morgan residence until 1943, when it was acquired by the U.L.C.A. The more modern five-story addition at the left, in the process of erection, is to be occupied January 1, 1958.

The United Lutheran Church of America is the direct successor and heir to three Lutheran bodies — the General Synod of the Evangelical Lutheran Church in the U.S.A., the General Council of the Evangelical Lutheran Church in North America, and the United Synod of the Evangelical Lutheran Church in the South — which merged into this united body in 1918.

This is the largest Lutheran body in the United States, with a membership of more than 2,270,000 persons.

*The Rev. Frederick H. Knubel, First President of
the United Lutheran Church in America*

The Martin Luther Film

The Martin Luther film is a successful contemporary full-length motion picture story of the Reformer which has won wide acclaim. It has been shown as a feature billing in theaters all over the country and prints may be purchased for church and educational use from its owners, the Lutheran Church Productions, Inc.

The Martin Luther Film

The Martin Luther Film

The Martin Luther Film

The Unitarian Church

Unitarianism may be traced back as far as Paul of Samosata (Bishop of Antioch, *ca.* 260-272), and to the views of some Arians in the fourth-century disputes about the Trinity. Unitarians have disavowed the doctrine of the triunity of God and thus affirmed Jesus and the Holy Spirit as less than coequal with the God of Unity.

The Socinians of Poland held similar views. In 1774 a Unitarian Church was organized in England under Theophilus Lindsey. Many Anglican divines of that day were Arian in their unofficial views. In America many of the Protestant clergy have privately affirmed a theology more akin to Unitarianism than Trinitarianism, the official theology of the Protestant churches.

The first church in America to affirm openly the Unitarian position was King's Chapel in Boston, which in 1785 revised its liturgy, omitting the Athanasian and Nicene creeds and other specifically Trinitarian passages. This step was taken under the leadership of James Freeman. Thus, one of the oldest Episcopal churches in New England became "the first Unitarian church in America." (See picture of King's Chapel, p. 240.)

Fourteen years after Martin Luther posted the Ninety-five Theses on the doors of the castle church of Wittenberg, Michael Servetus (1511-1553), "the father of Unitarianism," issued his controversial and hotly contested book *On the Errors of The Trinity*. For his disagreement with the dogma of the Trinity as that dogma was set forth by contemporary theologians, both Protestant and Catholic, Servetus in 1553, having been found guilty of heresy on charges brought against him by Calvin, was burned at the stake in Geneva along with his works.

The leader of the Unitarian movement in Poland was Faustus Socinus (1539-1604). Although successful at first in winning converts and establishing churches, he was persecuted and in 1658 the Polish Diet passed a decree of banishment against all who subscribed to what was known as the "Socinian heresy." Strong Unitarian movements developed during the Reformation period in both Poland and Transylvania where Francis David, a Hungarian, led the movement, converting John Sigismund, King of Transylvania who became the first and last Unitarian king in history.

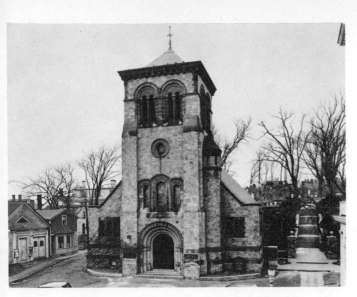

The First Parish (Unitarian) in Plymouth, Massachusetts, is believed to be the oldest continuous church in America. Organized by the Pilgrims who landed in Plymouth in 1620, as a noncreedal church holding a non-Trinitarian covenant, it has been Unitarian since early in the nineteenth century.

In 1819 William Ellery Channing (1780-1842), delivering a sermon in the Unitarian Church in Baltimore, defended the liberal position against the many attacks that were being made on it. In his famous sermon Channing gave the first important statement of American Unitarianism, that is that the authority considered ultimate was not the voice of the past as revealed in Scripture but the voice of experience and reason. Later, in 1838, in his address to the Harvard Divinity School, Ralph Waldo Emerson made explicit what had merely been implicit in Channing's Baltimore sermon. Traditionally up to this time Unitarians had not denied the ultimate authority of the Bible, rather appealing to the Bible in stating their position.

The Old Ship Meeting House organized in 1635 by religious dissenters from Hingham (Massachusetts) and built in 1681, became Unitarian when Ebenezer Gay, who for sixty-nine years served as minister of the church, took a liberal stand on the doctrine of the Trinity as early as 1740. The church, which is an outstanding example of original colonial architecture, was constructed with medieval Gothic beams combined with a roof built like the inverted hull of a ship.

Theodore Parker

Parker (1810-1860) was a popular preacher, attracting thousands to Boston Music Hall. He was a philosophical theologian unafraid of new learning. Along with Emerson his influence was great within Unitarianism, although he remained a Congregationalist in some of the accepted ideas of the times.

Present headquarters of the American Unitarian Association which was organized in 1825. In 1884 an event of fundamental importance took place. At the meeting of the National Conference of Unitarians, the American Unitarian Association was in effect transformed into an association of churches. The way was charted so that within a few years the Unitarian churches had the controlling voice in determining the policies and shaping the activities of the association.

World's Parliament of Religions, the Columbian Exposition of 1893

A Free Religious Association to promote religious liberalism in America and to redeem the Unitarian Church from orthodoxy was organized in 1866. With its major purposes achieved, the movement declined in the 1880's.

The crowning achievement of the Association was the convening of the Parliament of Religions at the Chicago World's Fair in 1893. Two volumes of papers were published in the same year, which had a wide circulation and influence.

Pictured here is one of the sessions of the Parliament.

Interior of King's Chapel, Boston, Massachusetts

Group of Foreign Delegates, Boston International Congress of Religious Liberals, September 22-27, 1907

A fourth International Congress, held under the auspices of the International Council of Unitarian and Other Liberal Religious Thinkers and Workers. This Council was organized in Boston, May, 1900, "to open communication with those in all lands who are striving *to unite pure religion and perfect liberty,* and to increase fellowship and co-operation among them."

Congresses were held in London (1901), Amsterdam (1903) and Geneva (1905), representing five hundred to a thousand members of fifteen nationalities and from some twenty-five religious communions.

The Reformed Presbyterian Church
(The Covenanter Church)

The Reformed Presbyterian Church of North America was organized as the Reformed Presbytery of America in 1774 by ministers of the Reformed Presbytery in Scotland and Ireland. The name probably indicated the Church of the Scottish Reformation, or the Church of the Reformation with the Presbyterian form of government. The synod was constituted in 1809. The Church's Terms of Communion acknowledge the Westminster Confession of Faith and the Catechisms; the duty of public covenanting; the obligations of past covenants, and, in particular, of the American Covenant of 1871. From the emphasis on the covenants, past and present, came the more familiar name, the Covenanter Church, or the Covenanters.

The Church has never been large, and now numbers about five thousand communicant members. It has been a missionary Church at home and abroad, and has been active in education. It gave leadership and effective service in the antislavery struggle.

"The basic belief of Covenanters, which has kept them a separate denomination, is the lordship of Jesus Christ in the life of the individual, the church and the nation, and the specific applications of that belief which it makes." Members do not belong to oath-bound secret societies. The Church in its praise service uses only the Psalms of the Bible, sung without instrumental accompaniment. It practices close communion. Since the nation does not acknowledge Christ's sovereignty, members practice political dissent, neither running for political office nor voting in political elections. The Church is pressing for a Christian Amendment to the Constitution.

Covenanters Worshiping by the Banks of the Whitadder

Old Greyfriars Church, Edinburgh

First International Convention of Reformed Presbyterian Churches in Scotland, Ireland and America, 1896, to celebrate the tercentenary of the National Covenant, signed in this church in 1638.

Martyr Memorial Services were conducted on a Sabbath at some thirty-seven places in Scotland; a convention was held in Glasgow, and one public meeting in Edinburgh. A second international convention was held in 1938.

Coldenham Church

Near Newburgh, New York. Probably the oldest continuing congregation; formerly "Wallkill," from the river. John Cuthbertson, first Covenanter minister to come to America, visited here in 1753 and ten later times. Organized 1769, reorganized 1798. This building erected 1838, remodeled some years ago. First settlement in 1748 by James Rainey family.

The Rev. Robert James Dodds

He and the Rev. Joseph Beattie went to Syria in 1856 for the Church's first permanent mission station at Latakia, Syria. Born at Freeport, Armstrong County, Pennsylvania, August 29, 1824. Died at Aleppo, Syria, December 11, 1870.

242

Stone for Hugh McMillan

A loyal Covenanter elder in Rocky Creek congregation, Chester District, South Carolina. Born 1787 in Ireland. Brought by parents that year to America. Father of two ministers. Buried in "Brick Church" cemetery.

Geneva College, Beaver Falls, Pennsylvania

Founded at Northwood, Ohio, 1848. Removed to Beaver Falls in 1880.

The first building erected there.

Reformed Presbyterian Theological Seminary, Pittsburgh, Pennsylvania

Seminary organized 1810 at Philadelphia. Located at different places. In Allegheny and Pittsburgh, Pennsylvania since 1856. In present location since 1923.

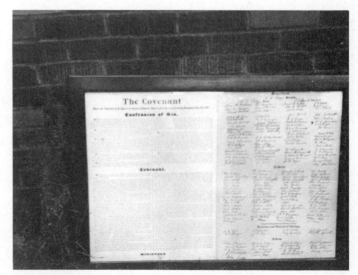

Covenant of 1871, the American Covenant

The Covenant, sworn and subscribed to by the Synod of the Reformed Presbyterian Church in North America, at Pittsburgh, Pennsylvania, May 27, 1871. Signed by seventy-seven ministers, eight licentiates and students of theology and nineteen elders not members of the synod.

The Church of England in America—
The American Episcopal Church

An early leader in the development of an autonomous American Episcopal church was William White (1748-1836), a chaplain of the Continental Congress and a rector in Philadelphia. He was a "chief architect" bishop of the church. His idea was an organization on a diocesan and national basis, bishops to be obtained to serve out of this frame of reference (in opposition to the view, "bishops first"). In 1782 he issued an epochal brochure entitled *The Case of the Episcopal Churches Considered*.

Samuel Seabury (1729-1796) was chosen bishop in 1783 by Connecticut clergy and sent to England for consecration. The Archbishop of Canterbury refused and Seabury turned to the Scottish Episcopal Church, where he was consecrated in 1784.

In the conventions of 1785 and 1786 two American bishops in the English succession were secured. In 1786 Parliament passed an act authorizing persons to be consecrated outside "His Majesty's dominions." There was much strife in carrying out "proper" authorizations. In 1789 the General Convention framed a constitution, revised the Prayer Book and achieved national unity. Seabury was recognized as a bishop. The American succession of bishops was made secure in later agreements and consecrations.

High Church and Evangelicalism were two schools of thought, represented by Bishop John Henry Hobart (1775-1830) and Bishop Alexander Griswold (1766-1843) respectively. These two schools persist to this day.

The General Theological Seminary, founded in 1817 and removed to New York in 1821, reflected Bishop Hobart's High Church views. The Evangelicals were Calvinists: the Bible first, the Church second.

There were no schisms in the Episcopal Church in spite of different emphases. In 1830 the Episcopal Church in America was a small organization. From then on its increase in size and spread in influence were phenomenal. A more aggressive missionary program was developed. A Reformed Episcopal Church developed in 1873, which conducted a seminary in Philadelphia.

Ruins at Jamestown, Virginia

Only the tower remains of this historic church, a reminder of the religious commitment of the first English colonists in America. In the woods of Jamestown the first Protestant service was held in America (1607), the service of the Church of England. Captain Smith undertook the erection of a barnlike structure for worship, with the Rev. Robert Hunt as minister. Great were the vicissitudes of this early colony, including famine and war with the Indians. Reconstruction of the early house of God followed its destruction. Here the Indian girl, Pocahontas, was baptized in 1614 and then immediately married to a colonist. The wooden structure was succeeded in 1639 by a brick church. A civil war — the first in America — brought destruction to the edifice, except for the tower and a few chimneys. It is now an "ancient" American landmark.

St. Luke's Church, Smithfield, Virginia

St. Luke's, erected in 1632, is the oldest church in America, often referred to as "Old St. Luke's." In 1957 this church celebrated its 325th birthday, on the occasion of the Jamestown Settlement Festival, commemorating the 350th birthday of that settlement.

Now a national shrine, St. Luke's was in a state of collapse as late as 1954, but is now restored. It is the only original Gothic church remaining within the borders of the U.S.A. A temporary chapel preceded it, served by the Rev. William Bennett. The early settlers came from Essex, England, in 1619. In 1637 this region became known as the Isle of Wight.

Bruton Parish Church, Williamsburg, Virginia

When the seat of the state government was moved from Jamestown to Williamsburg in 1699, Bruton Parish Church began to take on wider significance as the place of worship of officials in Colonial Virginia. The name reverts to Sir Thomas Ludwell, who was born in Bruton, Summerset, England, and whose tomb lies here. Preceding his death in 1678 there was an earlier edifice; and after him another. The mother country lay close to the hearts of the people of this parish. Yet love for the new country took hold in the days of the American Revolution to supplant the older ties. Students of William and Mary College were early given recognition by a reserved section in the gallery of this church. In 1905 was begun the work of restoring the edifice to its original form, much after the pattern of the building of 1715.

245

Trinity Church, New York City

In the churchyard of New York City's Trinity Episcopal Church lie buried many famous Americans: Alexander Hamilton, Judge Watts, Captain James Lawrence and Robert Fulton among them. From its beginnings this church owned a large section of land and "Queen's Farm" (from Vesey Street to Christopher Street, from Broadway to the Hudson River). Such holdings gave rich opportunities to serve other parishes and organizations of the city. Trinity Church's original edifice dates back to 1697. Destroyed in 1776 by fire, a new building was erected. In 1841 a third building, the present imposing structure, was started. Trinity Church is regarded as the mother church of St. Paul's, St. John's and St. George's.

St. Peter's, Albany, New York

The Church of England held its first American service in Albany in 1704. Its first church was dedicated in 1715. Queen Anne, a patroness, called the church "the little Chapel of the Onondagas." Lord Howe, killed in the Battle of Ticonderoga in 1758, is buried in its chancel. A new building was dedicated in 1802. A third followed in 1859. This church is a mother church of New York Episcopalianism.

St. Michael's, Marblehead, Massachusetts

The cornerstone of this church was laid in 1714. Sea captains, loyal to the Church of England, were in the majority on the original roster of members. Nearly all the materials used in constructing the edifice came from England. Some beautiful English appointments were ruined by patriots of the American Revolution in their wrath against this English church. Here in 1786 chanting of the service was introduced, an innovation in American Protestant churches. The church was vacated for a period from lack of support, until in 1883 the whole Episcopal Church in the United States rallied to restore it to life. It contained at one time the organ originally in New York's St. Paul's Church, the instrument on which the inaugural march was played when George Washington took the oath of office as first President of this commonwealth.

St. David's, Radnor, Pennsylvania

The cornerstone of this church was laid May 9, 1715. The main door faces the south, with the church laid out east and west, according to ancient church custom. Radnor is some sixteen miles from Philadelphia. Its predecessor on this site was a building of logs known as the "ancient Welsh Episcopal Church," first mentioned in 1700. During the Revolutionary War it was used by soldiers as a rendezvous, and British soldiers were interred in the adjoining graveyard. The custom of decorating the church with evergreens at Christmas, it is said, originated here in 1820.

Samuel Johnson

Born in Guilford, Connecticut, in 1696, Samuel Johnson attended the Saybrook Institution and became a tutor "when a college was located, after much controversy, in New Haven in 1718" (Yale).

A Congregationalist, he became a "convert" to the Anglican Church, involved with Timothy Cutler in the dark controversies between Congregational Separatists and the mother church. He became a missionary of the Anglican S.P.G. in Connecticut. (From Connecticut came the first American bishop, Samuel Seabury.)

In 1754 he became the first president of King's College in New York (now Columbia University). He died in 1772.

The Old North Church, Boston, Massachusetts

From its beginning this celebrated church has had a distinguished list of clergymen and members. Its third minister was the famous Increase Mather, known throughout the colonies; Henry Ware began his pastorate here in 1840; Emerson began his attendance in 1829. The American crusade against intemperance is linked with this church.

Its organization began (in 1723) with the secession of members from "the First Church" in Boston, standing for political as well as religious independence. A previous building was destroyed by the British, who used it as firewood. Known as "Christ Church, Salem Street, Boston" and "The Old North Church of Paul Revere," this church was founded as a colonial mission of the Anglican S.P.G.

Timothy Cutler

On September 12, 1722, Yale held its first commencement with a graduating class of eight. The president was the Rev. Timothy Cutler (1684-1765), who with one other tutor constituted the faculty. It was a commencement of bad feeling. Cutler had decided to leave the Congregational fold and become an Episcopalian. It was a time of church strife and rancor, and church leaders were tossing aside allegiances.

Cutler became a first minister of the Old North Church, or Christ Church, Salem Street, Boston. He went to England for "proper" ordination, giving joy to the hearts of loyal Anglicans and bitterness to Dissenters and Separatists. He was rector of this church from 1723 to 1765.

Tower of Old North Church, 1740

For seventeen years Christ Church, built in 1723, had no spire. As early as 1737 plans were made "to further embellish" the church. A 190-foot wooden spire was raised in 1740. A Burgis-Price print of 1743 (here pictured) reveals the tower and the ornamental weathervane as they appeared then. The steeple was restored more than once. In 1912 descendants of Paul Revere were responsible for its restoration.

"The Branches"

One of the chandeliers, called "the branches," given by Captain William Maxwell in 1724. Wax candles are still used (in 1947) for lighting in this historic Old North Church.

This drawing is by Helen D. Foster.

"The Vinegar Bible," Given by King George II

Printed in 1717 by John Baskett. "The name comes from the misprint in the title at the top of the first column of the page where the major part of the twentieth chapter of St. Luke is printed, which reads, 'The parable of the vinegar' instead of 'The parable of the vineyard.' " It is still in the possession of the church.

An Attempt to Land a Bishop in America
(*A contemporary print*)

This amusing cartoon portrays the general attitude of New England colonists in their fear of the establishment of the temporal power of the Church of England in America.

The picture shows a crowd of excited colonists brandishing staves and clubs. One, a Quaker, holds a copy of Barclay's *Apology;* others are hurling copies of *Calvin's Works,* etc. On deck is an Episcopal carriage dismounted. An affrighted prelate is mounting the ropes. A grinning ape is ready to throw a missile at the bishop.

The controversies raged about the middle of the eighteenth century.

Paul Revere

On April 18, 1775, the Old North Church made history in America. On that evening Paul Revere had agreed to display a warning of the British march to Concord to destroy secreted military stores.

> If the British march
> By land or sea from the town tonight,
> Hang a lantern aloft in the belfry arch
> Of the North Church tower as a signal light:
> One if by land, and two if by sea,
> And I on the opposite shore will be
> Ready to ride and spread the alarm
> Through every Middlesex village and farm,
> For the country folk to be up and to arm!

The sexton, Robert Newman (1772-1804), and Captain John Pulling, Jr., a member of the vestry, slipped into the church at night. The sexton took lanterns from the closet next to the belfry door and went

> Up the wooden stairs with stealthy tread
> To the belfry chamber overhead;
> And startled the pigeons from their perch
> On the sombre rafters that round him made
> Masses of moving shapes and shade —
> Up the light ladder, slender and tall
> To the highest window in the wall!

Then Newman hurried down. Paul Revere mounted his horse and set off to warn the patriots.

Christ Church at this time had been closed for three years. Newman was appointed by the town in 1776 to "ring the bell of Christ Church at 1 o'clock and at 9 at night."

Paul Revere Pew

Paul Revere's son, Joseph Warren, bought this pew (No. 54) in 1808. It is still owned by his descendants.

Interior of Christ Church

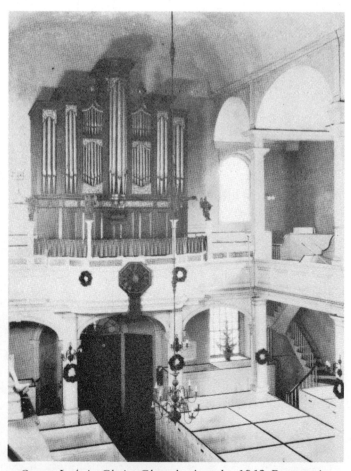

Organ Loft in Christ Church after the 1912 Restoration

This picture shows the "cherubim," the Avery-Bennett clock (erected in 1726) and the "branches" chandelier.

Bust of George Washington

This bust stands in a niche made by the window through which Sexton Robert Newman escaped after displaying the lanterns as directed by Paul Revere. It was presented to the church in 1815 by Shubael Bell, Esq., senior warden. It is reputed to have been modeled from a plaster bust of Christian Güllager (of Boston) in 1790. It has been called "the first memorial bust to Washington erected in a public place, the first memorial in New England and the second memorial in the country."

When General Lafayette was asked if the bust was a good likeness of General Washington, on his visit to the church in 1824, he replied, "Yes, that is the man I knew, and more like him than any other portrait."

Christ Church, Philadelphia

First among the churches of colonial America in association with the struggles for independence. Erected in 1727-1737, it was built of bricks brought from England. Sometimes referred to as "St. Benjamin's" because of Benjamin Franklin's interest in and association with this church. Franklin helped finance it and conducted a lottery to raise funds for its bells. On July 4, 1776 these chimes rang out loudly to spread the glad news of the signing of the Declaration of Independence in near-by Independence Hall.

Under its roof was perfected the organization of the Episcopal Church in America, 1785. From 1790 to 1797 General Washington attended services and held a pew here. Here also came to worship Betsy Ross, maker of the first American flag. In its churchyard lie buried Franklin and six other signers of the Declaration of Independence.

St. Paul's, Norfolk, Virginia

The churchyard of St. Paul's Episcopal Church is one of the most beautiful spots in all of Virginia. Here lie patriots of both the Revolutionary and Civil Wars. Here lie some of the pioneer Huguenots who first settled in Virginia. Here are the graves of the sons of Scottish and Irish patriots.

As early as 1739, soon after the establishment of the first settlement, its first walls arose. Rebuilt after the War of the Revolution and again after the Civil War, the later structures faithfully preserved the original lines.

252

King's Chapel, Boston, Massachusetts

The first building of the Protestant Episcopal Church in New England stood on Tremont Street, its cornerstone laid in 1749 by the governor of the Massachusetts Colony. The parish dates back to 1686 under the leadership of the Rev. Robert Ratcliffe.

King James II sent to the first chapel the gifts of a Bible and silver communion service. First called "Queen's Chapel" after Queen Anne, who had sent gifts of vestments. In the enlargement of the church building, each member was asked to pay for his own pew, resulting in a variety of styles. The interior, unlike simple Puritan meeting houses, was elaborately decorated, even with coats-of-arms. When a new church was built in 1749, King George III sent gifts, and having long been a protégé of the English royal families, it became known as King's Chapel, a favorite place of worship for those who affectionately remembered their English fatherland.

The steeple of this church was never finished, originally from lack of funds. It has been Unitarian since the early nineteenth century. (See "Unitarianism.")

St. Michael's, Charleston, South Carolina

This Protestant Episcopal Church edifice is one of the most striking examples of the type of building character-istic of the eighteenth-century British. Its tower consists of a series of chambers nestling one above the other. The cornerstone was laid in 1752 and the church opened for services in 1761. From England came its chimes and clock. During the Revolution the British tore off lead from the roof to make bullets.

St. Michael's, though suffering greatly from the effects of the Revolution, continued its work and became an increasingly popular shrine. The Freemasons and various political assemblies have met here. The Civil War also left its scars upon the church. Cyclone and fire contributed their damage in turn. It is now a landmark in Charleston.

Christ Church, Alexandria, Virginia

In the building of this church George Washington was intensely interested and gave generously to its construction. In 1765 the parish of Fairfax was created, of which Washington was for five years an active vestryman. The sale of tobacco (by tax) was one means of financing the building. The architect was of the family of Sir Christopher Wren. Washington paid almost $100 for a family pew. He presented the church with a handsome brass chandelier. In its historic records also appears the name of Robert E. Lee, who was baptized and confirmed in the parish.

The Little Church Around the Corner

A famous New York Episcopal church, the Church of the Transfiguration. The founder was the Rev. George Hendric Houghton who, after a ministry of half a century, died in 1897. His nephew, the Rev. George Clarke, was its second rector (died in 1923).

Pictured here is the Rev. George Hendric Houghton taken about the time the church was popularly rechristened "The Little Church Around the Corner."

Intersection of Fifth Avenue, Broadway and 23rd Street in 1850

Rector Houghton built his little church six blocks further north.

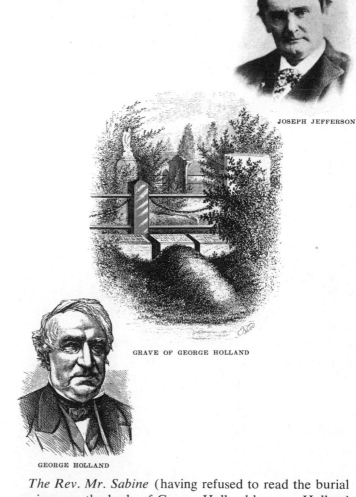

JOSEPH JEFFERSON

GRAVE OF GEORGE HOLLAND

GEORGE HOLLAND

The Rev. Mr. Sabine (having refused to read the burial service over the body of George Holland because Holland had been an actor): "I believe there is a little church around the corner where they do such things."

Joseph Jefferson: "If that be so, then God bless the little church around the corner."

The "Church Parade" on Fifth Avenue in the late Sixties

This song, sung by Wambold in Dan Bryant's Minstrels, spread to the variety theaters, and from thence to the homes of the nation. It was one of the song hits of the seventies.

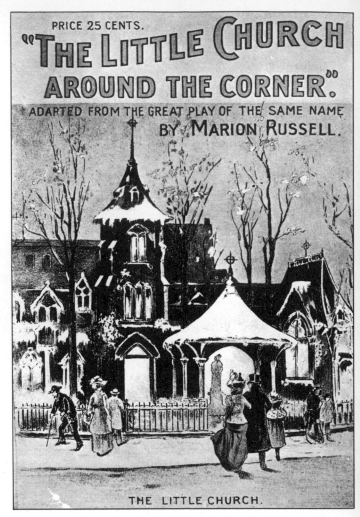

A Paper-Covered Novel Published in the Early Years of the Present Century

The picture on the cover is a copy of the old billboard lithograph that advertised the play when it toured the country.

A Scene Used Many Times on the Stage and Screen

The above picture shows the finale in *Sally,* a Ziegfeld production. The church is in the background, the wedding party before the lich gate.

Interior of the Church

George Clarke Houghton

Rector of the Little Church Around the Corner for over a quarter of a century.

For Better, for Worse

For a small wedding the chantry is used.

1890

1850

1860

1870

1910

1900

1920

Wedding Fashions, 1890-1920

1880

Wedding Fashions, 1850-1880

The Rev. Houghton performed over 7,500 ceremonies. He refused the ceremony to over 20,000 couples.

The Little Church Around the Corner, as It Appeared in 1925

Henry Codman Potter

Bishop Potter (1834-1908) has been called "The People's Friend," and "A Prophet of Social Reform." Rector at Grace Church, New York, 1868-1883, and Bishop of New York.

Phillips Brooks

Pictured here in his study is Phillips Brooks (1835-1892), "the greatest preacher the Episcopal Church has produced." Minister in Trinity Church, Boston, his sermons concentrated on the theme, "God is love." He became a bishop.

Samuel Hart

A first professor of theology at Berkeley Divinity School, a fine type of Anglican theologian steeped in the traditions of the English Church. "He was Connecticut condensed into one man." He was a secretary of the House of Bishops, his last official function at the General Convention in 1916.

The Universalist Church

The idea of Universalism stems from the teachings of Clement and Origen in the second- and third-century schools of Alexandria. These Church Fathers taught universal salvation under a God of love and justice.

The Englishman, James Relly (1722?-1778), author of a widely read treatise on "Union," a follower of Whitefield, a confirmed Universalist and critic of Calvinism, is regarded by the Universalists as one of the conspicuous progenitors of American Universalism, particularly through his influence on John Murray (1741-1815). Persecuted in England, Murray came to America in 1770, and began preaching Universalism on the Atlantic seaboard. His Calvinism took the form of believing that Christ's atonement is not limited to the elect.

For a time Murray served as a chaplain in Washington's army. In 1779-1780 his group organized its first meeting house, the mother church of the denomination, at Gloucester, Massachusetts.

James Relly

John Murray

FIRST CHURCH IN GLOUCESTER.

The Gloucester friends of Murray, in 1779, had formed themselves into what they considered an organization and built a plain little meeting house in which, on Christmas Day, in 1780, they held services. This was the first Universalist Church to be built in America.

In Philadelphia in 1790 the scattered Universalists joined in the adoption of a "Faith and Plan of Church Government." Self-government of each church was a basic tenet.

Dr. Benjamin Rush, cosigner of the Declaration of Independence, was the author of this 1790 Declaration. The whole human race is affirmed to a final restoration to happiness by the merit and efficacy of Jesus Christ and His Spirit.

Rush was a pioneer in the field of temperance education. He helped organize the first antislavery society. He also founded (1791) the First Day Sunday School Society, which became the first nonsectarian Sunday school in America.

Independent Christian Church, Gloucester, Massachusetts

The most vigorous intellectual and spiritual leader of Universalism was the clergyman and philosopher, Hosea Ballou (1771-1852). His famous publication, *Treatise on Atonement,* appeared in 1804. This marked a definite espousal of Unitarian thought.

Winchester, New Hampshire, Universalist Church

The first Avowal of Faith was adopted here in 1803: the Winchester Confession of Faith. Hosea Ballou was present and took a leading part in framing this confession. "A Unitarian creed in Trinitarian form," it has been called. "Neither this nor any other form of words shall be imposed as a creedal test" is the Universalist profession.

Clara Barton, Founder of the American Red Cross and a Distinguished Universalist

The Evangelical Church

Jacob Albright

Jacob Albright (1759-1808), son of German immigrants and a Lutheran, later a Methodist, associate of Asbury and Henry Boehm, became an evangelistic preacher among German-Americans, and in 1800 organized his three "classes" in eastern Pennsylvania. He became the founder of the Evangelical Church.

A division occurring in the Church in 1891-1894 led to the beginning of the United Evangelical Church, reunited in 1922.

The Evangelical United Brethren Church is the name of the merger, in 1946, of the Evangelical Church and the Church of the United Brethren in Christ.

The United Brethren in Christ

Phillip Otterbein

Phillip Otterbein (1726-1813), a missionary to America from the Reformed Church in Germany, assisted in the ordination of the Methodist Asbury. The latter was unfavorable to German-speaking societies. Together with Martin Boehm (1725-1812), evangelist and an expelled Mennonite, and others, he founded the (German) United Brethren in Christ. Both Otterbein and Boehm became bishops.

The name of the church was settled upon in 1800. It is Arminian in doctrine, mode of baptism being optional. Its headquarters are at Dayton, Ohio.

Now merged with the Evangelical Church.

The American Baptist Association

The churches of the American Baptist Association, composed of independent Baptist churches, among them "Landmark Baptists," "Missionary Baptists," "United Baptists," and some others, do not claim to be a part of the Protestant Church which began in the days of Martin Luther, John Calvin, and others.

It is their contention that these churches of the American Baptist Association began originally with Jesus Christ and the Apostles, and that when the Catholic Church movement got under way their churches immediately refused to fellowship it and were called through the centuries dissenters and nonconformists because of their rejection of the Catholic theory.

These churches affirm that their faith is represented in groups that were sorely persecuted by the Catholic Church, such as the Donatists in Africa, Novationists throughout the Roman Empire, Paulicians in Armenia, and later in Europe, and the Albigenses and Waldenses in Spain, France and other parts of Europe. They claim to be the direct successors of these Anabaptist groups, so-called for their insistence upon rebaptizing those who came to them from the Catholic Church.

The History of the Evangelical Churches of the Valleys of Piemont, originally published in 1658 in London, England, has recently been republished by the churches of the American Baptist Association.

This history contains much information about the Waldenses in these valleys, and gives their confessions of faith which are still acceptable to this group of Baptist churches today. The history gives vivid accounts of the persecutions which these people underwent, "All which are justified, partly by divers Ancient Manuscripts written many hundred Years before Calvin or Luther, and partly by other most Authentick Attestations: The true originals of the greatest part whereof, are to be seen in their proper Languages by all the curious, in the Publick Library of the famous University of Cambridge." (This quotation appears on the flyleaf of the history.)

The contents of the history was "Collected and compiled with much pains and industry, By Samuel Morland, Esq; During his abode in Geneva, in quality of His Highness Commissioner Extraordinary for the Affairs of the said Valleys and particularly for the Distribution of the Collected Moneys, among the remnant of those poor distressed People." (As it appears on the flyleaf of the history.)

The pictures are of drawings printed in this history of the persecutions suffered by the people who worshiped in the Valleys of Piedmont hundreds of years before Calvin and Luther, hence preceded the Protestant Church of their day. These are the people that the churches of this Baptist group claim as their predecessors in the faith.

The documentations referred to in this history are still in the museum in London.

The historical facts which accompany this drawing are as follows: "Jacopo Perrin, an Elder of the Church of Villaro, and David his brother, were taken prisoners in their beds, in a certain village called La Baudine, and carried from thence to Lucerna, where they were clapt up in the Marquess his preson, where they were most barbarously and inhumanely used; amongst other things, the bloody butchers of that place striped off the skin off their arms and legs by long slices, in the form of leather points, till such time as they had left the flesh quite bare, and at length they were miserably starved to death in the same prison, where their carcasses were suffered to lie and putrefy."

"Giovanni Pelanchion, a young man about 25 years of age, having been taken prisoner, and made his escape, was afterwards retaken by the soldiers, who tied one of his legs to the tail of a mule, and so dragged him violently through all the streets and corners of Lucerna; and because the poor wretch sometimes lifted up his head and hands through the great pain and anguish that he suffered by the grating of his body against the ragged flints in the streets, the hard-hearted villains battered and bruised his body with stones and brick-bats as he passed along, crying that he was possessed with a devil which kept him from dieing. After this they cut off his privy members, and violently crammed them into the poor creatures mouth, and down his throat to stop his breath: At last they chopped off his head, and dragged him to the rivers brink, there left him unburied. This cruelty has been divers times verified in public (with great regret) even by several of the Catholics, as likewise by many of the poor Protestants themselves who were then prisoners, and were made to look on this doleful spectacle."

264

Rendered in current English, the story accompanying this picture reads:

"Margarita Revel of La Cartere of the age of fourscore and five years, the Mother in Law of Captain Paolo Genoulat, and Maria di Pravillerm of the age of ninety years and blind, both of S. Giovanni, were taken, and in a most barbarous manner burned alive in the place called Les Vignes, on the one side of Angrogna; which was seen and hath been attested by Judith Grand, and by the wife of Matthieu Jordan of La Torre, as also by Maria daughter of Jacobo Davide. In like manner were handled Madona Lena, and Jeanna Batzan, both of La Torre, the last ninety, and the first eighty years of age, and blind."

An example of martyrdom suffered by the Waldenses or Anabaptists.

The Disciples of Christ

THE DISCIPLES OF CHRIST OR "CHRISTIAN CHURCHES"

There were two basic convictions in the minds of the founders of this church: (1) the Church should be a unity; (2) divisions are due to "human opinions" added to simple basic Christian requirements. First a "movement," then a separate religious body. It was Congregational in polity.

Thomas Campbell of the Irish Secession group of Presbyterians came to the U.S.A. in 1807. His son Alexander (d. 1866) helped to form the Christian Association at Washington, Pennsylvania, in 1809. In 1811 the organization began associating with Baptists (the Campbells holding to "believers' baptism"). Barton Stone (Presbyterian) and others were in union, some practicing immersion. Stone favored the name "Christian," while Campbell favored "Disciples." Both names were used. It was in the Middle West that the organization prospered most.

Progressive and Conservative groups developed.

Characteristic doctrines: rejection of creeds; New Testament emphasis; belief in the Divine Sonship of Jesus as basic; the Lord's Supper celebrated each Lord's Day as a memorial feast rather than as a sacrament.

In 1893 Herbert L. Willett suggested the establishment of a seminary in connection with a university. Result: the Disciples Divinity House near the campus of the University of Chicago (1894). There were other such affiliations.

The Campbells, Father and Son

LEFT: Thomas Campbell (1763-1854). RIGHT: Alexander Campbell (1788-1866).

A Map of "The Campbell Country," Showing the Brush Run Church Location, Birthplace of a Constituted Campbellite Church

Alexander Campbell Mansion, Bethany, West Virginia

Barton W. Stone (1772-1844)

The Cane Ridge Meeting House in Kentucky

Ordained to the Presbyterian ministry, Barton W. Stone went west from Maryland, where he was born, and eventually served churches at Concord and Cane Ridge, Kentucky. Pictured here is the church where he began his ministry. The basis of unity, he came to say, was not doctrine but love and good will.

Walter Scott

Walter Scott (1796-1861), originally a Presbyterian, was born in Edinburgh. In 1818 he came to New York and moved later to Pittsburgh. His famous "five-finger exercise" outlined the steps to conversion (still repeated by some Disciples to this day): faith, repentance, baptism, remission of sins, and the gift of the Holy Spirit. Another step, confession, was added later. Scott was a flaming evangelist on the Ohio frontier.

The Churches of God in North America (General Eldership)

Reared in the German Reformed faith, John Winebrenner (1797-1860) served the Salem Reformed Church, Harrisburg, Pennsylvania. A dispute with his vestry caused his removal. In 1823, when he was not permitted to serve in his parish church, he and his loyal followers met out-of-doors to hold services. Thus was initiated the group now known as the Churches of God in North America.

Winebrenner was too fraternal with other religious groups to remain in favor with his conservative church of that day. A convinced revivalist and evangelist, his field of work seemed cut out for him apart from the conventional and formalist ways of his ecclesiastical household. The name "Church of God" was chosen for his newly formed group on the principle of "Bible names for Bible things." Believers became "Saints." The Church was said to possess "ordinances." No creed — only the Bible. "Eldership" corresponds to the use of the word "conference." No officials or bishops in the Church.

Winebrenner was an author, and editor of *The Church Advocate,* one of the older religious journals in America, and president of the First General Eldership in 1845.

The one and only condition to membership in the church is regeneration — a cardinal doctrine of this group. Immersion and washing of the saints' feet are also typical practices of the group.

The Old Log Building First Used by the Salem Reformed Church

John Winebrenner

The Campus and Administration Building of Findlay College, Opened in 1882

The Church of Jesus Christ
of Latter Day Saints (The Mormons)

This church looks back to its organization in 1830 by Joseph Smith (born in 1805 in Sharon, Vermont), who in 1820 had a vision at Palmyra, New York; and to the leadership of Brigham Young (born in 1801 in Whittingham, Vermont), who headed the migration of the earlier followers of Smith from Illinois to Utah, present headquarters of the church.

Its doctrine of polygamy and celestial marriage in the plural, advocated by Young, caused a national controversy and in 1890 a prohibition of the practice by government manifesto.

It is a highly organized body. There is a first presidency of three men, twelve apostles, a presiding patriarch, seven presidents of seventies, and a presiding bishopric of three.

Its priesthood is of two orders: the higher or Melchizedek and the lower or Aaronic (temporal affairs). In areas there are divisions of war, stake and mission. Tithing is practiced by the faithful.

The two sacraments of historic Christianity are observed. Such doctrines as the Trinity, atonement by Christ, prophecy, healing, and the gift of tongues belong to its traditional faith. The Bible as the Word of God has a companion Word in the Book of Mormon, which the Angel on September 21, 1823 showed to Joseph Smith in the form of plates, and which was published under Smith's memorial inspiration in 1830.

The story of the Mormon trek westward is one of tragic romance.

Facsimile of a Portion of the Gold Plates, as Said to be Represented on the Paper Which Joseph Smith Gave to Martin Harris, the Prophet's Scribe

Joseph Smith, the Prophet

Organization of the Mormon Church

The "Church of Christ" was organized on April 6, 1830, in the house of Peter Whitmer in Fayette, Seneca County, New York — "exactly 1800 years to a day from the resurrection of Christ." The chosen six "entered into covenant to serve the Lord" and "partook of the sacrament of the Supper." Joseph and Oliver, his scribe, ordained each other as spiritual teachers of the Church.

They then laid hands upon the others, to receive the "gift of the Holy Ghost."

The six: Joseph Smith, the prophet; Oliver Cowdery, his scribe; Hyrum Smith, an elder brother of Joseph; Peter Whitmer, Jr.; Samuel H. Smith, a younger brother of Joseph; and David Whitmer.

Soon after the organization of the church, the prophet received a revelation to move his group from Fayette to Kirtland, Ohio. This was in 1831. A small temple was erected in Kirtland.

Then another revelation came, pointing to Missouri. The "Lamanites," or American Indians, were to be conquered by conversion. A temple on a hill in Independence, Missouri, became the "Land of Zion", the holy site for the chosen people, the New Jerusalem, the Garden of Eden. The temple was dedicated on August 3, 1831.

The next year hostility against the saints began by stoning, shooting of livestock and burning of haystacks. Revelations came to the prophet to stand firm. Jackson County citizens declared a manifesto for the removal of the saints immediately. Then a mob took over. Joseph Smith organized his followers into a military organization. This added fuel to the fire. In the spring of 1834 the saints were finally expelled from Jackson County.

The march westward over bleak prairies is a testimony to the sincerity, devotion and fortitude of the saints. Three years of peace were enjoyed in Clay County, in Far West, Missouri. Then the militia moved in. Smith and others were taken prisoner and condemned to be shot. Spared by men who refused to carry out the order, the settlement burned, they began another exodus — this time to Nauvoo, Illinois (1839).

The Temple at Kirtland, Ohio

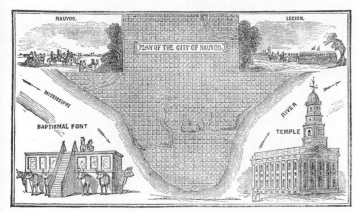

The Home of the Saints in Illinois

Massacre of Mormons at Haun's Mill, Missouri

Joseph Smith had reached the home of the saints in Missouri after three months' travel from Kirtland. The massacre at Haun's Mill took place on October 29, 1838, as a consequence of the governor's order of expulsion or extermination.

The Assassination of Joseph Smith

Joseph Smith had acquired the titles of Prophet, Seer, Revelator, Mayor and Lieutenant General of the Nauvoo Legion. The latter title, secured from the Illinois Legislature, was higher than that of the incumbent major-general, Winfield Scott, then commander of the U. S. Army. But Smith was in danger of his life from foes within and foes without. He had fled with some of his cohorts across the Mississippi when the word came that he must return to Nauvoo to take charge of the flock. He did and suffered arrest. In an upper room of the red sandstone jail (today a shrine) in Carthage, Illinois, his end soon came. A mob stormed the building. Brother Hyrum was shot and Joseph drew his own gun and fired

at the assailants. Two shots pierced him as he flung himself in a desperate leap from the window. His body was partially mutilated. The date was June 27, 1844.

Three nights after the martyrdom of Joseph Smith, a certain Anson Call received in a dream word from the prophet that there were to be glorious days ahead. There were other "manifestations" from the deceased leader.

Upon Brigham Young the mantle of leadership now fell. Young had been healed by the prophet, and he had suffered along with the others in the westward marches. His apostolic career, Mormons hold, was foreordained even before the revelation at Palmyra. In 1836 Joseph Smith had predicted Young's mission.

Where now? The twelve fasted and prayed. Brigham had a vision of a mountain in the Far West, whose location was not geographically clear. Mormons believe that divine inspiration guided their leader and his followers to Salt Lake. The trek west began.

On July 24, 1847 Brigham Young's wagon halted at a place in full view of the Great Salt Lake Valley. He was lifted into a vision by the magnificent sight — it appeared to be the same as in the former vision. "It is enough. This is the right place. Drive on," said the new prophet.

The Mormons celebrate ths date annually, a date more important to them than the Fourth of July.

Brigham Young (1801-1877)

President of the Mormon Church, 1844-1877.

Ruins of the Temple at Nauvoo

The Exodus from Nauvoo

Even while preparations were being made to leave, the temple at Nauvoo was completed and dedicated. A revelation had been received that this temple must be completed — if not, the Church would be rejected. Then began the siege of the town and, later, the destruction of the temple (1848).

The Trek to the Far West

273

The Mountain Meadows Massacre

The saints at Salt Lake were confronted with emigrants from Missouri and neighboring states on their way to southern California. Their memory of their own persecution by Missourians made them furious at the intrusion and the arrogance of the interlopers was too much for gentle handling. When the emigrants reached the Mountain Meadows, "redskins" (Indians and disguised Mormons) attacked and massacred the entire lot, save a few children. This was in 1857.

To this day phantom gunfire echoes and screams of women and children are said to haunt the ears of travelers passing that way.

John D. Lee, for the part he played in the massacre, was returned to the site and shot (1877).

Triumphal Passage of United States Troops Through Salt Lake City

In 1857 President Buchanan ordered an army to Utah. The Mormons resented the incursion of the Federal Government upon their own sovereignty, since they regarded themselves as an autonomous theocratic state. Sporadic pillages by the Mormons on the U. S. troops followed. Prophet Young concluded that he could not whip the United States Army, so he planned a flight.

Finally, Young surrendered the Territorial Seal and received the new governor with courtesy. Without further opposition General Johnston paraded triumphantly through the streets of Zion (Salt Lake City) in the spring of 1858.

Tribute Is Paid to Brigham Young in His Travels

Brigham Young is a symbol of the struggles of pioneer days and the building of an empire. He is a beloved figure in the eyes of Latter Day Saints. He led to the building of a self-sustaining agricultural empire. When the cornerstone of the Salt Lake Temple was laid, he proclaimed his desire for a building substantial enough to endure for a thousand years. The church was envisaged as a monopoly of power, in commerce and trade as well as in spiritual matters. Even the minerals of the earth were believed to be under angelic care.

Young's name is associated especially, in the minds of non-Mormons, with the theory and practice of polygamy. He even provided extra wives as a reward for devotion to the work of the Lord. There is no godliness without progeny. Procreation is an immutable law of God. Bodies must be supplied for the myriads of angels awaiting incarnation.

Young was showered with adoration by his followers. Flowers were strewn on streets at his visitations.

The Brigham Young House

It has been rumored that Brigham Young had an immense number of wives, that he lived in gorgeous Oriental style.

T. B. H. Stenhouse, a Mormon elder and missionary for twenty-five years (and author of *The Rocky Mountain Saints*), remarks that such rumors are "purely imaginative. There are probably *only* nineteen 'sisters' who call him 'husband.' "

On September 25, 1890, Wilford Woodruff, fourth president of the Church, under Federal pressure issued the manifesto which suspended the practice of polygamy. It was a bitter pill to swallow, since the practice had religious sanction and strong sentimental and social ties.

Brigham Young's Handwriting

An Early Drawing of Salt Lake City, Viewed from the North

Design of Salt Lake Temple

Mormon Temple and Tabernacle, Salt Lake City, Utah

Built of solid granite taken at great expense and labor from the Wasatch Mountains some fifty miles away, the present Mormon Temple is an extraordinary achitectural monument to the zeal and dedication of the enthusiastic, missionary-minded followers of Brigham Young. The timber had to be hauled by oxen from a canyon twenty miles away. Its cornerstone was laid by the founder in 1853 and the construction continued for twenty years, at a cost of some four million dollars.

The Tabernacle seats some eight thousand people. Its organ is one of the largest in the country. Its shape is like the back of a turtle, the roof supported by forty-four sandstone pillars, wall to wall.

Two Other Mormon Temples

Temple at Manti, Utah.

Temple at Mesa, Arizona.

Mormonism has split into other, separate organizations, though the main body continues at Salt Lake City.

The Church of Christ (Temple Lot), organized in 1830, has its headquarters in Independence, Missouri. This group followed the leadership of Joseph Smith and the remnant Latter Day Saints in Bloomington, Illinois.

The Church of Jesus Christ (Bickertonites), followers of Joseph Smith, Jr. and William Bickerton, who denounced Brigham Young, has its present headquarters at Monongahela, Pennsylvania.

The Church of Jesus Christ (Cutlerites), reorganized in 1853 in Iowa, has been centered in Minnesota since 1864. Alpheus Cutler, appointed successor to Joseph Smith, was their leader.

The Church of Jesus Christ (Strangites), whose leader was James Strang (d. 1856, a martyr), began their separate existence in Burlington, Wisconsin.

The Reorganized Church of Latter Day Saints, now at Independence, Missouri, claims the true succession to Joseph Smith.

The Lutheran Church—Missouri Synod

A present membership of over two million members makes this independent body one of the largest Lutheran groups in America.

In 1847 congregations in Missouri, Michigan and Ohio organized the synod, with the Rev. Carl Ferdinand W. Walther its first president. It maintains the most extensive system of parochial schools in American Protestantism, its institutions numbering over a thousand. It maintains two theological seminaries, with an enrollment of some twelve hundred.

A large number of Germans left Saxony and landed in New Orleans in January, 1839. Under the leadership of the Rev. Stephan they came up the Mississippi to St. Louis. Some remained here; most, however, moved on to Perry County, establishing a center there. During their first year they built a log college and a seminary. C F. W. Walther became the minister of Trinity Church in St. Louis and began to publish a magazine, *Der Lutheraner*. This magazine inspired the Rev. Friedrich Wyneken to home missionary service.

Another group of Lutherans under the leadership of the Rev. A. Kramer settled at Frankemuth, Michigan in 1845. These two groups were responsible for the founding of the synod. They immediately committed themselves to remain united in doctrine and to publish sound Lutheran books and papers.

The Church accepts as its confession of faith all the symbols contained in the Lutheran Book of Concord of 1580, the doctrinal decisions of the symbols being binding because "they are the doctrinal decisions of Holy Scripture itself." It thus affirms that the prophecy regarding the Anti-Christ has been fulfilled in the Pope of Rome and his dominion; rejects "the whole of Millennialism"; affirms that the New Testament teaches the abrogation of the Sabbath and all holy days as prescribed observances, that such days are ordinances of Christian liberty; affirms that the ministry is a divine ordinance with powers conferred by "the Word of God"; rejects the view that the grace of God is communicated by an immediate operation apart from external means; and affirms that the Holy Scriptures are a unique revelation and thus "differ from all other books in the world," rejecting the view that only parts of the Scripture are the Word of God. It is a strongly "confessional" church.

Pioneer Leaders of the Missouri Synod

Top: C. F. W. Walther (1811-1887), university student at Leipzig, influenced by Pietism and shaken by rationalism, a student of Luther's works, ordained in Saxony. He welcomed the opportunity of emigration and, with others, the prospect of founding an ideal Lutheran church in America. The father and organizer of the "German Evangelical Lutheran Synod of Missouri, Ohio and Other States," he wrote model church constitutions and interpreted Lutheran doctrines. A professor of theology at Concordia Seminary and its president.

Bottom: F. C. D. Wyneken, a vigorous missionary for the Church.

The Perry County Log Cabin College, Second Location

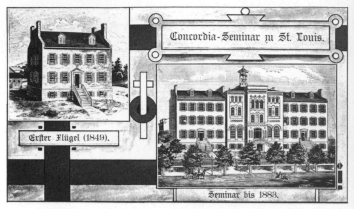

Concordia Seminary, St. Louis, Missouri
(Nineteenth-century picture)

Now one of the largest Protestant seminaries in the United States.

Concordia Seminary, Springfield, Illinois

Its first home was in Fort Wayne, Indiana. It was established in 1846.

Concordia College, Fort Wayne, Indiana

A first "gymnasium" of the church. Other educational institutions were established at St. Paul, Minnesota; Seward, Nebraska; Milwaukee, Wisconsin; Addison, Illinois; Concordia, Missouri; Bronxville, New York; Winfield, Kansas; New Orleans, Louisiana; Portland, Oregon and East Oakland, California.

The Seal of the Church

Missouri Synod Parochial Schools

The founders of the Missouri Synod, arriving in America at the time of the gradual introduction of public schools, established their own parochial schools and teacher-training institutions. Missouri opened its first public school in 1838 in a two-room building in St. Louis, the same year the Saxon Lutherans sailed for America. State normal schools were practically unknown when the Saxons began teacher training in 1843. It was a new adventure for the German immigrants. What was needed, they believed, was systematic Christian training of the youth and instruction in German.

Pictured here is the Lutheran High School, St. Louis, Missouri.

The Seventh-Day Adventists

The second coming of Christ — an ancient Christian hope — was given a renewed emphasis in Scripture study in the early decades of the nineteenth century. The "last days" or "end of the age" was envisioned anew by Protestants of many denominations.

In America in the early 1840's an extensive Second Advent movement developed. William Miller, a licensed Baptist minister, was the recognized leader. It was prophesied that the Second Advent would occur "about the year 1843."

The seventh-day Sabbath observance had begun at Washington, New Hampshire. This, together with a renewed emphasis on spiritual gifts and prophecy and the Advent doctrine, slowly grew into a distinct church movement. *The Advent Review and Sabbath Herald*

(1850) became the forum of such views. In 1855 headquarters were established in Battle Creek, Michigan, where in 1860 the name "Seventh-day Adventist" was officially adopted by a conference. In 1901 a General Conference co-ordinated the various phases of the movement. In 1903 the general headquarters was moved to Washington, D. C.

"The hour of God's judgment" is a characteristic doctrine. Missionary zeal on a world-wide program and the practice of tithing are among its distinctions. Its members are among the most liberal givers of any major denomination. Membership runs around 275,000. There is no formally adopted creed. They affirm, in practice, "conscientious co-operation" in patriotic matters.

Bettmann Archive

Followers of the prophet, William Miller, were called "Millerites." He predicted the Second Advent would occur specifically between March 21, 1843 and March 21, 1844. His associates, after their disappointment, reset the date to October 22, 1844. Daniel 8:13-14 was the source text for the prediction.

Of great historical significance to Seventh-day Adventists is the ship *Pitcairn,* which was built as the result of contributions of nickels, pennies, dimes and dollars by thousands of church members throughout the United States to serve as a missionary ship for the tiny Central Pacific island which is now inhabited entirely by Seventh-day Adventists. In 1890 the *Pitcairn* was built and launched to carry the Advent message to the South Pacific islands. It sailed from San Francisco, California, October 20, 1890.

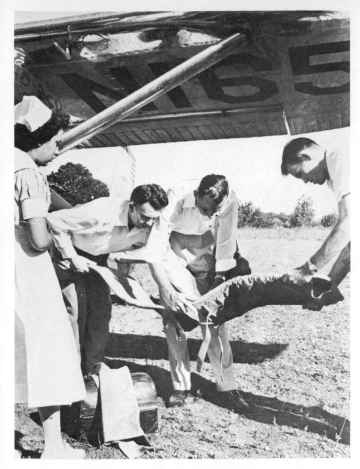

Tied up to a floating native village in the Pacific islands is a Seventh-day Adventist missionary ship which carries medical supplies and other equipment to help build a better life for thousands of remote peoples in the vast Pacific area. A fleet of twelve ships operated by Seventh-day Adventists are currently at work in the Pacific island area.

Dr. David Zinke, assisted by medical students of the Seventh-day Adventist College of Medical Evangelists, prepares a lightweight stretcher on which a patient will be placed and strapped to his airplane to be flown to the church's Montemorelos Hospital and Sanitarium. A typical Seventh-day Adventist medical missionary doctor, Dave Zinke uses fifteen remote airstrips throughout central Mexico to bring in emergency medical cases to the hospital's modern facility.

International headquarters of the Seventh-day Adventist denomination. The first General Conference of Seventh-day Adventists was organized at Battle Creek, Michigan, on May 21, 1863 by twenty delegates from six church conferences. An executive committee of three persons was named. In 1903 the denominational headquarters was moved from Battle Creek to its present location in Takoma Park, Maryland, a suburb of Washington, D. C.

The Young Men's Christian Association

The Y.M.C.A. was founded in London on June 6, 1844. Leaders were George Williams and Edward Beaumont, two young drygoods clerks. It began and continued as a religious movement of laymen, aimed to help young workers who had become, at the beginning of the Industrial Revolution, indifferent to religion. No formal religious creed was urged upon its members, other than "to exert a Christian influence in the sphere of their daily calling." In spirit it was an evangelical, ecumenical and even puritanical movement.

Within a decade the "Y" had spread through England, to the Continent, Canada and the United States. Education soon was added to its functions. The first World Conference was held in Paris in 1855. The gymnasium became a focal point of activities. Members included non-Christians (India's thirty thousand members are Hindu in religious faith, and many Japanese remain loyal Buddhists). In 1955 there were some 2,230,000 members in the United States. Catholic youth here joined despite the Vatican's warnings.

World membership in 1955 was 4,242,819. Over five thousand full-time secretaries are engaged as professionals, over eight thousand headquarters buildings are in operation.

The red triangle is its familiar seal, symbolizing spirit, mind and body.

At the Centennial International Convention of the Y.M.C.A.'s of the United States and Canada, June 21-24, 1951, the following were among the topics discussed by leaders (showing the wide variety of interests of the Y.M.C.A.): "Beliefs That Matter"; "The Y.M.C.A. and the Churches"; "Being a Christian in Politics and Government"; "Being a Christian in Business and Industry"; "Making Democracy Work"; "Being a World Citizen"; "Every Man's Occupation a Christian Vocation"; "World Peace and World Unity."

George Williams (1821-1905), a Founder of the Y.M.C.A.

St. Helen's Baptist Church, Montreal

Where the first Y.M.C.A. in North America was organized on November 25, 1851.

A Gospel Wagon

Used in the early religious work of the Y.M.C.A.

Old South Chapel, Boston

Where the first Y.M.C.A. in the United States was organized on December 29, 1851.

A Y.M.C.A. Tent in the Association's First Services to the Armed Forces in 1862

The Boston Association's Gymnasium in the Early Days of Y.M.C.A. Physical Education

The first Y.M.C.A. building to contain a gymnasium was erected in New York in 1869.

Debating was an early informal educational activity in many Y.M.C.A.'s.

In 1887 the first national Y.M.C.A. physical education director was appointed. Four years later, directly as a result of the widening physical education program, basketball was invented by a Y.M.C.A. secretary.

Organized camping, as it is known today, was instituted by a Y.M.C.A. layman in 1885.

Y.M.C.A. formal educational institutions have 100,-000 students. The Y.M.C.A. operates twenty-four formal schools of college level.

John R. Mott

Honorary Life President of the World's Alliance of the Y.M.C.A., Mott was born in 1865, was converted under a Quaker evangelist and early in his student days took active part in Y.M.C.A. activities. In 1946 he received the Nobel Peace Prize. He died in 1955. He has been called "the greatest Christian statesman of his time." His thought moved in terms of the world.

The Famous Y.M.C.A. Hotel in Chicago

World service of the Y.M.C.A. is based on the philosophy of bridging differences between all races, creeds and nationalities, coming to grips with the basic problems of health, education, economic welfare and spiritual growth and the principle of helping people to help themselves.

The Y.M.C.A. Hotel, advertised as having 1,800 rooms, has been "home" to thousands of transients.

The Y.M.C.A. Symbol

The Evangelical Lutheran Joint Synod of Wisconsin and other States

This body of Lutherans looks back to an earlier organization of Lutherans who inaugurated a Wisconsin Synod in Grace Church, Milwaukee in 1849. John Muehlhaeuser was a leader and first president of the synod. Adherence to the Scriptures as the verbally inspired and inerrant Word of God has characterized this group as "a truly orthodox Lutheran church." Three groups, from Wisconsin, Minnesota and Michigan, merged in 1892. In 1917 occurred the larger amalgamation. One of the serious controversies with other groups occurred over the doctrine of election.

Pictured here are John Muehlhaeuser and Grace Church, Milwaukee.

The Gemeinde Blatt

A Lutheran church paper, 1865, first issue published in Watertown, Wisconsin.

Adolf Hoenecke

The Seminary in Wauwatosa, Dedicated in 1893

The Rev. Adolf Hoenecke "was not only a part of the history of the Lutheran Church of his time; he also helped make that history." The history of the Wisconsin Synod is the story of his mature life. He died in 1908.

NIVGOSDZANN, DJIVGONAAIY'	EARTH AND SUN

1

Nivgosdzann, djivgonaaiy',
Ya:, tsi'ivlqsovs/zae dabigha,
Da.naesh(iv hik'eh) bae.binash(ni/:
Ayinla/nh, Ann - shi)Ta/.

2

Da(adza.yu Nbi)at'ae'ht,
Nbi)yulhi shilq"goliv";
Ihidna-zhi' shilq"djihh"goago),
Yati' nzhoni N"yae.yalqti'.

3

Oyiv(lqts'av, shizha/zhae, Nsshilqnni,
shi(ni)Ta/ nshqliv", shonhdlav!
Nih hik'eh) Shi(bilq noqgizhgae
Jesus nzhogo ana"godla/.

4

Ani/ta) shilq"gozhov(, oshdlavgo;
Nih shi)Ta/! Nbilq"dishni:
Da(adzav.yu anashdalq-yu
Shiya.gozhov(goh N"ahgolqsivh.

1

Earth and sun, the sky above me,
All the lights in heaven's hall,
Looking at them I remember:
'Tis my Father who made all.

2

Everywhere His power is with me,
Is the Spirit from above
Life, true life, He sets before me,
Speaking with His Word of Love.

3

Hear, my child, He says, O listen:
Trust in Me, your Father true;
Whatsoever stood between us -
Jesus righted all for you.

4

Now I do rejoice, believing:
Father mine! to Him I say;
And His blessing will be with me
Wheresoever on my way.

Niv-gos dzann, djiv go na-a-iy', ya: tsi'ilq sovs sae da-bi gha, da-naesh-
iv hi k'eh, baebi nash(ni: A-yin-la/n h-Ann shi) Ta/, A-yin-la/nh, Ann shi, Ta/.

A Hymn in Apache Language

Among the missionary enterprises of the Evangelical Lutheran Joint Synod of Wisconsin and other states is the Apache Indian Mission.

The Finnish Evangelical Lutheran Church (Suomi Synod)

Suomi College and Theological Seminary

Finns came to America in the 1850's. Fourteen years later their real immigration began, largely from northern Norway and settling in Minnesota, Iowa and other Midwestern areas. The copper country in northern Michigan attracted a large group. Near Hancock, at Quincy, they organized their first church in 1867 with other Scandinavian groups.

One group favored the revival lay preacher movement led by the European, Lars Laestadius (1800-1861). The other was content with the more conservative Lutheran heritage. The latter group organized in 1890 in what is today the Suomi Synod.

In 1946 Suomi College and Theological Seminary celebrated its golden jubilee. Old Main was dedicated in 1900, where today the Finnish culture continues to be remembered.

The Baptist General Conference of America

On Friday the thirteenth, 1852, in Rock Island, Illinois, the first Baptist church of this General Conference was formed. Its leader was Gustaf Palmquist (1812-1867), school teacher, evangelist and musician. One of these early baptismal services occurred "in the spacious and beautiful baptistry which the mighty river provided." Other early leaders were Anders Wiberg, theologian, author and preacher, and F. O. Nilsson, exiled Baptist leader from Sweden.

In February, 1854, the Chicago Rock Island Railway tracks, the first to reach the Mississippi, were brought to Rock Island. At New Sweden, Iowa, the first church building was erected in the same year. Other early pioneer churches were erected in Minnesota. Palmquist returned to Sweden after five years of pioneer work.

The Baptist General Conference (organized in 1879), with a current membership of some 60,000 persons, operates Bethel College and Seminary in St. Paul, founded in 1871 by John Alexis Edgren. Present headquarters are on the North Side in Chicago.

Gustaf Palmquist, on Sunday, August 8, 1852, baptized three fellow Swedish immigrants in the Mississippi, near Rock Island, Illinois, and thus initiated the Swedish Baptist communion, now the Baptist General Conference of America.

The Swedish Baptists began in 1852 by immersing their members in the waters of the Mississippi. Painting by the pastor-artist, Reynold Lund.

Anders Wiberg, Pioneer Leader of Swedish Baptists in America

*Fredrik Olaus Nilsson, Pioneer Leader of Swedish
Baptists in America*

*Swedish Immigrants in Iowa Campaigned for Lincoln's
Election (1861)*

WITH GRATITVDE TO GOD

AND TO THE BAPTISTS OF SWEDEN.
THE BAPTIST GENERAL CONFERENCE
OF AMERICA IN ITS CENTENARY
YEAR OF 1952 PRESENTS THIS
PLAQVE TO BETELSEMINARIET
IN HONOR OF THESE PIONEERS

GVSTAF PALMQVIST
ANDERS WIBERG
F·O·NILSSON
J·A·EDGREN

*Plaque Presented to the Bethel Seminary in Sweden in
1952, the Centennial Year of the Baptist General
Conference of America*

The Young Women's Christian Association

The world-wide Young Women's Christian Association had two separate beginnings a century ago. Each took place in England in 1855 and both were efforts by women to improve the situation of their fellow women created by the Industrial Revolution and the Crimean War. One was Emma Robart's Prayer Union; the other was the General Female Training Institute founded by the Hon. Mrs. Arthur Kinnaird. The first was a concern for the spiritual welfare of women and girls of every kind; the second came into existence primarily to house nurses returning from the Crimean War. In a few years these two merged under the name of the Y.W.C.A.

Meanwhile, a parallel need for women working in the industrial centers of America was met by Mrs. Marshall O. Roberts' Ladies Christian Association in 1858 and by Boston's organization of a Y.W.C.A. in 1866, inspired by Mrs. Lucretia Boyd. The pattern of the Y.M.C.A. was followed in organizational enterprises.

There are today Y.W.C.A.'s in sixty-six countries. Three million members are counted in the United States alone.

The fields of interest are varied: teen-agers, families, education, Christian guidance, interracial relationships, working standards, foreign contacts, and so on. Although the Y.W.C.A. is of Protestant origin, it has a membership including young women of all races and creeds.

Mrs. Caroline D. Roberts

A founder of the Y.W.C.A. in the United States (New York City Association).

The Industrial Revolution was a time of change for women. In London two groups of women met in 1855, one to pray for "Our Princesses . . . domestic servants and factory girls," the other to found a home for nurses returning from the Crimean War.

Throughout those early years of change in the status of women the Y.W.C.A. spread and grew, providing care, protection and religious influence. It pioneered with a program of housing, health, education and recreation. Young women, venturing fearfully into the world as wage earners, found security in Y.W.C.A. boarding houses. Suitable recreation and social gatherings were planned for them and noon meetings held in their places of work, such as the munitions factory — probably turning out Civil War bullets — above. They were taught skills to help them find better jobs, given motherly advice on personal problems, and spiritual guidance by devout Y.W.C.A. workers of the day.

Y.W.C.A. Art Class of the Eighties

Reflecting the scope of early Boston and New York programs.

1880. This was why the Y.W.C.A. was needed in the big cities. Mothers of small-town daughters heading for the bright lights and new careers for women, were happy to know that their daughters could be safely housed in a Y.W.C.A. residence.

Always a pioneer, the Y.W.C.A. was among the first to teach business girls to deal with the "exacting" typewriter.

Y.W.C.A. parlors were always popular with young women. Here they had a chance of meeting their friends "to gather for a sing" around the piano or just relax with a good book, quite often the Holy Bible.

Today, Y.W.C.A. lounges in residences throughout the country are still popular with girls and young women. Traditionally, in every Y.W.C.A. a lounge is to be found with a piano, and at every Y.W.C.A. residence desk, the Holy Bible.

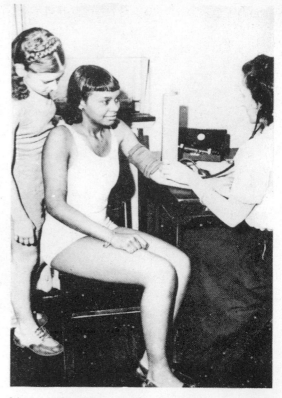

Health examinations are a regular part of Y.W.C.A. procedures aimed at the goal of physical and mental well-being.

Reaching High

The tall candle which this young Y-Teen is lighting symbolizes the worshipful spirit in which teen-age girls throughout the country enter the Y.W.C.A. There are games and parties for Y-Teens, coed groups and sports and arts and crafts, but when they elect officers these young people install them with candlelight services of reverence and dedication to an ideal.

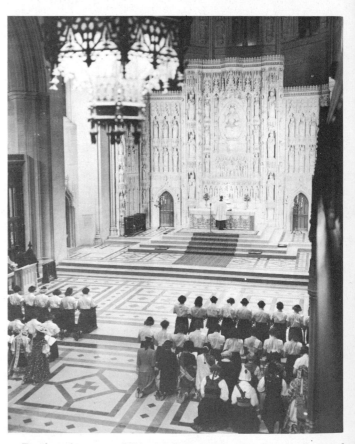

During the annual World Fellowship Week, members of Y.W.C.A.'s from sixty-six countries come together to rededicate themselves to the abiding Christian purpose of this largest women's organization in the world.

Round the World

Four of the fifteen young women participating in the Y.W.C.A.'s 1954 program in international relations at the grass-roots level take a global look to show the wide-spread emphasis of the work of the Young Women's Christian Association of the U.S.A. The work-study project, made possible through a designated grant, took the young women to local Y.W.'s throughout the United States. In the scene above, from the left, are Eleni Kalfoglou, of Greece; Ling Siok Ting, of Ipoh, Malaya; Margaret Ohn Bwint, of Burma, and Angelita M. Pulgado, of the Philippines.

The Twain Meet

Kipling to the contrary, East and West meet on the steps of the National Cathedral in Washington, D.C., through the auspices of the Y.W.C.A. A Y-Teen from America presents contribution raised by Y.W.C.A. of this country to a Y-Teen from Burma to aid in the Association's work there. Occasion is the annual worship service at the cathedral which launches World Fellowship Week each November.

Vesper Time

Y-Teens lead evening devotionals at a Y.W.C.A. summer camp. In its threefold program for youth, a healthy body, mind and spirit, the Y.W.C.A. emphasizes the importance of worship in the life of each individual.

The Christian Reformed Church

The historic roots of the Christian Reformed Church are to be traced to the Dutch immigrants from the Reformed Church of the Netherlands. In that country, a group of congregations seceded from the State Church in 1834 in reaction to ecclesiastical reorganization and doctrinal latitudinarianism. These churches of the secession and the churches founded a half-century later under the impetus provided by Abraham Kuyper provided the founders and a large measure of the continued growth of the Christian Reformed Church in America.

Discouraging conditions in the mother country led to large-scale emigration to the United States, beginning in late 1846. Under the leadership of Dr. Albertus C. Van Raalte, a colony was founded in Western Michigan, where the city of Holland was founded. These settlers soon organized ecclesiastically, and in 1850 were taken into the Reformed Church in America. This union of 1850 was unsatisfying to some from the first, on the scores of alleged doctrinal laxity and un-Reformed practices in the older American denomination. By 1857 this dissatisfaction had grown to such proportions that four congregations seceded and formed the new denomination now known as the Christian Reformed Church, in which allegiance is expressed to the Belgic Confession (1561), the Heidelberg Catechism (1563), and the Canons of Dordt (1618).

The Christian Reformed Church is organized according to the Reformed or Presbyterian system. The three recognized offices are ministers, elders and deacons. Each congregation possesses a large measure of autonomy.

The largest concentration of Christian Reformed churches and members is to be found in western Michigan, as has been the case ever since the founding of the denomination.

The First Christian Reformed Church Building at Graafschaap, Michigan

This old log structure shows the type of building used by the Dutch settlers in western Michigan a century ago. The building pictured was the only one belonging to members of the Christian Reformed Church when they formed their denomination in 1857 and it was replaced a few years later by a large wooden church structure which still stands. The denomination celebrated its centennial in 1957; several of its early meeting places were in log structures like the one pictured.

An Early Synod of the Christian Reformed Church

This photo was taken nearly a century ago in front of what was then the Spring Street Church in Grand Rapids, Michigan, one of the first congregations of the Christian Reformed denomination which in 1957 celebrated its centennial.

Church at Englewood, New Jersey

This building shows the influence of the early Dutch colonial architecture. It is the oldest church building of a Christian Reformed Church, and the congregation was one of those of the Classis Hackensack (of German origin) which joined with the Christian Reformed Church late in the nineteenth century.

A View of the Historic Building of the Ninth Street Christian Reformed Church, Holland, Michigan

It is commonly known as the Van Raalte Church, in honor of the leader of the Dutch settlement in western Michigan. The front part of the building, with its pillars, is part of the original structure built more than a century ago.

Calvin College and Seminary

Photo shows main building of Calvin College on its present campus in Grand Rapids, Michigan. Several other buildings, a library, dormitories, Calvin Seminary building, a science building and a Commons building, surround this. Founded in 1876, Calvin College and Seminary today has an enrollment of more than sixteen hundred students and is growing rapidly.

Eastern Christian High School, Paterson, New Jersey

One of the several schools for secondary instruction, or Christian high schools, to be found in many sections of the United States and Canada. The one pictured is a new building in Paterson, New Jersey, and similar ones are found in Michigan, Illinois, Iowa, Minnesota, California and several other states.

A Typical Christian Grammar School in the Midwest

It is one of more than 200 such schools supported in the United States and Canada by people of the Christian Reformed Church. The schools have their own organization called the National Union of Christian Schools.

The United Presbyterian Church of North America

This Church proudly proclaims its direct descent from the heroic Covenantors of Scotland. The Scottish Covenants are dated approximately from the middle of the sixteenth to the middle of the seventeenth centuries.

The first period is that of the Covenant of 1557, in the days when attempts were made to crush the Reformation in Scotland. George Wishart, preacher, was burned at the stake in 1546. A year later John Knox was condemned to the French galley service. Two years prior to his return to Scotland, a band of Protestant leaders entered into a covenant to remain loyal to the Word of God.

The second period is that of the Covenant of 1580 — the "King's Confession," signed by King James and persons of all ranks, for the principles of liberty, justice and defense of the Evangel of Christ.

The third period is that of the National Covenant of 1638. In the old Greyfriars Churchyard a vast crowd of persons of all classes, incensed at the attempt to force an episcopacy on the Presbyterians of Scotland, particularly a new Service Book, pledged their loyalty to "true religion." The Scottish people were granted civil and religious freedom after a victorious battle with the English.

The fourth period is that of the Solemn League and Covenant of 1643, subscribed by English and Scots during the feud between the King and the English Parliament. After the Civil War and the dethronement of the King (Charles I), under Cromwell Presbyterianism flourished in Scotland.

From the reign of Charles II (1660-1685) to that of James II (1685-1688) is the period of heroism of the Scottish Covenantors. In the days of the persecution during these reigns the United Presbyterian Church had its beginnings. The Martyrs' Monument in Greyfriars Churchyard records: "From May, 1661, to February, 1688, were one way or another murdered and destroyed for the same cause about eighteen thousand, of whom were executed in Edinburgh about one hundred of noblemen, gentlemen, ministers and others — noble martyrs for Jesus Christ."

Two years after the Revolution of 1688 Presbyterianism was re-established in Scotland. Many entered the Established Church there. Others, however, formed separate religious societies as dissenters. Among the latter was formed a presbytery in 1743.

Many of the ancestors of the United Presbyterian Church came from Ireland, though most are of Scottish origin. About 1720 began the emigration to America of these Scottish and Irish Reformed Presbyterians. In 1743 at Octorara, Pennsylvania, they renewed their covenant vows. The Rev. John Cuthbertson of the Reformed Presbytery of Scotland came to America in 1751, an event which led, in 1774, to the formation of the First Reformed Presbytery of America (near Harrisburg, Pennsylvania).

Meanwhile, other dissenters voiced protest against the Established Church of Scotland, notably the Rev. Ebenezer Erskine. This group formed the "Associate Presbytery" in 1733. Two years later the Associate Church came to America and formed an organization in Pennsylvania.

The union of these groups came about in 1782. Three groups emerged after this date: the Union Church, i.e., the Associate Reformed Presbyterian Church; the non-Union Associate organization, i.e., the Associate Presbytery; and the Covenanter Church (still in existence). In 1858 the United Presbyterian Church was formed by a merger of the first two of these bodies.

This church body joins other Presbyterians in acknowledging the Westminster Standards of Faith, including the catechisms. Their own early "Articles of Testimony" included their distinctive convictions against secret societies, for closed communion and the use of the Psalms in worship. A revised testimony was affirmed in 1925. Today there is a plan for union with the Presbyterians in America of the established tradition.

It is a militant church against moral and social evils and well known for its missionary zeal.

The Old Grass Market, Edinburgh

Many suffered martyrdom here. As James Renwick was murdered, his last words were: "I shall soon be above these clouds. Then shall I enjoy Thee and glorify Thee, O my Father, without interruption forever. I die in the faith that Thou wilt not leave Scotland, but that Thou wilt make the blood of Thy witnesses the seed of Thy Church."

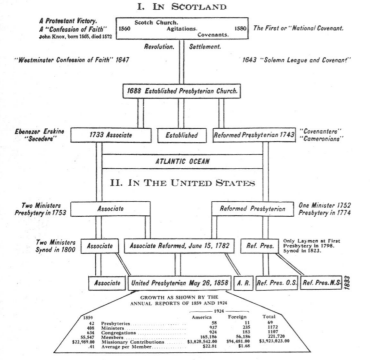

Genealogy of the United Presbyterian Church
(Prepared by the Rev. J. W. Ashwood in 1924)

The Martyrs' Monument, Greyfriars Churchyard, Edinburgh

298

Cairney Bridge Memorial, Where in 1733 the Seceders Met and Organized the "Associate Presbytery"

The Rev. Joseph T. Pressly, First Moderator of the United Presbyterian General Assembly

Old Associate Seminary, Service, Pennsylvania

Established in 1794. This picture was taken when the building was a hundred years old.

Colleges of this Church: Westminster (1852), Monmouth (1856), Muskingum (1837, 1888), Tarkio (1883), Sterling (1887). Its seminaries: Xenia (1794), Pittsburgh (1825).

The Free Methodist Church of North America

This Church had its origin at Pekin, New York in 1860 as a result of the efforts of several ministers and laymen of the Genesee Conference of the Methodist Episcopal Church to restore and maintain what they held were original and essential principles of Methodism. Among these principles were: doctrinal fidelity to the Wesleyan position on Christian perfection; simplicity and piety of life; and simplicity and freedom of Spirit in worship.

The naming of this branch of the Methodist family was influenced by its maintaining, on the basis of principle, free seats in a day when churches generally, especially in towns and cities, sold or rented pews.

The church in its beginnings, while holding that sound doctrine is essential to right living, nevertheless recognized that creedal affirmations are of little worth unless they are demonstrated in daily living. Accordingly, to this day the denomination insists upon a witness of life as well as a confession of faith on the part of its members.

World Headquarters: Winona Lake, Indiana.

Bishop B. T. Roberts

By choice of his fellows, leadership of the church came to this gifted graduate of Wesleyan University who had advanced views on church government, including lay participation, ordination of women and free pews. In all three he anticipated later developments in major Methodism. In doctrine he was conservative, in method evangelistic.

Free Methodist Church

The site of the orchard where the decision was made to organize the Free Methodist Church. Picture of youth on a pilgrimage to this site (near Pekin camp ground).

The movement was centered first in western New York, later in Illinois.

Historic Albion Church

Built in the late fifties as a non-pewed or "Free" Methodist church (independent), this church early became a part of the new denomination. It is in service today, the original pulpit furniture still in place.

Educational Beginnings

In 1866 Bishop Roberts established what is now Roberts Wesleyan College at North Chili, New York. Classes began in a former tavern (here pictured) while the first school building was being erected. Free Methodism now has three senior colleges, five junior colleges, a Bible school, and affiliation with Asbury Theological Seminary, Wilmore, Kentucky.

Free Methodism's World Headquarters

Winona Lake, Indiana, is the administrative center of the church's world-wide activities. Pictured here are the denominational office building and the headquarters church.

The Augustana Lutheran Church

Lars Paul Esbjörn

Founder of the Swedish Lutheran Church in America. Liberal in spirit, Swedish born (1808), Pietist, Lars Esbjörn emigrated, along with others, to this country in 1849 to minister to his people who had come earlier. He settled in Andover, Illinois and joined the Norwegians in forming a conference, "The Lutheran Synod of Northern Illinois." He was a trustee of Illinois State University and a Scandinavian professor at that institution. He served as a teacher at Augustana Seminary in Chicago and returned later to Sweden to re-enter the state church.

Eric Norelius

The choice of the name "Augustana" for the newly founded Swedish Lutheran church body in 1860 at Jefferson Prairie, Clinton, Wisconsin was suggested by Eric Norelius, an early religious leader among Swedish immigrants. He served as president of the Augustana Synod for nineteen years.

Tuve Nilsson Hasselquist

An early leader among the Swedish Lutherans of America, Hasselquist (b. 1816) came to this country (in 1852) an ordained Lutheran minister, beginning his work as pastor in Galesburg, Illinois. He was the first president of the Augustana Synod (1860-1870) and president of and professor in Augustana College (1863-1891). Although theologically conservative, he was of a free spirit with strong leanings toward Pietism. As editor of the Swedish periodical, *Augustana,* he exerted great influence within his denomination.

The Modest First House of Hasselquist in Galesburg, Illinois
(From the Mementos of the Rev. C. E. Cesander to whom this picture was given by Hasselquist.)

Erland Carlsson — Immanuel Lutheran Church, Chicago

A commanding figure in the early days of the Augustana Lutheran Synod, serving as its president (1881-1888). He came to America in 1853, settling in Chicago, serving for twenty-two years as minister of the Immanuel Lutheran Church. His work was notable in social service, guiding Swedish immigrants to opportunities for work and security, counseling them against fraudulent schemes and religious fanatics. In 1854 the terrible cholera year occurred with its high mortality rate. Tireless were his efforts to alleviate the sufferers. In 1857 a severe financial depression hit the country, and a great exodus to the country on the part of city people seeking sustenance impoverished the church. Up to 1854 men worked for fifty cents a day and women took in washing for ten to twenty-five cents a day. The pastor's support did not come on a salary basis until 1857, when $350 per annum was voted.

In this church's basement was initiated the beginning of the Swedish press in America.

A daughter church — Salem — was organized on Chicago's South Side in 1868, and another — the Gethsemane — in 1870. Even so, over a thousand communicant members continued in the mother church. Immanuel Church needed a larger building and in 1869 a stately structure was erected at Sedgwick and Hobbie streets on Chicago's North Side. It was the synod's most imposing edifice. Then in the Chicago Fire the church was reduced to ashes. In the midst of the ensuing tragedy, with the church in undeclared bankruptcy, Erland Carlsson rallied his people, first to clear away the debris and salvage whatever remained, and then to undertake with unbelievable energy the work of gathering funds for a new building. He visited Sweden in 1873 for solicitation of funds. In 1875 the new church was dedicated, to which a new minister, the Rev. C. A. Evald, was called to carry on spiritual and executive leadership.

Thousands upon thousands of Swedish immigrants who passed through Chicago have received through the Rev. Carlsson and Immanuel Church the counsel, assistance and spiritual care so desperately needed.

Born in 1822 in Sweden, Immanuel's dynamic pastor died in 1893 — a truly remarkable pioneer minister in American religious history.

Birthplace of the Augustana Synod

A rural church, Jefferson Prairie, Clinton, Wisconsin, 1860. Thirteen Norwegian and forty-nine Swedish congregations were represented at its initial meeting.

The College at Springfield, Illinois

Called "Illinois State University," it opened in 1852 and was sponsored by English, German, Swedish and Norwegian Lutherans.

A.

B.

C.

D.

Immanuel Lutheran Church, Chicago

A. The old church on Superior Street.
B. Interior, before the Chicago Fire.
C. Exterior of the church at Sedgwick and Hobbie streets, before the Chicago Fire.
D. The church in ruins.

Immanuel Lutheran Church, Chicago

The new church at Sedgwick and Hobbie streets, as it appeared in 1928 in connection with the 75th Anniversary Celebration.

The Present Immanuel Church, Located at Elmdale and Greenview Avenues. A New Centennial Church

Augustana College and Theological Seminary
(Illustration from an earlier period.)

Professor Esbjörn, professor at Illinois University in Springfield, hoped to found a Lutheran college in Chicago. To that purpose he and his Swedish students moved to Chicago, welcomed by the Immanuel Church and its minister, the Rev. Erland Carlsson. For three years (1860-1863) his hopes seemed to be in the process of realization when, against his wishes, the small school was moved to Paxton, Illinois, attracted by a proposition made by the Illinois Central Railroad. For twelve years the college was located in Paxton. The colony there did not materialize and a new location was sought. The first buildings were erected in Rock Island, Illinois, in 1875. "Old Main" (on the right), erected in 1889, is a landmark along the Mississippi.

The Augustana Church has mothered this institution as a synodical unit until recent times when the college became separated from the school of theology. Other colleges of the church, some of which have had only a brief life, were mothered by sectional conferences within the Church, e.g., Gustavus Adolphus in St. Peter, Minnesota, Minnesota College in the Twin Cities, Wahoo in Nebraska, Lund Academy in Minnesota, Hope College in Fergus Falls, Minnesota, North Star in Warren, Minnesota, Round Rock in Texas, Upsala College in East Orange, New Jersey and Bethany College, Lindsborg, Kansas.

Conrad Emil Lindberg

One of the outstanding theologians of his day in the Swedish Lutheran Augustana Synod. His *Dogmatics* set the standard of conservative theological thinking for Lutheran ministers of the church for some thirty years. His theology was highly systematic and set squarely in the history of dogma. Professor of Augustana Theological Seminary. (His dates: 1852-1930.)

Gustav A. Andreen

President of Augustana College and Theological Seminary from 1901 to 1934. He was among the few of the Augustana Lutheran ministers of his day to have an earned Doctor's degree (Yale) and directed the college to competitive high standards among American educational institutions.

Olof Wilhelm Ferm

Typical of many of the Lutheran clergy who worked quietly and anonymously in organizing and serving parishes before and during the turn of the century, the Rev. O. W. Ferm (1853-1911) also served the Augustana Lutheran Synod nationally by pioneer leadership in the early period of the organization of its Ministers' Pension and Aid Fund. (Today this Fund is one of the strongest of such undertakings among Protestant bodies.)

[The Rev. O. W. Ferm is the father of the author of this book — EDITOR'S NOTE.]

The Famed Oratorio Society (Organized in 1882) of Lindsborg, Kansas, at Bethany College

Known nationally for its rendition of *The Messiah*. From this cultural center on the plains have also gone forth the art works of Birger Sandzen, including paintings and etchings of the Rockies and the Southwest.

Jenny Lind

The celebrated Swedish Nightingale, touring America, gave generously to the missionary and education funds of the Swedish immigrants.

Emmy Christina Evald

Daughter of the pioneer Swedish Lutheran minister, the Rev. Erland Carlsson of Chicago, wife of his successor at Immanuel Lutheran Church, the Rev. Carl A. Evald, Emmy Evald, born in 1857, was the leading figure (and a founder) of the Augustana Synod's Women's Home and Foreign Missionary Society. This was the first Swedish-American women's society, dedicated to the development of the intellectual and moral stature of women. She presided at the Lutheran Women's Auxiliary at the World Congress in Chicago.

The Salvation Army

William Booth (1829-1912), a minister of the Methodist New Connection in England, founded this organization, which today has grown into a world-wide operation touching eighty-five countries and colonies. Originally no separate organization was planned; rather it was to be supplementary to the work of the churches.

The East London Mission was a first venture. When Booth's converts were refused membership in the established churches, he held services for them as a group outside the church. Beginning in 1865, the movement was named the Salvation Army by him thirteen years later. It was organized along semimilitary lines, with uniforms, ranks, strict training and discipline, as an army that was fighting for peace and love. General Booth believed that a starving man must be fed and from this conviction grew a vast program of social welfare which spread all over the world. The Army was established in the U.S.A. in 1880. It has been described as "Christianity in action."

Among its many famous organized activities may be named: Harbor Light Corps — Skid Row; Home League and League of Mercy; Golden Agers Club; Anti-Suicide League; Christmas Cheer; Family Welfare; Day Nursery Care; Emergency Housing for Women and Children; Youth Activities; Summer Camps; Booth Memorial Homes and Hospitals; Missing Friends Bureau; Prison and Police Court Work; Emergency Disaster Service; Service to Armed Forces; Hotels for Rehabilitated Men; Officers Training School; and others.

Lieutenant Eliza Shirley, a girl of sixteen, active in the Salvation Army in England, conducted an open-air meeting with her parents in Philadelphia on a Sunday afternoon, October 5, 1879 — the first Salvation Army meeting in the United States. She wrote to General Booth for officer reinforcements. In 1880 the first official party, consisting of seven officers commanded by Commissioner George Scott Railton, landed in New York.

Many times these pioneers were banned from street meetings and subjected to ridicule, abuse and even jailed.

General William Booth, Founder

The Salvation Army Creed

What the Salvationist BELIEVES

THE following are the principal doctrines held and taught by The Salvation Army:

WE BELIEVE that the Scriptures of the Old and New Testaments were given by inspiration of God and that they only constitute the Divine rule of Christian faith and practice.

WE BELIEVE there is only one God who is infinitely perfect, the Creator, Preserver and Governor of all things, and who is the only proper object of religious worship.

WE BELIEVE that there are three persons in the Godhead, the Father, the Son and the Holy Ghost, undivided in essence and co-equal in power and glory.

WE BELIEVE that in the Person of Jesus Christ the Divine and human natures are united so that He is truly and properly God and truly and properly Man.

WE BELIEVE that our first parents were created in a state of innocency but by their disobedience they lost their purity and happiness and that in consequence of their fall all men have become sinners totally depraved and as such are justly exposed to the wrath of God.

WE BELIEVE that the Lord Jesus Christ has by His suffering and death made an atonement for the whole world so that whosoever will may be saved.

WE BELIEVE that repentance toward God, faith in our Lord Jesus Christ and regeneration by the Holy Spirit are necessary to salvation.

WE BELIEVE that we are justified by grace through faith in our Lord Jesus Christ and that he that believeth hath the witness in himself.

WE BELIEVE that continuance in a state of salvation depends upon continued obedient faith in Christ.

WE BELIEVE that it is the privilege of all believers to be "wholly sanctified" and that their "whole spirit and soul and body" may "be preserved blameless unto the coming of our Lord Jesus Christ" (I Thessalonians 5:23).

WE BELIEVE in the immortality of the soul, in the resurrection of the body, in the general judgment at the end of the world, in the eternal happiness of the righteous and in the endless punishment of the wicked.

Captain James Kemp, "Ash-Barrel Jimmy" — First
Convert of the Railton Party

Typical Early Poster Inviting the Public to Attend
a Salvation Army Function

Lining up for the Easter Parade, Salvation Army Style,
New York, 1892

Preaching the Gospel

A Salvation Army Lassie of 1898 Sells The War Cry
in a City Slum

With the Royal Service Men — Brussels Leave Hostel

The Salvation Army at Kaulewela, Honolulu

Street scenes like this are familiar to all Americans as today's Salvation Army members carry on the spirit of William Booth to "bring God to the people."

Familiar Scene on any American Street During the Pre-Yuletide Season

The Evangelical and Reformed Church

The Reformed Church in the United States, formerly the German Reformed Church, adopted this title in 1869. In 1934 and 1942 a merger with the Evangelical Synod of North America was effected, the name of the union becoming the Evangelical and Reformed Church. A leader of the union was the Rev. George W. Richards, for many years president of the Reformed Church Seminary in Lancaster, Pennsylvania.

The pioneers of the Evangelical Synod came to the United States in the nineteenth century, representing the Evangelical Union Church of Prussia (1817), set up by mandate of King Frederick William II. The center of the Reformed pioneers in the earlier period was Philadelphia, and the majority of the Reformed churches were located in Pennsylvania. The center of the Evangelical Synod was St. Louis, Missouri and the Mississippi Valley.

Zion Reformed Church, Allentown, Pennsylvania

The earliest settlers in and about Allentown, Pennsylvania were from the Palatinate and Switzerland. Here the Reformed faith became focused. Beginning with a log house in 1762, there followed a succession of church buildings, culminating in this old stone church completed in 1840. During the Revolution the famous Liberty Bell in Independence Hall was brought here and secreted under the floor of the church.

The Church of Christ, Scientist (Christian Science)

Christian Science is a religious system which rests upon the Bible as its ultimate authority and includes spiritual healing as an indispensable part of its teachings and practice.

The discoverer and founder of Christian Science, Mary Baker Eddy, was born in Bow, New Hampshire in 1821. Always a deeply religious person, she experienced a remarkable physical healing through spiritual illumination in 1866. This caused her to search the Bible intensively for the metaphysical laws governing healing. The results of her study and demonstration were set forth in the Christian Science textbook, *Science and Health with Key to the Scriptures,* first published in 1875.

In 1879 a small group of twenty-six people under the leadership of Mrs. Eddy voted to "organize a church designed to commemorate the word and works of our Master, which should reinstate primitive Christianity and its lost element of healing" (*Manual of the Mother Church*). In 1892 this church took its present form as "The Mother Church, The First Church of Christ, Scientist," in Boston, Massachusetts, with its branch churches and societies in various parts of the world. Today there are more than 3,200 such branches in forty-six countries, and together they constitute the Church of Christ, Scientist.

The former home of Mary Baker Eddy, the discoverer and founder of Christian Science at 8 (now 12) Broad Street, Lynn, Massachusetts, was the early headquarters of what has since become the world-wide Christian Science movement. Mrs. Eddy occupied it from 1875 to 1882, during which time she completed the manuscript of the first edition of the Christian Science textbook, published in 1875 with the title *Science and Health,* later to become known as *Science and Health with Key to the Scriptures.* In this house she also prepared the manuscripts of the second and third editions of the textbook and had them printed and distributed; practiced Christian Science healing; taught her classes in Christian Science; was ordained pastor and conducted the services of the early church she established before providing for the present form of government under the *Manual* of the Mother Church.

In this little attic room in Lynn, Massachusetts, Mary Baker Eddy completed the Christian Science textbook, *Science and Health with Key to the Scriptures,* in 1875. At that time Mrs. Eddy was compelled to rent out the rest of the house in order to secure an income, except for the front parlor on the first floor in which she taught some of her early classes in Christian Science. From these modest beginnings emerged the world-wide movement of Christian Science.

First Church of Christ, Scientist, Oconto, Wisconsin

The first Christian Science church edifice to be built. This edifice, which seats one hundred people, was erected in 1886. The first service was held on October 31, 1886. Seven years prior to its erection, Mary Baker Eddy had founded the Church of Christ, Scientist, in Boston, Massachusetts. Other Christian Science churches also had been established in different parts of the United States before this church was built.

Original Edifice of the Mother Church in Boston, Massachusetts

At about the time of its completion, December, 1894. It was dedicated on January 6, 1895, one week after its completion and opening service. Nearly six thousand persons attended the five dedicatory services held in the edifice, which seats one thousand. The inscription on the frontal tablet reads: "The First Church of Christ, Scientist. Erected Anno Domini, 1894. A Testimonial to our Beloved Teacher, the Reverend Mary Baker Eddy: Discoverer and Founder of Christian Science: Author of its text-book Science and Health with Key to the Scriptures: President of the Massachusetts Metaphysical College, and the First Pastor of this Denomination."

Mary Baker Eddy, Discoverer and Founder of Christian Science

Mrs. Eddy speaking from the balcony of "Pleasant View," her home at Concord, New Hampshire, to ten thousand Christian Scientists, in June, 1903. Mrs. Eddy spent seventeen years of extremely active "retirement" at Concord, establishing the various activities of the Christian Science movement. In 1908, at the age of eighty-six, Mrs. Eddy returned to the environs of Boston for the last three years of her life to establish *The Christian Science Monitor*.

The Extension of the Mother Church on Dedication Day, June 10, 1906

Thirty thousand Christian Scientists from all over the world took part in the six successive services held that day. Four years before, in her Message to the Mother Church for 1902, Mrs. Eddy referred to the need for a larger edifice and at the annual meeting of the church it was voted to raise any part of $2,000,000 necessary to provide an auditorium to seat four or five thousand persons. On June 2, 1906, eight days before dedication, the treasurer announced "that sufficient funds have been received for the completion of the church building, and the friends are requested to send no more money to this fund" (*The First Church of Christ, Scientist, and Miscellany* by Mary Baker Eddy).

Jehovah's Witnesses

During the 1870's Charles Taze Russell (1852-1916), dissatisfied with current "sectarian" explanations of Scripture, initiated a Bible class in Allegheny, Pennsylvania. The Second Coming and the millennial reign were topics of early interest in this group. In 1879 the publication of *The Watchtower* and an organization were begun. The World War (1914) was taken to mark the end of "Gentile Times" prophesied thirty-five years earlier. Today *The Watchtower* has a circulation of three million copies in forty-five languages.

Russell was the first president of the organization, now known as "The Watch Tower Bible and Tract Society." J. F. Rutherford (1869-1942) succeeded him in leadership. The slogan set up in 1922 was "Advertise, advertise, advertise the King and the Kingdom." *Awake!* is the magazine which first appeared in 1946. Headquarters are in Brooklyn, New York. Since 1942, N. H. Knorr has been the leader-president.

Jehovah is God's name. The true church has Christ as its head. There are 144,000 associates with Christ, resurrected to the heavens as kings and priests with Him. With the Church are "the great crowd" of all nations who participated in heralding the news of the Kingdom. The faithful will survive the end of the present order under Satan. Christ will reign a thousand years in an age of bliss under Him on this earth. All will then be united in one true worship. After the millennium Christ will "turn all mankind over to His Father." This, in part, is the "Biblical faith" of Jehovah's Witnesses.

Charles Taze Russell, President of the Watch Tower Bible and Tract Society from 1884 to 1916

Joseph Franklin Rutherford, President of the Watch Tower Bible and Tract Society from 1916 to 1942

Convention Held at Columbus, Ohio, in 1931

It was here at the Ohio State Fair Grounds on July 26 that the name "Jehovah's Witnesses" was adopted by unanimous resolution. About fifteen thousand were present.

Nathan Homer Knorr (b. 1905), President of the Watch Tower Bible and Tract Society Since 1942

Headquarters of the Watch Tower Bible and Tract Society in 1909 in Brooklyn, New York

Formerly the Henry Ward Beecher home, it was purchased when the Society moved from its original quarters in Allegheny, Pennsylvania.

"Bethel," International Headquarters of Jehovah's Witnesses, Brooklyn, New York

The Watch Tower Bible and Tract Society was organized in 1884 in Allegheny (now Pittsburgh), Pennsylvania. Headquarters were moved to the Henry Ward Beecher home, purchased in 1909. In 1929 a nine-story building was constructed to replace the original accommodations and in 1949 the present ten-story addition was made. Besides the administration offices of the Society, this building also provides living quarters for the entire family of 480 who carry on the work of the home and the Society's Brooklyn printing plant.

Printing facilities of the Watch Tower Bible and Tract Society are housed in these two modernly equipped buildings at 117 Adams Street, Brooklyn, New York. At first some printing was done in the basement of the headquarters building at 124 Columbia Heights. Later a small factory was leased on Myrtle Avenue. In 1922 a larger one was obtained at 18 Concord Street. This was soon outgrown and in 1926 property was purchased at 117 Adams Street where an eight-story building was constructed in 1927, a four-story addition made in 1937 and a nine-story annex built in 1949. In 1956 a second building of thirteen stories was erected, doubling the existing facilities. The Society also owns and operates printing plants in fifteen other countries.

The Watchtower, *Official Magazine of Jehovah's Witnesses*

First published in July, 1879; a total of six thousand copies was distributed. The first issue is here shown surrounded by a few of the forty-five languages in which it is currently published. Circulation has reached three million copies. Pictured here are the following languages: Norwegian, English, Original Copy, Cinyanja, Afrikaans, Twi, Tagalog, German and Japanese.

International Convention at New York City, July 26, 1953

Attendance in and around Yankee Stadium was 116,802. An overflow audience at a temporary trailer city set up in New Jersey was connected by direct wire to swell the total attendance to 165,829. Over ninety lands were represented.

New World Society Assembly of Jehovah's Witnesses, July 19-26, 1953, at Trailer City, Home for 45,000 Witnesses for Eight Days

Jehovah's Witnesses Practice Mass Immersion

Responding to a call for immersion given to the throngs at the Yankee Stadium mass meeting, 4,640 candidates were immersed in Riverside Cascade Pool at 134th Street near Broadway, New York City. Twelve special buses, each carrying sixty persons, operated a shuttle service from the stadium to the pool. Seventy men working in shifts did the immersing, July 19-26, 1953. The above picture is typical of such immersions.

Campus of the Watchtower Bible School of Gilead

Organized in 1943. More than two hundred missionaries are trained here each year and sent to foreign countries. Currently 1,245 are active in a hundred lands, while 573 are engaged in various forms of administrative work in the United States.

The Evangelical Covenant Church of America

The Evangelical Covenant Church of America is a continuation of a Lutheran lay movement that developed in Sweden a century ago and was perpetuated by Swedish immigrants in America.

Organized as a denomination in 1885, the Covenant is noncreedal but subscribes officially to this "article of faith," that the Bible is "the only and the sufficient rule for faith and conduct."

The American beginnings of the Covenant are found in the simple preaching of the gospel among Swedish settlers by laymen or colporteurs of but small formal training, particularly in the Midwest: Illinois, Minnesota, Iowa, Nebraska, Kansas. This preaching emphasized conversion and a pietistic "growing in faith." Membership in the churches that were established (in 1910 there were over 400, 303 of which were officially affiliated with the Covenant) required that the individual be conscious of his having been "born again unto a living hope."

Typical of the "Mission Friends," as the early Covenant people were called, were the "mission meetings," preaching and Bible discussion conferences, held regularly in various localities in the Midwest as well as in the East. Particularly popular were outdoor meetings in the summertime. A cross section of such an audience in 1905 or 1906 in what was then a Chicago suburb is shown here. Third from the right in front is the Rev. C. A. Bjork, president of the Covenant, 1885-1910; next to him, fourth from the right, is Prof. A. W. Fredrickson, president of North Park College, 1905-1909.

A Group of Early Covenant Preachers at a Ministers' Conference in the 1890's

At right in front is the Rev. C. A. Bjork, president of the Covenant; third from right is the Rev. Nils Frykman, composer of numerous Swedish hymns and gospel songs many of which are even now used, in translation, in Covenant churches throughout the country.

A school for the training of preachers was established by the Covenant in 1891 in Minneapolis with the Rev. David Nyvall as president. This group is the first class of ministerial candidates; the photo was taken in 1892 at the end of the first school year. Mr. Nyvall is seated in the center. The only surviving member in 1957 is the Rev. K. E. Peterson (third from the right, standing) now living in retirement in Minneapolis.

In 1889 Dr. P. P. Waldenström, leader of the "Mission Friends" in Sweden and later president of the Covenant church there, came to America and traveled widely among the Covenant churches. A committee met him in New York upon his arrival and this group picture was taken at that time. Dr. Waldenström is seated at the right, the Rev. C. A. Bjork at the left. Second from the left, standing, is Prof. David Nyvall; in the center the Rev. E. G. Hjerpe, who became Bjork's successor as president of the Covenant, serving from 1910 to 1927.

The school which the Covenant started in Minneapolis in 1891 was moved to Chicago in 1894, where it became North Park College. Its main department was still the theological seminary but general education courses were now added. This picture, taken in the spring of 1895, shows the student body grouped at the front entrance of what is now "Old Main." (Notice the full beards and generous mustaches of some students.) On the balcony at top right are the entire faculty: J. A. Lindblade, David Nyvall and Axel Mellander (right to left).

Dr. Paul Peter Waldenström

Dr. Waldenström (1838-1917) is regarded as the theologian and Bible interpreter of the revivalist, nonconformist, "Mission Friend" movement in Sweden. His interpretation of the Atonement (1872) was largely accepted by the Mission Friends. (The Atonement is not something objective, something once for all accomplished. In the New Testament it means *purification* and is a term wholly inapplicable to God as the object. It means taking away sin by forgiveness and is therefore not a work accomplished but a divine grace offered to sinners through the Savior and accomplished wherever man accepts it in faith and identifies himself with the Savior.) Dr. Waldenström visited America three times. (In 1889 he was awarded an honorary doctor's degree by Yale University.) His books were read and studied by the Covenant people in America and his influence upon their religious thinking was profound.

He was the honored guest of the Covenant when it celebrated its twenty-fifth anniversary in 1910, his third and last visit to this country.

The Rev. Carl August Bjork

The Rev. Carl August Bjork (1837-1916), born in Sweden, came to Swede Bend (Ridgeport), Iowa, in 1866, a cobbler by trade. In 1868 he helped to organize there the first "society" of Swedish Mission Friends, the "mother church" of the Covenant. (The "North Side Church" in Chicago was organized in December of the same year.) He served as the first president of the Covenant — from its organization in 1885 to 1910.

The Rev. Erik August Skogsbergh

The Rev. Erik August Skogsbergh (1850-1939) came from Sweden in 1876 to Chicago and became a pioneer in the Covenant work. An eloquent speaker and gifted singer in the years of his strength (the photo is from the time of his arrival in Chicago), he was regarded as the greatest preacher among the Swedes in America. He served as pastor of Covenant churches in Minneapolis and later in Seattle; in both places he was instrumental in erecting large "tabernacle" churches.

The Rev. Erik Gustaf Hjerpe

The Rev. Hjerpe (1853-1931), preacher and organizer, served churches in Galesburg, Illinois, New Britain, Connecticut, Jamestown, New York and Chicago. He was the second president of the Covenant, serving from 1910 to 1927.

The Rev. David Nyvall

Rev. Nyvall (1863-1946), son of a well-known Mission Friend lay preacher in Sweden, educated at Uppsala University, came to America in 1886. In 1891 he became the organizer of the Covenant school in Minneapolis which in 1894 was moved to Chicago to become North Park College. Eloquent speaker, profound thinker, energetic educator, prolific writer, he served the Covenant as president of North Park College, 1891-1905, 1912-1924, and continued as teacher there up to 1938.

The first publishing activity of the "Mission Friends" was a Swedish periodical called *Missions-Wännen* (established in 1874), the printing and distributing of tracts, and the publication of a Swedish hymnal. The offices shown here were located at what was then 144 Chicago Avenue, Chicago. The publishing of the periodical was later taken over by a private company, and the paper is still published in the Swedish language at the same place. Second from the right is the Rev. Otto Högfeldt, who was editor of the paper for over fifty years. The Covenant as a denomination established its own organ in 1894 *(Missionären);* in 1911 the Swedish forerunner of the present official denominational paper, *The Covenant Weekly,* was established.

The first denominational institution of the Covenant was the Home of Mercy, hospital and old people's home, in Chicago, established in 1886, the year after the Covenant was organized. It was housed in a former residential structure on Foster Avenue near the present California Avenue, and was the forerunner of the present Swedish Covenant Hospital and the Covenant Old People's Home.

Covenant Church in Swede Bend, Iowa

The earliest Covenant church buildings in rural areas were of the plain, unadorned "meeting house" type which the immigrants had known in Sweden — as unlike the temples of worship of traditional architecture as possible. This is the "church" in Swede Bend, Iowa, the cradle of the Covenant in America. Built in 1868 it is still used by the rural congregation.

Swedish Mission Tabernacle, Chicago

In the larger cities more imposing brick churches were built by Covenanters, often of the "tabernacle" or auditorium (music hall) type. The Swedish Mission Tabernacle in Chicago was built in 1877 at LaSalle and 30th Streets. Here the historic conference was held in 1885 when the Evangelical Covenant Church of America was officially organized. The building, still used as a church, is now occupied by a Negro Baptist congregation.

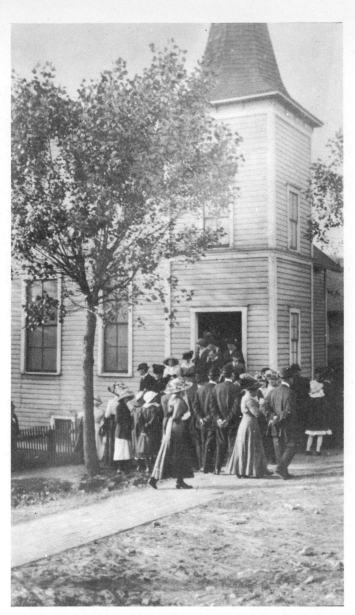

Covenant Church in Johnsonburg, Pennsylvania

Many small-town Covenant churches, usually frame structures of simple design but more "church-like" than the older meeting houses, were built in the 1880's and 1890's. The Covenant church in Johnsonburg, Pennsylvania, built in 1890, is typical of these immigrant churches.

Covenant Church in Fort Dodge, Iowa

The Covenant church in Fort Dodge, Iowa, built in the first decade of the 1900's, shows the more attractive style. Such neat Swedish houses of worship are numerous throughout the country, but particularly in the small towns of the Midwest.

The Volunteers of America

Founded in 1896 as a "completely American and democratically administered religious social welfare organization," by Ballington and Maud Booth, this body emerged from the Salvation Army as an independent body. It repudiated the system by which the entire Salvation Army "was ruled from London headquarters." It operates nineteen children's, emergency, maternity and old-age homes, twenty-seven summer camps and many other forms of social welfare.

Maud Booth

Maud Booth, the "Little Mother of the Prisons." As a leader of the Volunteers of America, she was prominent among those who were largely responsible for the adoption of the parole system, the elimination of the striped uniform, the lockstep, the ball and chain, the silent system and enforced idleness in prison. Mrs. Booth followed General Booth in top command. Her death occurred in 1948.

Ballington Booth

Ballington Booth, the first elected commander-in-chief of the Volunteers of America, with the title of "general." His father was General William Booth. General Charles Brandon Booth, his son, has been commander-in-chief since 1949.

The Lutheran Free Church

Besides adhering to the unaltered Augsburg Confession and Luther's Small Catechism (as well as the ancient symbols of the Christian Church), this Church omits reference to the other historic Lutheran confessional statements. The congregation is held to be "the right form of the kingdom of God on earth" and thus, as a group, only a free association of churches (not a synodical body). It has never adopted a church constitution. The chief seminary and college is Augsburg in Minneapolis. The church dates back to 1897 as "crystallized in the Lutheran Free Church" movement.

Its ancestral origin is Norwegian. Prominent in the history of this evangelistic church were George Sverdrup (1848-1907), the "father" of the Church, and Sven Oftedal (1844-1911), both of whom served as Augsburg College presidents. Its constituency is chiefly in the North Central states, the far Northwest coast and Western Canada.

The Hauge Lutheran Church near Mt. Horeb, Wisconsin (Restored)

Organized in 1852, this is the oldest congregation in the Lutheran Free Church.

George Sverdrup

Sven Oftedal

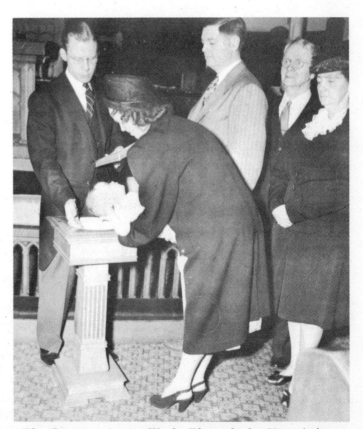

The Congregation at Work, Through the Use of the Sacrament of Baptism

329

The Church of the Nazarene

This church was organized at Pilot Point, Texas, in 1908, when three independent Holiness groups merged under this name. A previous merger took place in 1907, when Holiness groups from the East and West united to form what was then called the Pentecostal Church of the Nazarene. At Pilot Point a third Holiness group was added, known as the Holiness Church of Christ.

The present membership (1957) of the denomination is 280,000, with international headquarters in Kansas City, Missouri. In doctrine this body is in accord with the earlier emphases of Methodism, with stress on holiness or sanctification, baptism with the Holy Spirit and the pentecostal power of Christian experience.

The Rev. Phineas F. Bresee

Founder of the Church of the Nazarene in the West, (California).

A group of men from the Holiness groups in the East and West at the union which formed the Pentecostal Church of the Nazarene. The picture was taken in Chicago at the First General Assembly in 1907.

The first meeting of the Board of General Superintendents elected at the second union in 1908 at Pilot Point, Texas. Left to right: E. P. Ellyson, P. F. Bresee, H. F. Reynolds.

Fowler Memorial Administration Building, Eastern Nazarene College, Wollaston, Massachusetts

One of six liberal arts colleges in the United States fostered by the Church of the Nazarene.

International Headquarters Offices of the Church of the Nazarene, Kansas City, Missouri

Completed in 1956 at a cost of $400,000.

Nazarene Theological Seminary, Kansas City, Missouri

Graduate school for ministers and missionaries in the Church of the Nazarene. Completed in 1954 at a cost of $450,000.

The opening service of worship and communion at the Fourteenth General Assembly of the Church of the Nazarene, June 17, 1956, held in Kansas City, Missouri, at which time twelve thousand persons crowded the Municipal Auditorium.

Mr. R. R. Hodges, Assistant to the General Secretary

Pointing to the map showing the distribution of 4,435 churches of the Church of the Nazarene in the United States, Canada and elsewhere.

The Pentecostal Holiness Church

Two Holiness groups, known as the Pentecostal Holiness Church and the Fire Baptized Holiness Church, as organizations date back to 1898-1900. In 1911 a consolidation in the present denomination occurred at Falcon, North Carolina. The Articles of Faith stated their distinctive doctrines: "entire sanctification — an instantaneous, definite, second work of grace"; "the Pentecostal Baptism of the Holy Ghost and fire" appropriated by "faith on the part of the fully cleansed believer, and the initial evidence of the reception of this experience is speaking with other tongues as the Spirit gives utterance"; divine healing; the "imminent, personal, premillennial second coming."

Over 1,112 churches form this international body.

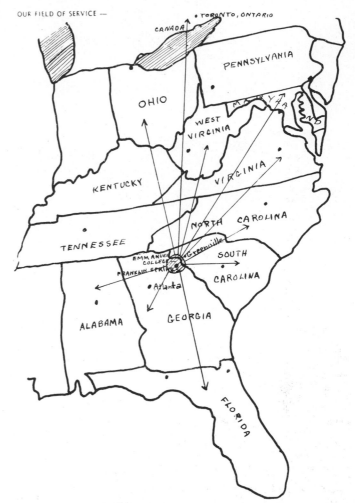

At Franklin Springs, Georgia, the Pentecostal Holiness Church owns and operates the fully accredited Emmanuel Academy and College. The official Church organ, *The Pentecostal Holiness Advocate,* is also located here. Other Bible schools are located in Oklahoma City, Greenville, South Carolina and Madera, California, and an orphanage in Falcon, North Carolina.

Graduation Day on the Lawn of Emmanuel College

The Church of the Lutheran Brethren

Bible School and Seminary at Fergus Falls, Minnesota

Organized in Milwaukee, Wisconsin in 1900, this church group looks back to the free church movements in nineteenth-century Europe for its spiritual origins. The Haugean revival in Norway and the revival under Oslo's teacher of theology, Gisle Johnson, were particularly their avowed progenitors. Georg Sverdrup of Augsburg Seminary in Minneapolis is acknowledged as an inspiring influence. The publication *Broderbaandet* (begun in 1899) by K. O. Lundeberg of Kenyon, Minnesota, resulted in the organization of several independent congregations. The Lutheran Brethren have held that a church should consist of people separated from the world. They have also favored Presbyterian polity.

At Fergus Falls, Minnesota, this church has fostered a Bible school and seminary (pictured here). Many missionary enterprises have been nourished at this and other of its schools.

deriolda jɛuta fi paulus tam tesalonikna

1

paulus hidi silvanus hidi timoteus tam tapna fi tesalonikna hɛi alauna bumna hidi bum-sumuna yesu kristu: θugɔta tigia hidi tɔita.

2 numaa gidɛb alauna dɔk-dɔk kigi kaf, hɛi li ma numaa faraa kigia hɛi sidauta fumaa. kɛi numaa faraa dɔk-dɔk kɛi lita figia hɛi fida hidi lɔpna hɛi ti-kamda hidi ŋalda hɛi cubta kud θeeta hɛi bum-sumuna fɛia yesu kristu fɔk ir alauna fɛia buia. 4 kɛi numaa wee, nigia sa filɛki gɔina, nigi bɔsimaana, sa alauna ti kigina. 5 kɛi labara ma firina fumaa ma tigia hɛi yɔbɔin hauadi, mei hɛi donota hɛi ŋusta pɛldɛta hidi wida gɔi gasi ŋolo, ki nigi wi kau ir na-na numaa pɔi jargia kɛi dɛkgia. 6 nigi modi sa θi kudmaana kud bum-sumuna kau, hɛi li ma nigi fum yɔbɔina kud semalda ŋolo hidi firita hɛi ŋusta pɛldɛta. 7 ta-ta pɔita figi li ŋaa kɛi sa fina kaf hɛi makedonia hidi akaia fi ðugia kɛi θi kudgia. 8 kɛi gɔi figi pa del yɔbɔina fi bum-sumuna kalɛi gɔi, hɛi makedonia

From the first edition of the New Testament in Masana (Africa), the translation of which was completed in 1945 by Mr. Revne. One of many of the missionary enterprises of the Church of the Lutheran Brethren.

Modern Revivalism

Dwight L. Moody

An evangelist of magnetic power was Dwight L. Moody, who started a tidal wave of religious revival in the late nineteenth century. He was not an ordained minister. Born in Northfield, Massachusetts, in 1837, he was a shoe clerk and salesman. With Ira D. Sankey, "the singer of salvation hymns," he conducted revivals in England (1873) and from coast to coast in America. He died in 1899. Nonsectarian and interdenominationalist, he carried on his preaching in homely, neighborly manner. His influence endures to this day.

*"Gospel Wagon" of the Early 1900's —
Moody Bible Institute*

"Moody Bible Institute was founded, under God, in 1886 by the great evangelist D. L. Moody, a man of great vision and faith. In 1888, he knelt on a lot near LaSalle Street and Chicago Avenue and asked the Lord to give it to him so that he could build a dormitory for men. God answered that prayer, and a year later a new structure was ready to serve as dormitory, office and classroom."

Auditorium, the Old Chicago Avenue Church

Interviewed by newspapermen in 1890, Mr. Moody was asked what studies he proposed to have taught in his four-year-old training school. He answered: "First, I shall aim for a sufficient knowledge of the English Bible; so far as may be, a practical mastery of it. Second, I would have workers trained in everything that will give them access practically to the souls of the people. And third, I would give great prominence to the study of music, both vocal and instrumental. I believe that music is one of the most powerful agents for good or for evil."

Graduating Class, 1955, in Torrey-Gray Auditorium

The Missionary Technician — Flight Section

The Moody Bible Institute's experienced instructors and the best of equipment assure the future missionary pilot of the best training.

Billy Sunday

Born in Ames, Iowa, 1862, he became America's most conspicuous evangelist in his time. He played baseball with Chicago, Philadelphia and Pittsburgh teams. He "got religion" on a Sunday after hearing a mission band sing near a Chicago saloon. He became a Y.M.C.A. secretary and coached baseball at Northwestern University. He turned to professional evangelism, employing street language and acrobatic gestures. He would stand on chairs while speaking, tear off his coat. One of his unconventional prayers ran thus: "How are things in heaven, God? They are mighty rotten down here." On occasion he would turn boxer on the public platform, sparring with an imaginary devil. In 1920 he was rated a millionaire. He made his home in Winona, Indiana. His wife was referred to as "Ma Sunday." He died in 1935.

Above is a 1922 photograph of Sunday. The second picture is Sunday and his trombonist, Homer Rodeheaver, in 1916, as viewed by a Boston *Herald* cartoon.

"I'll fight till hell freezes over" — Billy Sunday

"The Old-Time Religion"

"I am an old-fashioned preacher of the old-time religion, that has warmed this cold world's heart for two thousand years."

— BILLY SUNDAY

Gypsy Smith

An English boy to whom Ira Sankey (famous teammate of Dwight L. Moody) said, "The Lord make this boy a preacher." Gypsy Smith was a gypsy who had never slept under a roof until he was seventeen. He taught himself to read with the aid of a Bible given him by an elderly lady who purchased some clothespins from him. He felt the call to preach and served in a Christian mission under William Booth (before the founding of the Salvation Army).

He made some thirty-five visits to the United States as an evangelist. He carried with him till his death in 1947 two willow clothespins made by his father.

"I learned religion by living it," he once said. "The message of love and hope — that is all the world needs."

Smith is credited with having preached to more people and having brought about more conversions than any other figure of his time.

The Tabernacle at Scranton, Pennsylvania

This is typical of the auditoriums erected for Sunday's campaigns. The term "sawdust trail" comes from the practice of covering the floor with sawdust to deaden the sound of feet. A door was placed at the end of each aisle as an escape from possible fire.

340

A Billy Graham Crusade, Madison Square Garden, 1957

This contemporary evangelist has for ten years conducted crusades in the United States, Glasgow, London and over the air. The above crusade is a million-dollar enterprise.

A night audience of 18,500.

The Assemblies of God

The "one great Christian experience which has brought together all component parts of the Assemblies of God movement" is "the Baptism in the Holy Ghost accompanied by speaking in tongues as the Spirit gives utterance (Acts 2:4)." This pentecostal experience is the reason for the distinct existence of this body.

Organized in 1914 at Hot Springs, Arkansas, as the General Council of the Assemblies of God, the Church was born in a widespread revival movement with intense missionary zeal in the conviction of "the imminent return of the Lord Jesus." No one founder is claimed. Its beginnings are "Pentecostal outpourings" in widely separated places. In Topeka, Kansas, in 1901 occurred a revival which initiated groups in Kansas, Oklahoma and Texas.

The First General Council came in response to a call for a general meeting by the Rev. E. N. Bell and some others. Some three hundred ministers and delegates responded from groups all over the U. S. A. The form of government is Congregational. Headquarters are in Springfield, Missouri. Some eleven Bible colleges and institutes are associated with this denomination; some 400,000 persons are members.

Pictured above is a camp meeting scene in Houston, Texas, somewhere between 1906 and 1907. Many of the persons who attended these services also participated in the early revivals which led to the organization of the Assemblies of God.

The group of some three hundred ministers and their wives pictured above attended the organizational meeting of the Assemblies of God in Hot Springs, Arkansas, April 2-12, 1914. At this meeting a general organization for the church was agreed upon.

Members of the first executive board of the Assemblies of God selected at the organizational meeting in April, 1914, included: First row (left to right): T. K. Leonard, E. N. Bell, C. B. Fockler. Second row (left to right): J. W. Welsh, J. R. Flower, Secretary; D. C. Opperman, H. A. Goss, and M. M. Pinson.

The International Church
of the Foursquare Gospel

Aimee Semple McPherson is the founder of this pentecostal church. Born in 1890, she was a missionary in China and evangelist in foreign lands. In 1921 she had a vision of the establishment of the Foursquare organization. Angelus Temple at Los Angeles, a million-and-a-half-dollar structure seating more than five thousand, is the fruition of her dream. Sister McPherson organized the church in 1927 on an international basis (now with more than six hundred branch churches). A commissary operates to feed and clothe and find employment for the needy. Since 1923 the Prayer Tower has continued a twenty-four-hour schedule of prayer in two-hour shifts of women praying in the daytime and men at night. Besides her literary authorship, Sister McPherson composed songs (among them, "Calvary's Crimson Rose" and "Why Are They Whipping My Jesus?") and operas.

Some five thousand students have graduated from the L.I.F.E. (Lighthouse of International Foursquare Evangelism) Bible College. The word "Foursquare," a Biblical term, means the Gospel that faces east, north, west and south.

Four symbols: Cross (symbol of salvation through the Blood of Christ); Dove or Torch (the Holy Spirit); Cup (Divine Healing); Crown (Second Coming of Jesus Christ).

Rolf K. McPherson, son of the founder, succeeded to leadership after the death of his mother in 1944.

Angelus Temple, Los Angeles, California

344

Angelus Temple, Los Angeles, California

Fifth Annual Convention of the Pentecostal Fellowship of North America, 1952.

The American Lutheran Church

This is a united body of Lutherans formed in 1930 and consisting of the merger of the Buffalo, Iowa and Ohio synods. The occasion was the four-hundredth jubilee year of the Augsburg Confession.

The former Iowa Synod had been founded in 1854. The Rev. W. Loehe of Neuendettelsau, Germany, was the spiritual father of this group. The Fritschels (Sigmund and Gottfried), teachers of ministers, were among the pioneer leaders.

The former Buffalo Synod had been organized in 1845. The Rev. J. A. A. Grabau was the leader of this immigrant group of Prussians. Grabau had been strongly opposed to unionism.

The former Joint Synod of Ohio and Other States dates back to 1818. At the time of the merger in 1930 this synod was the fourth oldest Lutheran body in the U.S.A. The spiritual fathers in Germany were the Franckes (August and Gotthilf) and in America, the Henkels and others.

The first president of this federated body was the Rev. C. C. Hein (1869-1937). Two seminaries are under the sponsorship of the American Lutheran Church: Capital University Theological Seminary at Columbus, Ohio (1830), and Wartburg Theological Seminary at Dubuque, Iowa (1854), the latter absorbing St. Paul's Luther Seminary (1932). Liberal Arts colleges are Luther (Regina, Canada), Capital, Texas, and Wartburg (Waverly, Iowa).

Mees Hall, Capital University, after Chapel

The Rev. C. C. Hein, First President of the American Lutheran Church

The Independent Fundamental Churches of America

Organized in 1930 at Cicero, Illinois by representatives of various independent churches, with headquarters in Chicago. One of the founders is the Rev. William Mc-Carrell, whose Independent Cicero Bible Church may be taken as representative. A graduate of the Moody Bible Institute (now also an instructor), the Rev. McCarrell was ordained by the Congregational churches (1915) but separated from that group in 1918.

The church at which he has been pastor continuously since his graduation "never engages in reform movements," "eliminates worldly methods of finance," "stands a testimony to the reality of prayer, power of the Gospel ... blessedness of the evangelistic and missionary note, the wisdom of separation from the world" and affirms what it calls "Christian Fundamentals."

This church has a unique "Fishermen's Club" (an organization of men for "soul-winning" work with over 100,-000 personal visitations), a Cicero Gospel Truck, a Cicero Gospel Tent, a Cicero Summer Bible School and a "growing Foreign Missionary Family." Branch chapels have issued from this church.

The Rev. William McCarrell

Cicero Gospel Truck

From 1921 to 1929 over twenty thousand men have stepped forward to receive Gospels, promising to read them. The truck ministry extended throughout Chicago, parts of Illinois and other states.

Cicero Gospel Tent

Here "ringing testimonies and Gospel songs sounded forth." For years it stood on the corner of 23rd Place and 52nd Avenue.

Frontier Christianity and America's "Hillbilly" Christians

Culver

Shakers, the United Society of Believers

Pictured here is a Shaker meeting house, *ca.* 1850.

In derision (because their bodies quivered in the excitement of spiritual ecstasy), these people were called "The Shakers." The group dates back to mid-eighteenth-century England and Jane Wardley's exhortations to her Quaker friends. Ann Lee (1736-1784) was an early leader. In 1774 she and others came to America, settling at Watervliet, New York. Communistic societies were founded in New York, New England, Kentucky, Ohio and Indiana. Mother Ann, from 1837 to 1848, "manifested herself in a Second Coming." The congregations sang wordless songs and marched to the accompaniment by hand motions. They believed in communication with spirits.

An African Church Meeting, Cincinnati, Ohio, 1853

Baptism in Kansas

Picture Post, August 10, 1946

America's "Hillbilly" Christians

The South has its own religious character in the "hill-billies" who take their faith in an unsophisticated yet reverent way. Theirs is an uninhibited expression of religion as a personal possession.

Pictured here is "The Preacher" who talks of hellfire. He can drive mules and make applejack on weekdays but glows when from a pulpit he describes the torments of the damned.

The Congregation Sings of Glory

Hillbillies take their religion as they take their liquor — hard. Men and women sit apart.

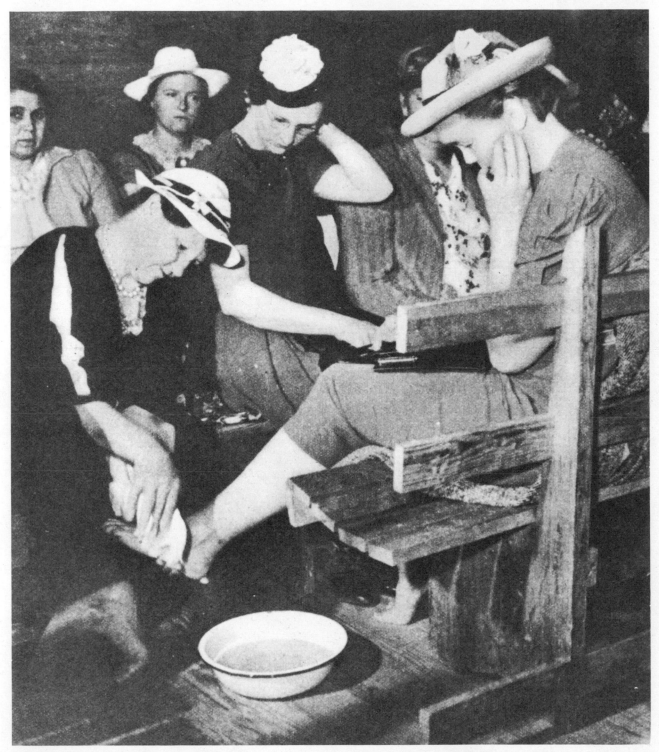

"The Foot Washin'" — *A Characteristic of Hillbilly Services*

It is a tradition among Baptists in the Southern Uplands. Only those who have been baptized "all over" may wash each other's feet.

Backwoods Converts Are Reborn at Camp Meetings

Revival meetings sometimes reach the highest pitch of emotional excitement as religious ecstasy takes hold of the converts.

Services begin early and often last all day, followed by a picnic dinner and a social get-together, at which neighbors who seldom see each other during the week renew friendships and exchange local news.

Modern hill folk sing up-to-date tunes from paper-back hymnals.

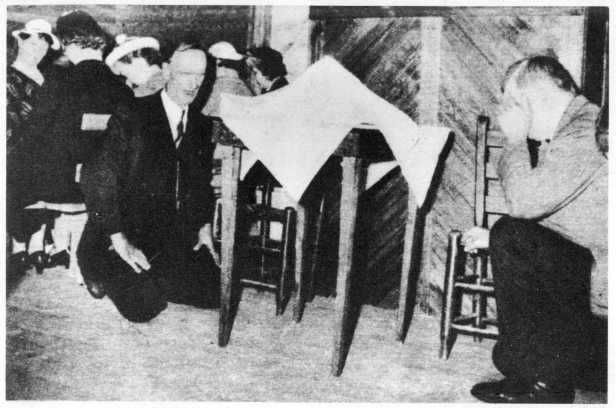

To the Hardshell, Praying Is an Affair of Struggle and Tears

It's the singing and preaching that usually count among the Hardshell Baptists. The "Big Pray" comes once a year, at Communion.

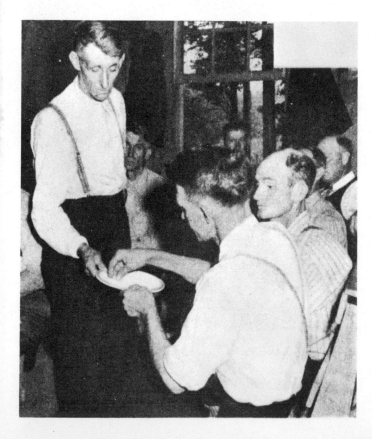

The Meeting Ends with a Love Feast

They came early. They have sung and been preached at all day. Worn out but still singing, they shake hands before going home.

Each Communicant Breaks Bread

It is a simple, shirt-sleeves-and-braces ritual. Each man talks of God in a familiar manner.

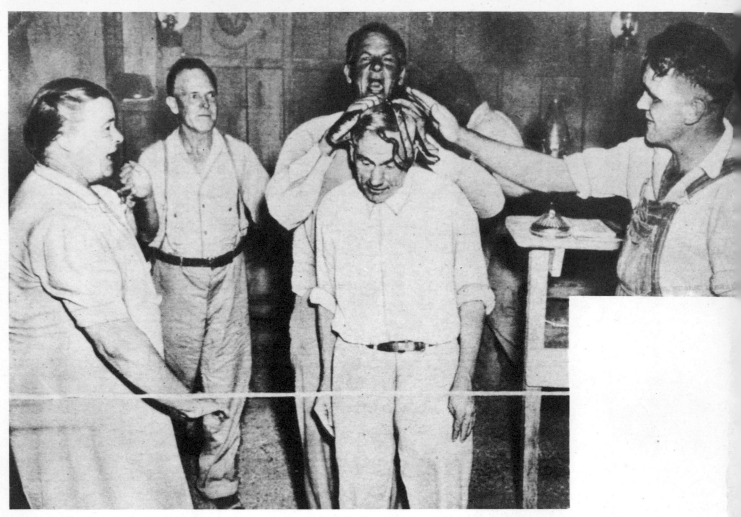

Snake Service

Demonstrating their faith, members of the Dolly Pond Church of God in the Grasshopper community northeast of Chattanooga, Tennessee, handle poisonous snakes during a revival meeting in their small house of worship.

The believers fondle the snakes, coiling them about their heads during the service, in a roped-off part of the church.

Snake-Handling Sect

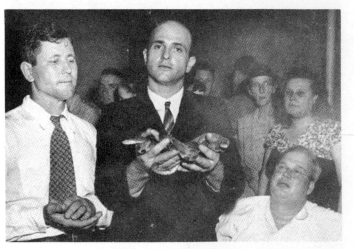

Tension Mounts

A revival meeting in the Southern U.S.A. Rhythmic beating, hand-clapping, dancing and music increase emotional excitement. Poisonous snakes are then taken out of their boxes. Photo by consent of the minister.

The Protestant Ecumenical Movement

The World Council of Churches was established at Amsterdam, Holland, in 1948. Many different types of Christian traditions are represented among the 165 Protestant, Anglican and Orthodox member church bodies from more than fifty countries.

The World Council of Churches is not a super-church, but it aims to bring the churches into living contact with each other and to promote the study and discussions of the issues of church unity. The Council desires to serve the churches, which are its constituent members, as an instrument whereby they may bear witness together to their common allegiance to Jesus Christ, and co-operate in matters requiring united action.

Formation of Universal Christian Conference for Life and Work, at Stockholm, Sweden, 1925

A forerunner of the World Council of Churches.

Participants in the Second World Conference on Faith and Order, Held at Edinburgh, in 1937

The Establishment of the World Council of Churches at Amsterdam, 1948

After a long interruption due to the war the Churches find the way back to each other. This new beginning is at the same time the end of long discussions: the World Council of Churches is established.

The Five Presidents of the World Council of Churches at the Time of the Constituting Assembly at Amsterdam, 1948

From left to right: Bishop Eivind Berggrav (Church of Norway), the Most Rev. Athenagoras (Greek-Orthodox Church), the Rev. Dr. Marc Boegner (Reformed Church of France), the Very Rev. G. K. A. Fisher, Archbishop of Canterbury (Anglican Church), and Bishop G. Bromley Oxnam (Methodist Church, U.S.A.).

The New Presidents of the World Council of Churches Elected at the Second Assembly at Evanston, 1954

They represent different types of Christian tradition and different parts of the world. They are (from left to right): Bishop Otto Dibelius, president of the Council of the Evangelical Church in Germany; Bishop Sante Uberto Barbieri, Methodist, Buenos Aires (Argentina); the Bishop of Chichester, the Right Rev. G. K. A. Bell, Anglican (United Kingdom); Juhanon Mar Thoma, Metropolitan of the Mar Thoma Syrian Church of Malabar, South India; the Very Rev. John Baillie, Presbyterian, Church of Scotland, Edinburgh; Archbishop Michael, New York, of the Greek Orthodox Archdiocese of North and South America, and the Right Rev. Henry Knox Sherrill, New York, presiding bishop of the Protestant Episcopal Church in the U.S.A.

Executive Staff Members of the World Council of Churches
in Front of the Council's Headquarters
at Geneva, Switzerland

From left to right: Dr. Leslie Cooke, Associate General Secretary, Director of the Division of Inter-Church Aid and Service to Refugees, British, Congregational Union of England and Wales. Dr. Willem A. Visser 't Hooft, General Secretary of the World Council of Churches, Dutch, Dutch Reformed Church. The Rev. Francis House, Associate General Secretary, Director of the Division of Ecumenical Action, British, Anglican Church. The Rev. Robert Bilheimer, Associate General Secretary, Director of the Division of Studies, American, Presbyterian.

The World Council of Churches in Action

Within a few yards of the Austro-Hungarian frontier guard post workers of the Refugee Service provide hot food to newly arrived Hungarian refugees.

*Bishop George K. A. Bell and Bishop Lajos Ordass at
the Meeting of the World Council of Churches
in Galyatetö, Hungary, August, 1956*

Picture Credits*

1. Picture Department, New York Public Library.
2. *L.* and *L.R.*—Picture Department, New York Public Library.
   U.R.—The Iona Community, Glasgow, Scotland.
3. *L.L.*—J. A. Wylie, *The History of Protestantism,* London: Cassell, Petter & Galpin.
4. *T.*—D. Bernhard Rogge, *Das Evangelium in der Verfolgung,* Stuttgart, Verlag von Friedrich Bohnenberger, 1924.
5. *U.L.*—J. A. Wylie, *op. cit.*
   L.L.—Picture Department, New York Public Library.
6. *T.*—Friedrich Oehninger, *Geschichte des Christentums in seinem Gang durch die Jahrhunderte,* Konstanz, Carl Hirsch.
   B.—Percy Dearmer, *Everyman's History of the English Church,* London, A. R. Mowbray & Co., Ltd., 1900.
7. *T.*—F. C. Happold, *Everyone's Book about the English Church,* London, Faber & Faber.
8. *T.*—Julius von Pflugk-Harttung, *Im Morgenrot der Reformation,* Stuttgart, Wilhelm Herget Verlag, 1924.
   B.—Adolf Keller and George Stewart, *Protestant Europe: Its Crisis and Outlook,* New York, George H. Doran Co., 1927.
9. *L.*—Karl Kaulfuss-Diesch, *Das Buch der Reformation,* Leipzig, Voigtländers, 1917.
10. *T.*—D. Bernhard Rogge, *op. cit.*
    B.—J. A. Wylie, *op. cit.*
11. *T.*—The Moravian Church in America.
    B.—Friedrich Oehninger, *op. cit.*
12. The Moravian Church in America.
13. *T.*—Friedrich Oehninger, *op. cit.*
    B.—The Moravian Church in America.
14. *L., U.R.,* and *L.R.*—Friedrich Oehninger, *op. cit.*
15. *T.*—The Moravian Church in America.
    C.L. and *L.L.*—Friedrich Oehninger, *op. cit.*
    L.R.—C. Werckshagen, *Der Protestantismus am Ende des XIX Jahrhunderts,* Berlin, Verlag Wartburg.
16. *U.L.*—N. V. Wallington, *Historic Churches of America,* New York, Duffield & Co., 1907.
    L.L., U.R. and *L.R.*—The Moravian Church in America.
17. The Moravian Church in America.
18. *U.L.* and *U.R.*—Julius von Pflugk-Harttung, *op. cit.*
    L.L. and *L.R.*—Eugen Diederichs, *Deutsches Leben der Vergangheit in Bildern,* Jena, Verlegt bie Eugen Diederichs, 1908.
19. *U.L., U.R.,* and *B.*—Eugen Diederichs, *op. cit.*
20. *T.*—Secured by the author on a European tour, 1956. *L.L.*—Eugen Diederichs, *op. cit.*
    L.R.—Julius von Pflugk-Harttung, *op. cit.*
21. Julius von Pflugk-Harttung, *op. cit.*

22. *U.L., L.L.,* and *U.R.*—Julius von Pflugk-Harttung, *op. cit.*
    L.R.—Paul Schreckenbach and Franz Neubert, *Martin Luther, Ein Bild Seines Lebens und Wirkens,* Leipzig, Verlagsbuchhandlung J. J. Weber, 1918.
23. *U.L.* and *L.R.*—Schreckenbach and Neubert, *op. cit.*
    C.L., L.L., and *U.R.*—Julius von Pflugk-Harttung, *op. cit.*
24. *T.*—Julius von Pflugk-Harttung, *op. cit.*
    B.—Schreckenbach and Neubert, *op. cit.*
25. *U.L.*—Schreckenbach and Neubert, *op. cit.*
    L.L. and *R.*—Julius von Pflugk-Harttung, *op. cit.*
26. *U.L.* and *U.R.*—Schreckenbach and Neubert, *op cit.*
    L.L. and *L.R.*—Julius von Pflugk-Harttung, *op. cit.*
27. *B.*—Julius von Pflugk-Harttung, *op. cit.*
28. Schreckenbach and Neubert, *op. cit.*
29. *U.L.* and *L.L.*—Julius von Pflugk-Harttung, *op. cit.*
    U.R. and *L.R.*—Schreckenbach and Neubert, *op. cit.*
30. *U.L.* and *B.*—Julius von Pflugk-Harttung, *op. cit.*
    U.R.—Schreckenbach and Neubert, *op. cit.*
31. *U.L.* and *U.R.*—Karl Kaulfuss-Diesch, *Das Buch der Reformation,* Leipzig, Voigländers Verlag, 1917.
    B.—Julius von Pflugk-Harttung, *op. cit.*
32. *L.*—Secured by the author on a European tour, 1956.
    R.—Julius von Pflugk-Harttung, *op. cit.*
33. Julius von Pflugk-Harttung, *op. cit.*
35-36. Schreckenbach and Neubert, *op. cit.*
37. Julius von Pflugk-Harttung, *op. cit.*
38. *L.* and *L.R.*—Julius von Pflugk-Harttung, *op. cit.*
    U.R.—Schreckenbach and Neubert, *op. cit.*
39. *L.*—Julius von Pflugk-Harttung, *op. cit.*
    R.—Schreckenbach and Neubert, *op. cit.*
40. *T.*—Julius von Pflugk-Harttung, *op. cit.*
    B.—Schreckenbach and Neubert, *op. cit.*
41. Schreckenbach and Neubert, *op. cit.*
42. Julius von Pflugk-Harttung, *op. cit.*
43. *T.* and *L.R.*—Julius von Pflugk-Harttung, *op cit.*
    L.L.—Schreckenbach and Neubert, *op. cit.*
44. *T.*—Schreckenbach and Neubert, *op. cit.*
    C. and *B.*—Secured by the author on a European tour, 1956.

*KEY

T.—Top	U.L.—Upper Left
C.—Center	C.L.—Center Left
B.—Bottom	L.L.—Lower Left
L.—Left	U.R.—Upper Right
R.—Right	C.R.—Center Right
	L.R.—Lower Right

Where no key is given, all pictures on the page are from the same source.

46. *U.L.*—Julius von Pflugk-Harttung, *op. cit.*
    L.L. and *R.*—Schreckenbach and Neubert, *op. cit.*

47. Gustav König, *Dr. Martin Luther, der Deutsche Reformator,* Berlin, Verlag von Reuther & Reichard.

48. *L.* and *U.R.*—Schreckenbach and Neubert, *op. cit.*
    L.R.—Julius von Pflugk-Harttung, *op. cit.*

49. *U.L., L.L.,* and *L.R.*—Schreckenbach and Neubert, *op. cit.*
    U.R.—Julius von Pflugk-Harttung, *op. cit.*

50. Julius von Pflugk-Harttung, *op. cit.*

51. *T.*—Schreckenbach and Neubert, *op. cit.*
    B.—C. Werckshagen, *op. cit.*

52. Schreckenbach and Neubert, *op. cit.*

53. Gustav König, *op. cit.*

54. Schreckenbach and Neubert, *op. cit.*

55. *T.*—J. A. Wylie, *op. cit.*
    B.—Karl Kaulfuss-Diesch, *op. cit.*

57. *U.L.* and *U.R.*—Julius von Pflugk-Harttung, *op. cit.*
    L.L. and *L.R.*—Schreckenbach and Neubert, *op. cit.*

58. Julius von Pflugk-Harttung, *op. cit.*

59. *U.L.*—Julius von Pflugk-Harttung, *op. cit.*
    L.L.—Friedrich Oehninger, *op. cit.*
    U.R. and *C.*—G. S. Facer, ed., *Erasmus and His Times,* London, G. Bell and Sons, 1951.

60-61. Schreckenbach and Neubert, *op. cit.*

62. *T.*—Schreckenbach and Neubert, *op. cit.*
    B.—Karl Kaulfuss-Diesch, *op. cit.*

63. Schreckenbach and Neubert, *op. cit.*

64. *T.*—Schreckenbach and Neubert, *op. cit.*
    B.—Friedrich Oehninger, *op. cit.*

65. *U.L.*—Julius von Pflugk-Harttung, *op. cit.*
    L.L. and *U.R.*—Schreckenbach and Neubert, *op. cit.*
    L.R.—Karl Kaulfuss-Diesch, *op. cit.*

66-70. Julius von Pflugk-Harttung, *op. cit.*

71. *L.*—Keller and Stewart, *op. cit.*
    R.—Friedrich Oehninger, *op. cit.*

72. *T.*—Friedrich Oehninger, *op. cit.*
    B.—C. Werckshagen, *op. cit.*

73. Friedrich Oehninger, *op. cit.*

74. *U.L.* and *B.*—C. Werckshagen, *op. cit.*
    U.R. and *C.R.*—Presbyterian Historical Society, Philadelphia, Pa.

75. J. A. Wylie, *op. cit.*

76. Secured by the author on a European tour, 1956.

77. *T.* and *C.L.*—C. Werckshagen, *op. cit.*
    L.R.—Friedrich Oehninger, *op. cit.*

78. Keller and Stewart, *op. cit.*

79-87. *The Mennonite Encyclopedia,* Scottdale, Pa., The Mennonite Publishing House.

88-89. Secured by the author on a European tour, 1956.

90. *L.* and *U.R.*—Secured by the author on a European tour, 1956.
    L.R.—J. A. Wylie, *op. cit.*

91-97. Secured by the author on a European tour, 1956.

98. *L.*—Secured by the author on a European tour, 1956.
    R.—Keller and Stewart, *op. cit.*

99-103. Secured by the author on a European tour, 1956.

104. *U.L.* and *L.L.*—Secured by the author on a European tour, 1956.
    U. R. and *L. R.*—C. Werckshagen, *op. cit.*

105. *U.L.* and *C.L.*—C. Werckshagen, *op. cit.*
    L.L., U.R., and *L.R.*—Secured by the author on a European tour, 1956.

106-107. Secured by the author on a European tour, 1956.

108. *U.L.* and *U.R.*—Secured by the author on a European tour, 1956.

    B.—C. Werckshagen, *op. cit.*

109. Secured by the author on a European tour, 1956.

110. J. A. Wylie, *op. cit.*

111. *U.L.* and *L.L.*—J. A. Wylie, *op. cit.*
    U.R. and *L.R.*—C. Werckshagen, *op. cit.*

112. *U.L.* and *U.R.*—C. Werckshagen, *op. cit.*
    L.L.—Secured by the author on a European tour, 1956.

113. C. Werckshagen, *op. cit.*

115. *T.*—Percy Dearmer, *op. cit.*
    L.L. and *L.R.*—Julius von Pflugk-Harttung, *op. cit.*

116. *L.*—F. C. Happold, *op. cit.*
    R.—Percy Dearmer, *op. cit.*

118. J. A. Wylie, *op. cit.*

119. *L.*—W. B. Carpenter, *A Popular History of the Church of England,* London, John Murray, 1900.
    R.—F. C. Happold, *op. cit.*

120. F. C. Happold, *op. cit.*

121. *L.*—F. C. Happold, *op. cit.*
    R.—D. Bernhard Rogge, *op. cit.*

122. J. A. Wylie, *op. cit.*

123. *U.L.*—Ibid.

125. *L.* and *U.R.*—D. Bernhard Rogge, *op. cit.*

126. *T.*—Percy Dearmer, *op. cit.*
    B.—J. A. Wylie, *op. cit.*

127. *U.L.* and *B.*—Percy Dearmer, *op. cit.*
    U.R.—C. Werckshagen, *op. cit.*

128. *U.L.*—B. W. Carpenter, *op. cit.*
    L.L.—Picture Department, New York Public Library.
    U.R.—J. A. Wylie, *op. cit.*

131. *L.L.*—C. B. Mortlock and D. Maxwell, *Famous London Churches,* London, Skeffington & Son, Ltd., 1934.
    U.R.—Keller and Stewart, *op. cit.*

133. *R.-1, 2,* and *4*—P. Hume Brown, *John Knox and His Times,* Edinburgh and London, Oliphant, Anderson & Ferrier, 1905.
    R.-3—Presbyterian Historical Society, Philadelphia, Pa.

134. *U.C.* and *U.L.*—P. Hume Brown, *op. cit.*
    B.—D. Bernhard Rogge, *op. cit.*

135. *B.*—P. Hume Brown, *op. cit.*

137. J. A. Wylie, *op. cit.*

138. C. Werckshagen, *op. cit.*

147. *T.*—Ozora S. Davis, *The Pilgrim Faith,* Boston and New York, The Pilgrim Press, 1913.

148. *C.L.*—"Magazine" of the *New York Times,* 1957.
    L.R.—Ozora S. Davis, *op. cit.*

150. *R.*—N. V. Wallington, *op. cit.*

151. *T.*—Picture Department, New York Public Library.
    B.—N. V. Wallington, *op. cit.*

152. *R.*—N. V. Wallington, *op. cit.*

154. *U.L.*—C. Werckshagen, *op. cit.*

159. *R.*—Langston Hughes and Milton Meltzer, *A Pictorial History of the Negro in America,* New York, Crown, 1956.

160-161. *Ibid.*

162. *U.L., L.L.,* and *U.R.*—*Ibid.*

163. *U.R.*—*The Call,* Minneapolis, Minn., June, 1957.

164. *R.*—Charles W. Wendte, ed., *Freedom and Fellowship in Religion,* Boston, Mass., International Council.

165. Friedrich Oehninger, *op. cit.*

167. *U.R.* and *L.R.*—Antonia H. Froendt, *The Huguenot-Walloon Tercentenary,* The Huguenot-Walloon New Netherland Commission, Inc.

168. *U.L.*—*Ibid.*

169. *L.L.* and *L.R.*—*The National Council Outlook,* The Reformed Church in America, New York, June, 1955.
U.R.—N. V. Wallington, *op. cit.*

170. *R.*—*The National Council Outlook,* The Reformed Church in America, New York, June, 1955.

175. *U.R.* and *L.R.*—Hughes and Meltzer, *op. cit.*

179. *R.*—Mrs. Hope Griswold Macintosh.

180. *L.* and *L.R.*—Friedrich Oehninger, *op. cit.*
U.R.—D. Bernhard Rogge, *op. cit.*

182. *U.R.* and *L.R.*—Arnold Lloyd, *Quaker Social History, 1669-1738,* New York, Longmans, Green & Co., 1950.

183. *U.L.*—*The Journal of the Friends Historical Society,* American Agency of Friends Historical Society, Philadelphia, Pa., 1932.
L.L. and *L.R.*—Arnold Lloyd, *op. cit.*
U.R.—Bernard Canter, *The Quaker Bedside Book,* New York, David McKay Co., 1952.

184. *L.* and *U.R.*—J. H. Price and S. R. Yarnall, *William Penn,* Philadelphia, The Religious Society of Friends, 1932.
L.R.—Stephen Hobhouse, *William Law and Eighteenth Century Quakerism,* New York, Macmillan Co., 1928.

185. *U.L.* and *R.*—Arnold Lloyd, *op. cit.*
L.L.—Bernard Canter, *op. cit.*

186. *U.L.*—Bernard Canter, *op. cit.*
U.R.—Stephen Hobhouse, *op. cit.*
B.—Friends Historical Library of Swarthmore College, Swarthmore, Pa.

187. *U.L.*—N. V. Wallington, *op. cit.*
C.L., U.R., and *L.R.*—Friends Historical Library of Swarthmore College, Swarthmore, Pa.
L.L.—Bernard Canter, *op. cit.*

188. *U.L.* and *L.L.*—David Hinshaw, *Rufus Jones, Master Quaker,* New York, G. P. Putnam's Sons, 1951.
U.R. and *L.R.*—Friends Historical Library of Swarthmore College, Swarthmore, Pa.

189. Friedrich Oehninger, *op. cit.*

190-199. Presbyterian Historical Society, Philadelphia, Pa.

200. *U.R.*—Wooster College, Ohio.
C.R.—Presbyterian Historical Society, Philadelphia, Pa.

201. *L.L.*—C. H. Parkhurst, *My Forty Years in New York,* New York, Macmillan Co., 1923.

202. *U.L.*—Picture Department, New York Public Library.

203. Lawrence W. Shultz, *Schwarzenau — Where the Brethren Began in Europe.*

204. *U.L., C.L.,* and *R.*—Lawrence W. Shultz, *Schwarzenau Yesterday and Today.*
L.L.—The Rev. Lawrence Shultz.

205. The Rev. Medford D. Neher.

206. National Association of Free Will Baptists, Nashville, Tenn.

208. *L.L.*—Percy Dearmer, *op. cit.*

210. *L.L.* and *L.R.*—Presbyterian Historical Society, Philadelphia, Pa.

214. *L.L.*—William Sargant, *Battle for the Mind,* New York, Doubleday & Co., 1957.

217. Elmer T. Clark, *An Album of Methodist History,* Nashville, Abingdon-Cokesbury Press, 1952.

221. *U.L.*—Elmer T. Clark, *op. cit.*
L.R.—Hughes and Meltzer, *op. cit.*

223. *C.*—Hughes and Meltzer, *op. cit.*

224. *L.L.*—Picture Department, New York Public Library.

U.R.—Hughes and Meltzer, *op. cit.*

225. *L.*—*The Philosophical Forum,* Boston, Mass., 1954.
R.—Elmer T. Clark, *op. cit.*

226-227. Krauth Memorial Library, Lutheran Theological Seminary, Philadelphia, Pa.

228. *T.*—D. Bernhard Rogge, *op. cit.*
B.—Krauth Memorial Library, Lutheran Theological Seminary, Philadelphia, Pa.

229-232. Krauth Memorial Library, Lutheran Theological Seminary, Philadelphia, Pa.

233. The United Lutheran Church in America, New York, N. Y.

234-237. Lutheran Church Productions, Inc., New York, N. Y.

238. American Unitarian Association, Boston, Mass.

239. *U.L., L.L.,* and *U.R.*—American Unitarian Association, Boston, Mass.
L.R.—C. Werckshagen, *op. cit.*

240. *U.L.* and *L.L.*—American Unitarian Association, Boston, Mass.

241. J. A. Wylie, *op. cit.*

242. The Reformed Presbyterian Theological Seminary, Pittsburgh, Pa.

243. *U.L., L.L.,* and *U.R.*—The Reformed Presbyterian Theological Seminary, Pittsburgh, Pa.
L.R.—The Rev. J. B. Willson, 2727 Fifth Ave., Beaver Falls, Pa.

244-246. N. V. Wallington, *op. cit.*

247. *U.L.* and *L.L.*—N. V. Wallington, *op. cit.*
R.—Mary Kent Davey Babcock, *Christ Church, Salem Street, Boston,* Boston, Christ Church.

248. *L.*—N. V. Wallington, *op. cit.*
R.—Mary Kent Davey Babcock, *op. cit.*

249-250. Mary Kent Davey Babcock, *op. cit.*

251. *U.L., U.R.,* and *L.R.*—Christ Church, Boston, Mass.
L.L.—Mary Kent Davey Babcock, *op. cit.*

252-254. N. V. Wallington, *op. cit.*

255-257. George MacAdam, *The Little Church Around the Corner,* New York, G. P. Putnam's Sons, 1925.

258. *U.L.*—George MacAdam, *op. cit.*
L.L. and *L.R.*—Charles Lewis Slattery, *Certain American Faces,* New York, E. P. Dutton & Co., 1918.
U.R.—Harriette A. Keyser, *Bishop Potter, the People's Friend,* New York, Thomas Whittaker, Inc., 1910.

259-261. Universalist Service Committee, Boston, Mass.

262. Elmer T. Clark, *op. cit.*

266. *L.*—W. E. Garrison and A. T. DeGroot, *The Disciples of Christ, A History,* St. Louis, Christian Board of Publication, 1948.
L.L. and *U.R.*—R. Frederick West and William G. West, *Who Are the Christian Churches and What Do We Believe?* Chattanooga, Tenn., 1956.

267. West and West, *op. cit.*

268. *The Church Advocate,* June 15-19, 1953, Harrisburg, Pa.

275. *R.*—J. F. Gibbs, *Lights and Shadows of Mormonism,* Salt Lake City, Salt Lake Tribune Publishing Co., 1909.

276. *T.*—N. V. Wallington, *op. cit.*
L.L. and *L.R.*—Austin and Alta Fife, *Saints of Sage and Saddle,* Bloomington, Indiana University Press, 1956.

277. *Synodalalbum,* St. Louis, Concordia Publishing House, 1911.

278. *U.L.*—*A Souvenir of Concordia Seminary,* St. Louis,

Index